PERSONAL FINANCE
FOR TECH PROFESSIONALS

"'No one tells you about these things,' is a phrase I've heard countless times from founders and early employees at start-up companies. Often it's said with regret—because a successful exit is just the beginning of the personal program, one that can crash or hang if stock options and other forms of compensation risk are not managed properly. This book changes that equation: read it and debug your own financial future."

ADAM FISHER, *bestselling author of* Valley of Genius

"The technology industry is characterized by intensive commitment from tech professionals to their careers, innovative equity-based compensation structures, and dynamic wealth formation. As such, it is no surprise many tech professionals are in search of guidance to face the daunting challenges and complexities of managing their personal financial affairs. Bruce Barton answers the call by providing you, in a comprehensive yet understandable narrative, the best practices in managing your personal finances, whether you are at the start of your career or preparing for retirement."

RUSTY THOMAS, *former KPMG Senior Partner and National Tax Lead: Technology Sector, Silicon Valley Office (retired 2017)*

"We all know working in the tech industry can be volatile. No matter whether a startup goes public, gets sold, pivots, or craters, the need to be informed and knowledgeable about your personal finances remains constant. Bruce Barton has done a magnificent job cutting through complex terminology to deliver lucid, bite-sized advice on how to build your wealth and thrive in the turmoil that is Silicon Valley."

JIM SMITH, *General Partner, Mohr Davidow Ventures*

"Between starting a company and having a family, it's hard to find time to devote to learning about personal finance. You could spend months researching and never figure out the important nuances of properly building your wealth. Bruce Barton has created an essential resource for tech entrepreneurs to quickly understand key issues concerning their financial well-being and take action. *Personal Finance for Tech Professionals* is everything you need, wrapped up succinctly in one place."

HERNÁN BOTBOL, *Argentinian entrepreneur and co-founder of Taringa!, now living in Silicon Valley and working on his latest startup*

**PERSONAL FINANCE
FOR TECH PROFESSIONALS**

an imprint of Mascot Books

www.amplifypublishing.com

Personal Finance for Tech Professionals: In Silicon Valley and Beyond

For more information, please contact:
Mascot Books
620 Herndon Parkway #320
Herndon, VA 20170
info@mascotbooks.com

Book design by Ricky Frame
Author photo by Carole Whitacre

Library of Congress Control Number: 2018909301
CPSIA Code: PRFRE1118A
ISBN-13: 978-1-68401-815-4

Printed in Canada

PERSONAL FINANCE *for*

TECH

PROFESSIONALS

in Silicon Valley and Beyond

BRUCE BARTON, CFP® CFA

Contents

1

Finally! A Personal Finance Book for Tech Professionals

Technology companies located in Silicon Valley and clustered in other tech cities throughout the United States are uniquely able to create wealth for their founders and employees. In addition to tech's well-known billionaires, some estimates put the number of tech millionaires in the tens of thousands. At a minimum, tech careers provide an opportunity for a secure financial future with compensation more than twice national average. In 2017, the average annual national wage was $54,500, while the average annual tech sector wage was $112,900, and California's tech workers earned even more that year with an estimated average of $161,900.[1]

Tech companies are, to a greater degree than other industries, meritocracies where employees are rewarded based on their contributions (as opposed to seniority, for example). The meritocratic environment creates financial opportunity, which attracts a large number of talented people. Over 11 million people work in the various industries and occupations making up the tech sector.[2]

Tech companies are the very definition of innovative, entrepreneurial, and productive. Employing just 7.2% of the American workforce, the tech sector directly contributes an estimated 9.2% to the U.S. economy.[3] The downstream value of new ideas and capabilities contributed indirectly by the tech industry to economic productivity and human welfare are enormous and, in fact, immeasurable. However, those tech careers are risky and prone to high expectations and high pressure, which can take a personal toll.

Tech industries can provide opportunities for building a solid financial life. But to take advantage of these opportunities and mitigate the impact of sudden short- or long-term unemployment, tech professionals need to know how to manage their finances. Tech professionals face unique financial issues and workplace pressures uncommon in other industries. They make high-stakes financial decisions that people in other careers do not make—for example, dealing with stock-based compensation. Surprisingly, there hasn't been a comprehensive personal finance resource available for this large and influential group of people, until now.

This book is written for technology professionals who want to build wealth, manage their finances well, and learn best practices for handling the unique financial issues people in their industries face.

Wherever You Are on Your Tech Career Journey

People working in technology companies typically fit into one of the following profiles arranged here in order of increasing risk and potential upside. Each profile suggests its own set of financial priorities.

Career builders are steadily expanding their networks in the increasingly flat hierarchical structures of larger, established tech companies.

- Career builders are often in high-profile positions and the job pressure and time commitment can be considerable.
- They are taking on increased responsibility, leading more and bigger projects or teams of people, or both. Ultimately they become senior managers and executives.
- Most of their compensation comes in the form of salary and incentive bonuses with some equity compensation, often in the form of restricted stock units at publicly traded companies.
- Increased responsibility is the primary driver of increased compensation.

- For career builders, slow and steady wins the race.
  They're not looking for a life-changing liquidity event.
  Instead, consistent large bonus payouts and ongoing
  restricted stock-unit grants (so-called evergreen grants),
  keep the wealth accumulation engine running over the
  long term. The risk of company failure is much less
  than with tech startups, and if a product or project
  isn't successful, there are other products and projects to
  move on to.

Individual contributors want to work in their area of interest
and expertise and don't really want to lead a project or manage a
team of people if they don't have to. These positions can be high
pressure, particularly around product or project deadlines.

- Individual contributors are good at their jobs and can
  be highly productive in a conducive work environment.
- At the height of their careers, they may be recognized
  experts within the company and industry.
- Individual contributors' compensation is driven by
  technical skill and productivity.
- Typically, compensation comprises salary and bonuses
  plus equity compensation.
- Established, publicly traded companies may offer
  restricted stock units while small, privately held startup companies may offer stock options. The amount of
  equity compensation depends on experience and ability
  to contribute.

Executives and managers in startup companies are working intensely on a relatively short-term project, initially spanning three to five years. The goal is to get the company through a set of milestones leading to a liquidity event for the investors. These are high-risk ventures, and there are many ways startup companies can fail, either in misjudging the market or not being able to complete product development.

- Startup company executives and managers typically receive an adequate salary but often less than they could earn in a larger company.
- The bulk of their earnings over their tenure with the company comes in the form of equity compensation, typically stock options, if all goes well.
- Startup company executives, managers, and senior staff are looking to earn life-changing money if the company's product or service is successful in the marketplace or if it attracts the attention of a larger company with a strategic need.

Entrepreneurs and founders start companies to pursue a technological or market opportunity and, hopefully, make a lot of money in the process. They come up with the idea and develop the plan to execute it. For founders, startups are where self-actualizing adventure and pursuit of wealth come together in one experience.

- Founders take most of the risk, sometimes working for months or years without salary to develop the product and company to the point it can attract investors.

- Company founders often contribute their own money to fund operations and pay for product development.
- Deciding how much of their personal assets to contribute and determining when it's time to stop funding the idea are crucial and often agonizing decisions that fall into two categories: 1) when it's clear the idea won't be successful and more money invested will be lost, and 2) when deciding how much of the company to sell to outside investors—owning a smaller fraction of a larger company can be worth more in actual dollars if outside funding can accelerate growth of the company.
- First time founders may have less personal net worth to risk than serial entrepreneurs who have had prior ventures that have sold or gone public.

A distinguishing feature among tech career profiles is the range of income possibilities and likelihood of earning those amounts. Whether you're on the hit-or-miss path through a succession of tech startups or you're steadily moving up in the corporate tech world, your income streams are what allow you to build wealth.

The range of financial outcomes along the startup path is much wider than that in established companies. If you're on the startup path, your income may be uneven with several low-to-moderate income years punctuated by large payouts every few years. In the startup world, more rolls of the dice increase your chances of hitting it big. You may need to work in three or four companies before being part of a group that makes it to a big acquisition or initial public offering. Many tech professionals prefer to work in startups because of the dynamic work environment and the chance to retire early.

If you're working in a larger, established tech company, your earnings are more regular and, hopefully, increasing. This is the less risky approach.

Both of these situations present their own unique financial challenges. You can use the information and guidance in this book to contend with either. If you're pursuing wealth in the startup gold rush, you can use the ideas in this book as your back-up plan to ensure you meet your financial goals in case the long odds of startup success repeatedly go against you. If you're pursuing a more traditional career in an established company, follow the principles in this book to steadily accumulate wealth and safely spend it in retirement. Whatever your career profile, following the best practices outlined in this book can help you not only feel secure in your financial future but also enjoy your life to the fullest today and reduce or eliminate the stress of money worries in your life.

If you make a lot of money early, that's fantastic. If good fortune doesn't strike right away, you'll get where you need to be anyway. As famous inventor, polymath, and founder of the United States Benjamin Franklin said over 200 years ago, "Industry, perseverance, and frugality make fortune yield."

What You Will Learn from This Book

This book covers unique personal finance issues faced by people working in technology industries. It's a curated discussion of important and frequently encountered issues—not an exhaustive list, which would span many books. Important topics covered include:

- **Stock-based compensation**, such as stock options, restricted stock units, restricted stock, and employee stock-purchase plans
- **Balancing spending** between your working years and retirement and tips for keeping spending under control
- How much you should be **saving for regular or early retirement** and the types of accounts you should be using
- **Investing** using an institutional approach, including techniques such as asset location and exploring private investments for accredited investors
- A host of **housing and real estate issues** in high-cost tech cities
- Taking care of yourself and **family matters** while dealing with overwork and stress
- Concepts and techniques for **reducing taxes**, including considerations for the 2018 tax law
- Making your **retirement** real by considering where you will live, what you will do, sustainable withdrawal rates, and order of withdrawal from your accounts
- Practical considerations for **initial public offerings (IPOs) and acquisitions** and their impact on your financial life
- Considering your **legacy and charitable giving** plans

The goal is to explain each issue so that newcomers to the topic can understand enough to take appropriate action, while also providing more substance to interested readers who are prepared to go deeper. However, the book **does not** cover basic topics such as banking, budgeting, credit scores, and time-value of money—there are plenty of excellent books and internet articles on these topics.

The book presents some individual topics at a short-term level, providing specific, detailed, and immediately actionable recommendations. It also gives voice to higher-level themes and considers future planning trade-offs that you might ruminate over for some time.

One of the important themes is that managing your finances is a continuous process. It involves a set of behaviors and actions implemented consistently over a long period of time, sprinkled with important decisions needing prompt attention occasionally that, as luck would have it, arise during the middle of an important project you're working on. For best results, you'll need to pay attention to your finances regularly.

Another unavoidable conclusion is that personal finance can be difficult. Some concepts are simple but not easy. For example, saving money is simple in concept but often not easy in practice, and changing your behavior or attitude can be difficult. Other concepts are downright difficult to understand, especially in the equity compensation and tax areas. The reality is that good management of your personal finances requires study, effort, and a fair amount of self-discipline.

There are at least three ways to use this book:

1. If you have urgent issues in your financial life or if you are about to meet with a financial advisor, read the chapters and sections you need right now. Each chapter stands alone, for the most part (which means some relevant information is repeated in more than one chapter). For example, if you have questions about your stock options or restricted stock units, or you

need to decide whether to participate in your employer's employee stock purchase plan, read Chapter 5 – Taking Stock: Equity Compensation. If your startup is about to be acquired, read Chapter 9 – Liquidity Events: IPOs and Acquisitions. Later, you can go back and read other chapters and sections to continue optimizing your financial situation or to consider longer-range planning issues.

2. If you don't have any urgent issues and want to get a fast start on improving your finances, use the checklist of recommendations at the end of each chapter and summarized in the Appendix. With the checklist as a guide, you can identify quick actions to consider taking right away. For example, the checklist includes having you consider whether to enroll in an employee stock savings plan, max out your 401(k), early-exercise stock options, make charitable contributions through a donor-advised fund, rebalance your portfolio, and more.

3. If you want to grow your financial literacy and develop a foundational understanding of financial planning, you can also read the book from start to finish. The material progresses roughly through the financial lifecycle for a tech professional. While the chapters and sections are written to be as stand-alone as possible, and to be useful as a reference resource, the approach and context for financial decision-making build through the book.

Meet Your Financial Guide

Behind any curated discussion there must, of course, be a curator. This book consists of the issues and topics I have dealt with often as both a tech professional myself and as financial advisor to families and individuals working in the tech industries. In a tech career spanning 15 years, I've worked as system design engineer, product manager, director of product management, and vice president of marketing. I've worked in three venture capital-backed tech startups, including one that went public, one that was acquired, and one that failed. My employers have also included large, publicly traded U.S. and foreign multinational companies. I have personally experienced nearly all of the issues covered in this book, many, unfortunately, before I had the benefit of the expertise you're about to receive.

While I was working in tech, my understanding of many of these issues was fuzzy. With an MBA in finance, I had a better shot than many of my coworkers at making good financial decisions, but even that training was lacking in some respects because the curriculum was centered on corporate finance, not personal finance. When I began my second career as a personal chief financial officer to families, I studied nights and weekends for five years to earn the top two credentials in the field: Certified Financial Planner (CFP®) and Chartered Financial Analyst (CFA). I wanted to make sure I knew what I was doing when giving advice to other people. It's one thing to make mistakes with your own finances—it's quite another to make mistakes with other people's money. With more specialized training in personal finance, I got more clarity. The fuzziness disappeared.

Now, after 15 years giving personal financial advice to families and individuals as a fiduciary acting only in their best interest, my views are clear and my understanding is sharp—some might even say opinionated.

No doubt I have formed opinions about the best way to do things. Those opinions and judgments are based on facts, evidence, and peer-reviewed research. I want to know that something works and is tested before general release. Having said that, there are many ways to accomplish your financial goals and many approaches to investments and personal finance. Finding an approach that works for you and sticking to it is the most important thing. Based on my training, research, and experience, the ideas here will work well for a majority of tech professionals.

I hope and expect the information presented in this book will be valuable to tech professionals managing their own finances and those working with a professional financial advisor or team of advisors. It includes the best practices of professional advisors and other personal finance experts. If you're managing your own finances, you can benefit from taking in the thought processes and specific advice of professionals and bringing that to your own situation.

Most importantly, the information in this book can help you recognize issues in your finances that you may not be aware of, or better appreciate the complexities of issues you have a surface familiarity with. It can also help you understand if and when you need to hire a professional advisor.

If you're working with an advisor, this information can help provide you with the language you need to communicate with your advisor. It will also help you to better understand your advisor's recommendations and provide a framework for you and your advisor to define and accomplish your financial objectives.

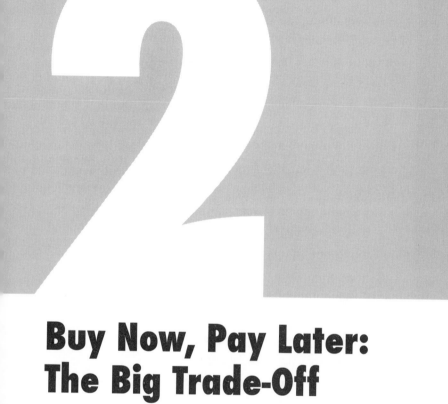

Buy Now, Pay Later: The Big Trade-Off

One of the surprising things you learn as a financial planner is that a significant proportion of families and individuals spend their entire after-tax income and then some. From household incomes of $100,000 to $1,000,000, the pattern repeats. You might reason that as household income rises, people are able to save more. While logically that is true, for many families and individuals extra saving does not happen. Instead, spending rises to the level of income in the absence of particular saving goals, such as early retirement or college funds.

Spending can become even more problematic for people who have met with some financial success and were able to retire early. Because their spending is no longer tethered to income, their frame of reference is lost and spending can rise above sustainable levels. In a memorable case many years ago, I was having trouble developing a workable financial plan for an early-retired couple with a $6-million investment portfolio. At first look, it seemed they had plenty of assets to remain retired. However, it turned out that their annual spending was over $500,000, which was not sustainable over a 50-year retirement. They needed to reduce spending.

Your behavior around spending has the biggest effect on whether you will achieve your financial goals.

You can't control stock market performance or control tax rates and rules. While you can exercise some control over your earning potential through your choices for education, profession, employers, projects, and career length, your income is largely determined by forces in the labor market, which are outside of your control. But, the one area in your financial life where you have near total control is your spending.

Your spending defines how well you will live in the future. Each and every day, you make important decisions about whether to consume now or save for later. Each and every day, you balance the big trade-off between leading a fulfilling life now and ensuring you can maintain a financially secure life into the future.

Happily, the ideas behind your personal finances are not difficult to understand. They can be described and summarized by a simple formula.

Income – Taxes – Spending = Savings

This simple formula describes flows of money over time: income flows in, while tax payments and money for living expenses flow out. Only the remainder, savings, is left to accumulate over time. Savings accumulate to become the assets you will draw on to pay your living and leisure expenses after your working years. The formula is the roadmap for the whole book. Most of the strategies we discuss in later chapters seek to improve the results of calculations using this formula, for example by reducing taxes, earning investment income, earning income from equity compensation, or spending wisely on housing.

You might argue that some items of spending have lasting value. That is certainly true. The payroll taxes for Social Security and Medicare pay for future benefits you may receive. Spending on education and training may allow you to earn higher income. However, for the most part, money spent on lifestyle expenses is gone. Money spent on experiences and services is gone. Money spent on purchases of household goods, such as clothes, furniture, and electronics have little value after purchase (particularly electronics, which lose value rapidly). Household items are worth only a few cents on the dollar after short use. These items become dead assets with no value in and of themselves and no ability to create income for you as investments would.

Success in the personal finance arena means many things to different people, but one thing most people would agree is that it means having enough savings to meet your living expenses in post-working years. The above formula can guide you in taking actions to build wealth. To build wealth you need savings. To increase savings, you can do one or all of the following:

1. Increase your income
2. Decrease your taxes
3. Decrease your spending

Those are your only three options. Unfortunately, it's not as easy as the formula suggests.

With hard work and good fortune you can increase your income over the course of your career. However, it's difficult to increase your income in the short run. Most people are already earning the maximum income available to them based on their education and experience. You can also increase the savings you have already accumulated by earning more investment income. However, in order to invest, you must first save. And there are limits on the amount your investments can earn because arranging your investments to increase their rate of return also increases their risk. There are limits on the amount of risk it is prudent for you to take, depending on your overall financial situation. You have even less control over the amount of tax you pay. Although there are sound tax planning techniques available to minimize your taxes, there is a limit to the amount of tax savings possible through good planning.

Which leaves us with the last term in our simple formula: spending. You have most control over this aspect of your personal finances, which makes it the most important. But while most people will readily agree that they should try to reduce taxes and earn more income, they are less willing to consider reducing expenditure or, if agreeable, unable to reduce spending in practice.

Current or Future Spending?

While the formula of Income − Taxes − Spending = Savings is simple, the consequences of its tight logic are profound. Let's rearrange the formula to illustrate another point.

Saving + Spending = Income − Taxes

In this version of our equation, the sum of savings and spending is equal to your after-tax income. (More generally, income can include both compensation income and investment income as follows: Saving + Spending = Compensation Income + Investment Income − Taxes.)

What you save over time, plus the investment growth on those savings, is what you will use to pay your living expenses after your working years. That is, your savings is what you will use to spend in the future. Using this idea, we can rewrite our simple formula again as:

Future Spending + Current Spending = Income − Taxes

Again, the right side of the formula is your after-tax income. Now the left side shows that your choice in deciding what to do with your after-tax income is to allocate that money to current spending or future spending. Whatever you don't spend now will be available to spend in the future. Your future self and future family will have access to funds for their current spending needs in the future.

What this illustrates is the continuous trade-off you make between current and future consumption: between spending now and spending in the future. It's a balancing act over your entire lifetime, with many course adjustments along the way. If you spend too much now, you may have to reduce your spending in the future. If you save too much now, you may unnecessarily give up enjoyable activities and experiences.

Spending Trajectories

Figure 1 below shows an example of spending over a lifetime and the consequences of an unbalanced trade-off between current and future spending. The solid line represents a hypothetical trajectory of spending over an individual's lifetime or a couple's joint lifetime. The shaded area represents retirement.

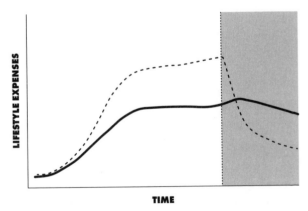

Figure 1

For proper comparison between pre-retirement and post-retirement spending, the illustration excludes taxes and retirement savings. Only lifestyle expense is shown.

In Figure 1, the solid line represents a good outcome—a comfortable life before retirement; responsible spending and ample saving during working years; sufficient assets to allow a fulfilling retirement with cushion to meet unexpected medical or care expenses late in life; and possibly money left over to leave to heirs.

In contrast, the dotted line shows a trajectory and outcome you want to avoid. With the dotted line, our hypothetical household increases spending more rapidly in early- to mid-career and sustains a high level of spending during peak-earning years. In fact, this household allowed its spending to increase during peak-earning years with its rising income. As a consequence, this household did not direct enough of its after-tax income to savings and investments. They have not accumulated enough assets to maintain their standard of living in retirement. They will be forced to drastically cut expenses in retirement, as shown by the sharp decline in spending in the shaded area. Their level of spending in retirement is also lower than that of the solid line household. They simply didn't save enough and they are forced to cut back. This situation is all too common yet completely avoidable.

Caring for Future-You

A growing body of research in behavioral finance indicates that we are simply not good at balancing now with later and taking care of our future selves. We have difficulty feeling a psychological connection to the future-us. And the longer the time into the future the less connected we feel. We feel connected to the people we will be next year but much less so to who we will be in 40 years. At the extreme, we feel our future selves are complete strangers. One set of behavioral finance researchers observed that "To people estranged from their future selves, saving is like a choice between spending money today or giving it to a stranger years from now."[1] Except for the most altruistic and charitable among us, it's difficult to forego current spending on ourselves in order to give money to strangers in the future, even if that stranger turns out to be us. These researchers are studying ways to increase savings by individuals, for example by helping them feel more connected to their future-selves and make better decisions around saving. In one set of studies, experiencing an aged version of themselves in virtual reality increased test subjects' tendency to allocate more money to retirement savings.

For more success with the continuous trade-off between spending now and saving for future spending, it is helpful to remember that the person you're saving for is the future-you. How does the current-you feel about how the past-you prepared for your current financial situation? Pretty good or could have done better? Can the current-you do a better job for the future-you? Does current-you need to make any changes to spending to take better care of future-you? What changes might be possible? Let's take a look now at how much you can spend and ideas for improving in that area.

How Much Should You Spend?

How much can you spend and still ensure you are saving enough to meet future spending needs in retirement? It's almost impossible to determine whether you have a good balance between spending and saving by reviewing your current spending in isolation. More information is required.

In some simple cases, it's easy to figure out whether spending is too high. For example, someone living from paycheck to paycheck and spending all of their after-tax income is not saving at all. Without savings, they won't have accumulated any assets to use to pay living expenses once they stop working (although Social Security benefits and Medicare benefits can help). This person needs to find a way to save some of their income.

At the other end of the income spectrum, a deca-millionaire Silicon Valley entrepreneur living comfortably on only a portion of the annual income from her investment portfolio, which continues to grow, is spending below her means. She doesn't need to save and could spend more.

These are the simple cases that don't require analysis. Most people have financial situations that fall in between these simple cases. Most people need to balance the amounts they are spending and saving.

Financial Modeling

In many cases, financial modeling will be required to strike the right balance between spending and saving over the course of your life, and to continuously adjust the balance based on changing circumstances. Spending is just one component of your financial picture. To determine whether your spending and saving are in balance, you will need to consider all of the following factors:

- Income: The money you receive from wages, investments, and other sources
- Taxation: The tax rates and rules used to calculate tax payments for income, payroll, property, and other assets

- Living expenses: The costs incurred in day-to-day life, including housing, utilities, food, healthcare, auto, and entertainment
- Assets: Anything you own that has a marketable value, including your home, other real estate, investments, savings, art, and antiques
- Liabilities: Mortgages, loans, leases, credit card balances, and other financial commitments
- Investment rate of return: The average amount your investments earn over a specific period and how much those earnings fluctuate
- Time until you plan on retiring: The number of remaining years of earned income you have to save for your retirement
- Anticipated expenses during retirement: How much you plan to spend annually after you stop working
- Estimated post-retirement years: The time you will need to rely on your savings and investment portfolio without income from work

Looking at any one of those variables by itself will not offer much value in determining whether your accumulated savings will allow you to meet your financial goals. Each factor will need to be quantified, and its relationship to the others determined, in order to appropriately evaluate each variable. That is the process of financial modeling.

Simple retirement planning calculators are available online that provide a basic level of financial modeling. Many of the personal finance and budgeting online apps and software include some financial planning features. There are also Excel spreadsheet templates available for personal financial planning.

However, unlike in the tax preparation arena, where the popular TurboTax® product allows individuals to prepare income tax returns with results comparable to that of professional preparers, there is no retail *financial planning* software or application of similar capability or quality. Software used by financial planners allows detailed modeling of the factors listed above, and it allows complex "what-if" analyses to study possible outcomes of various scenarios and the likelihood of achieving particular financial goals. If you have access only to simple retirement planning calculators for financial modeling, be extra conservative in the assumptions you make to give yourself more room for error.

Tracking Spending and Saving

One way to know where all your money goes is to track it. You can prepare a detailed budget each year and track your expenses compared to your budget. If you do track your expenses, that's fantastic. Keep up the good work. If you don't, that can be okay too. Honestly, budgeting is tedious, time consuming, and requires a comfort level with Excel spreadsheets or personal finance software, such as Quicken, that not everyone enjoys. Newer mobile and cloud-based applications, such as Mint.com and You Need a Budget™, promise to make budgeting less painful.

I'm often asked what amount is normal for a particular expense category—what percentage of the total budget an expense should represent. For example, how much do people spend on food each month? The answer is that there is no normal percentage for each category. Spending is a completely personal decision. Every person has different preferences for how they spend money. Each person makes their own individual trade-offs on how to spend a limited resource. Some people like to have new clothes, while others like to dine out. Some people want to have the latest electronics, while others enjoy exotic vacations. Some people contribute to charity.

The point is, it doesn't much matter what you spend your money on. What does matter is the total amount of money you spend because that determines how much is left to add to your net worth (or limit reduction in your net worth if you are spending down your savings in retirement).

If creating a budget and tracking spending by category helps you regulate your total spending, then use categories. Many people find this the most effective way to control their spending behaviors and ensure that they are saving enough.

However, if creating a budget and tracking your spending are difficult for you, there is another way to manage and track your spending. Track your savings instead. Tracking saving works nearly as well as tracking spending in meeting your savings targets for the year. It has the advantage that it's much easier to do—simply keep track of contributions to accounts where you save, whether that be bank checking and savings accounts, 401(k) plans, or brokerage accounts.

Budgeting

Conceptually, managing your spending is simple. Create a household budget (or "spending plan," if you prefer) that strikes the right balance between spending and saving. Spend money only on the amounts budgeted in each category. Review your expenses and savings periodically and make adjustments as necessary. If you have overspent in one category, look for ways to reduce spending in other categories such that you meet your overall spending and savings targets.

Budgeting sounds simple, but doing it is not always easy. Apart from the time-consuming mechanics of budgeting, there are the psychological and social factors that impede our efforts and may cause us to overspend:

- We buy on impulse.
- We think spending on material goods will make us happy.
- We have access to more and cheaper credit.
- We are influenced by what other people buy.
- We compete with people we know.

These factors seem to be present for everyone regardless of net worth and income. Being aware of how these factors impact your behavior is an important first step in countering their influences. Several threads of ongoing research have revealed important aspects of our behaviors related to spending.

Self-Control, Present Bias, and Advertising

Human beings have problems with self-control. In a now famous set of experiments from the 1970s, behavioral scientist Walter Mischel gave kids aged four and five a choice between receiving a small reward now and a larger reward a short time later. In the experiments, the kids could have one cookie at any time by ringing a bell, or three cookies if they could wait until the researcher came back into the room. If the researcher left a single cookie on a plate in front of the kids, the kids lasted barely a minute before gobbling it up. If the single cookie was out of sight, the kids lasted 11 minutes on average before ringing the bell. If the kids were told to think about something fun instead of cookies, they were able to wait even longer. Similar experiments have been conducted on rats and pigeons with similar results.[2] Some research suggests there may be an evolutionary advantage to impulsive behavior in animals such as feeding when food is present.[3] However, with respect to spending in modern human society, our apparent innate lack of self-control is unhelpful.

People have what behavioral economists call a "present bias." The goods and services we buy are worth more to us now than they will be worth to us later. We would much rather have tickets to see our favorite band now than three years from now. We are said to "discount" the value of purchases in the future. In fact, behavioral economists have learned through experiments with choices people make, that the value we place on purchases in the future drops off sharply as the time to purchase increases. We much prefer consumption now to consumption in the future, which helps to explain why we might have difficulty controlling spending.

Our present bias and lack of self-control make us susceptible to advertising and marketing messages calling on us to "buy now." Various sources estimate that the average American sees between 250 to 3,000 or more commercial messages every day, from email solicitations, to television commercials, to logos on buildings and clothes, to the collapsing air-man in front of the local car dealership. It's everywhere and it's non-stop. There is a reason advertisers spend hundreds of billions of dollars each year to message you: it works. And it is part of the reason you may be having trouble meeting your saving goals.

Spending and Happiness

Research on materialism and well-being consistently shows that people who are materialistic are less happy than less materialistic people.[4] Yet materialistic people believe that buying things makes them happy. Recent studies of the emotional impact of purchasing economically significant products has lessons for all of us.[5] People do experience a boost in happiness, particularly before (and somewhat after) acquiring new products. The boost in happiness is more pronounced for materialistic people than less materialistic people. Researchers believe that less materialistic people may derive more emotional fulfillment from interpersonal relationships, spirituality, experiences, and other intangibles than from acquiring products.

However, the positive feelings generated by product purchases are temporary—the happiness boost fades within a few weeks after purchase as the buyer adapts to owning the new product. Furthermore, materialistic people have high standards for their purchases and, as a result, are often disappointed because of it. They have a tendency to think purchases will alter their lives in some substantial way, and are quick to experience disappointment when they don't.

Understanding that purchase of products does not increase your long-term happiness can help you control your spending. Window shopping (or maybe Amazon scrolling) can bring happiness without busting your budget.

Social Spending

We humans are social creatures. A lot of what we do and think is in reference to others. More and more evidence provides support to the idea that the same is true of our spending.

One prominent sociologist's ongoing work suggests that one of the reasons we overspend is due to "reference group" comparison, and even competition.[6] Within reference groups—family, friends, coworkers, professional associates, neighbors, health-club members, and more—we compare our lifestyles and possessions. We compete for status. For many people, their reference groups include people who have net worth and incomes many times their own, and that's where problems begin.

Other researchers have documented that when lower income households are exposed to higher income households (and their spending habits) in the same geographic region, lower income households spend more of their current income.[7] The result is tremendous pressure to maintain a lifestyle that is financially out of reach.

Making matters worse, there is a "relentless ratcheting up of standards," i.e., the expectation that items you purchase will be an upgrade of what you previously owned. Millions of people in the United States struggle to keep up with the escalating expectations of consumerism. The outlook isn't good either. It's easier than ever to compare and compete with prevalence of social media.

So the next time one of your friends or family members posts about a luxury vacation they probably couldn't afford, go ahead and "like" it: then remember what a nice time you had on your last vacation that comfortably matched your financial situation.

Course Adjustment

If you can make it work for you, use a budget to set spending and saving goals. Wait for a cooling-off period before making unbudgeted purchases. Monitor your spending compared to your budget periodically. Or monitor your saving compared to the amount you need to save. Once you begin tracking your expenses or savings, you may find that you are spending more or saving less than you want. The good news is that most households can reduce their spending by 1–2% per year almost immediately with little effort. With modest effort, many households can reduce their spending by 5–10% per year.

Annual Expense Review

At least annually, put on your Chief Financial Officer hat and go through your family's expenses looking for items to cut or reduce.

Redundancy: The first thing to look for is wasted money. Are there services you are paying for that you no longer use or enjoy as you once did? Such services may include premium TV channels, phone app or website subscriptions for streaming music or video, extra credit monitoring, premium cloud storage, auto-ship beauty products, supplements, wine-of-the-month, specialty foods, or magazines. These are often billed directly to your credit card, so it's easy to lose track of them. Take a few hours one weekend to review and cancel the services and products that you are wasting money on.

Bill creep: The second thing to look for is any monthly bill that is creeping up over time above the general rate of inflation. In looking over your expenses for the last two or three years, are any services costing more, even though you haven't changed anything? If so, it's probably time to shop those services again. For example, the cost of auto, home, and umbrella liability insurance may be increasing, making it worthwhile to shop for insurance with different insurance companies. Using an insurance broker can be helpful when shopping around. Or maybe your cable TV bill has increased, and it's time to call the cable TV company and ask what new plans are offered that can reduce your monthly bill.

Bad deals: Related to bill creep is the fact that some services in competitive markets become less expensive over time. Mobile telephone service is an example. With extreme competition among wireless carriers, plans are getting cheaper and seemingly nonstop promotions can help you lower your bill or get more service for the same money. But you have to proactively shop your services periodically. Most service providers won't automatically reduce your pricing and switch you to the newer, cheaper service unless you initiate the change.

Luxury: Other suggestions from the "nice to have" but not "need to have" category of spending might be cutting house cleaning services from two days a week to one, or twice a month. Do you really need a gardening service or might it be nice to spend some time working in the yard on the weekend? Can you take bigger vacations every other year instead of every year? Can you cook at home one extra night per week instead of dining out? Can you downgrade your next car purchase one notch and wait an extra year or two before buying your next car? Can you sell the extra car you don't drive but are paying auto insurance for? These are small, incremental expense reductions that can add up to big savings over time.

Longer-Term Structural Changes

It may be that with annual expense reviews and one-time expense reductions you just can't reduce your expenses enough to allow you to reach your long-term financial goals, such as funding college education and retirement. In that case, you may need to look at making longer-term structural changes in your spending.

The cost of owning a home, including mortgage, property tax, insurance, and maintenance often consumes a large portion of a household's expense budget. And that's before taking into account the remodeling projects you're thinking about. Scaling back on the size of your home and your expectations for the quality of its finishes, or moving to a less expensive neighborhood, could help you reduce an entire set of expenses related to housing. There may be other structural changes which apply in your case.

Summary

- Spending is the most important aspect of your personal financial life to focus on because it is the area in which you have most control.
- Strike the right balance between spending and saving over your lifetime to avoid a sharp reduction in lifestyle at retirement.
- Use a budget to track your spending, or, if budgeting is difficult, track the amount you're saving instead.

- Be aware of behavioral biases that can increase your spending such as present bias (feeling that goods purchased now are worth more than goods purchased in the future), believing that buying things will make you happy, and social spending to keep up with a peer group.
- Use a "cooling off" period before making big, unplanned purchases.
- Conduct an annual expense review to look for money wasted on unused services, monthly bills that have crept up over time, better deals on your regular expenses, and ways to reduce spending on "nice to haves."
- If an annual expense review doesn't bring spending in line, consider longer-term structural changes to your spending, such as scaling back on your housing costs.

Even with all the helpful ideas, maintaining an appropriate amount of spending still can be difficult. Reframing the spending-versus-saving trade-off as an effort to increase your savings toward a positive goal, such as increasing your net worth, can make ongoing spending restraint more palatable. In the next chapter, we do just that by moving on to the rationale for and mechanics of saving.

Saving: Playing the Long Game

Each year in the media there are stories about people with modest incomes who saved money over many years and managed to accumulate millions of dollars to become wealthy. Each year in the media there are also stories about athletes and entertainers who earned millions of dollars and yet wound up broke. Both are re- markable achievements. These tales are important reminders of the differences between income and wealth, and the successful habits for building and maintaining net worth.

How much you earn is not the same as how wealthy you are. Income is a flow of money to you, such as salary and investment returns, during a particular period of time: weekly, monthly, etc. In contrast, your wealth is the total of your savings plus growth on your savings. It is measured by your net worth, which is the total of your assets minus the total of your debts. Your wealth, or net worth, is measure of a "store of value" as opposed to a flow. It's an accumulation.

Saving is the process of converting your income to net worth. Remember, savings are what's left of your income after you pay taxes and spend on lifestyle expenses. Savings are the portion of your income that you add to your net worth to keep building your wealth over time.

The key lesson here is that, ultimately, wealth depends how much of your income you save, not how much you earn. High income only helps you become wealthy if you are able to limit the amount of taxes you pay and save sizable amounts of your after-tax income instead of spending.

Why Save?

The short answer is that you need to accumulate enough assets (and/or pensions) during your working years to live on when you no longer can or want to work. You accumulate assets primarily by saving and investing during the accumulation phase of your financial life. Saving includes putting away regular amounts from your current income such as salary, bonus, and vested restricted stock units into retirement accounts and taxable brokerage accounts. Saving also includes putting away money from one-time or extraordinary events, such as the proceeds from the sale of stock options or restricted stock after your company goes public or is acquired.

There are two important reasons to take saving seriously.

Longer Lives

The amount of money you need to live on in retirement depends on how much you spend each year and *how many years you will spend that amount*, i.e., the years you will live after retiring from work. Therefore, life expectancy is a major consideration.

Life expectancy is a good-news-bad-news situation. The good news is we are living healthier and longer lives. The bad news is that a long life can put a strain on your financial resources if you are not prepared.

For the first time in human history, mass populations are living as long in retirement as the number of years they worked.[1] In 1900, life expectancy at birth in the United States was 47.3 years.[2] In 2012, life expectancy at birth in the United States was 78.8 years. That represents a tremendous achievement for our society. A large part of the improvement has come from reductions in infant mortality and eradication of diseases.[3]

Another measure of life expectancy is relevant here. When the Social Security program became law in 1935, a person 65 years of age could expect to live a further 13 years.[4] In 2015, that figure was 19.4 years.[5] That improvement of six years is a substantial increase and it may continue to rise.

Life expectancy varies considerably by region. In 2015, Silicon Valley had the second longest estimated life expectancy at birth of any metropolitan area in the United States. A child born in the area of San Jose, Sunnyvale, and Santa Clara could expect to live to be 83.3 years old, up from 82.7 years in 2014, when Silicon Valley had the longest life expectancy of any metro area in the United States.[6] Higher average incomes and healthier lifestyles were important factors in these results.

Some demographers foresee more improvement in life expectancy as advances in medicine and medical technology reduce and delay deaths from conditions such as heart disease and cancer, the two leading causes of death in the United States. Researchers have predicted that as many as half of babies born in industrialized nations in the year 2000 will live to be 100 years old.[7]

In planning how much to save, you need to consider recent improvements in life expectancy and likely continued increases. Planning to live until age 90 or 95 may be prudent; 95 or 100 may be safer still if you are in your twenties now, especially if you have a history of longevity in your family.

Living without an income for a long time can be difficult. Pulling off that feat requires careful planning, lots of saving, and vigilant attention to your investments, both while you are accumulating and spending down. Those who have not saved enough will have to work longer if they are able.

Shrinking Retirement Benefits

Income in retirement has traditionally come from pensions, Social Security benefits, and one's personal savings and investments. Unfortunately, the news on pensions and Social Security is not encouraging.

The number of large employers in the U.S. offering traditional pensions to new employees hit an all-time low of 24 in 2015, down from 246 in 1998.[8] Department of Labor statistics show that only about 8% of U.S. business establishments offer a pension benefit.[9] In tech companies, traditional pensions are rare to nonexistent.

At the same time, the forecast for the Social Security program is grim. The 2017 annual report from the trustees of Social Security program estimates that the program will reach insolvency in 2035, at which point benefits will be need to be cut by about 25% given current funding levels.[10]

With pensions a thing of the past, and the future of Social Security uncertain, taking care of yourself in retirement means focusing on your own saving and investments.

Guidelines for Saving

The popular press for personal finance is filled with suggestions for safe amounts to save, including simple rules of thumb ranging from 10% to 20% of your income. While these simple rules may work for some people in some situations, it can be difficult to know if they apply to you and your particular circumstances. Rules of thumb are particularly unreliable if you have a steep income trajectory or wide variability in income over your working career.

Rather than provide a simple rule of thumb, this section provides a set of guidelines based on your income and assets that can help you know whether you are on track with your saving. This "income replacement method," developed by industry researchers for determining safe saving rates, gives reasonable results for a wide range of incomes that apply to many people.[11] Assumptions are detailed so that you will know when the guidelines might not apply in your situation. *(While the guidelines can be a helpful starting place, an individual analysis from a professional may be the best way to determine more precisely what savings are sufficient to meet your retirement needs.)*

Income Replacement

Your replacement income is the amount of income you need to cover your living expenses in retirement. That amount is less than your income before retirement. That's because when you're working, you pay payroll tax and income tax on your income, and you are saving for retirement. Once you're retired, those expenses are reduced or eliminated: you will no longer pay payroll tax or save for retirement, and your income tax will be lower, possibly much lower.

Also, you may find that you reduce your spending in retirement while maintaining your standard of living. For example, you may spend less on clothes and transportation for work, and you may eat more meals at home. Your home loan may also be paid off by the time you retire, which reduces your expenses even though you continue to live in your home.

A portion of your pre-retirement income may be replaced by monthly Social Security benefits and potentially other pension income (if you're lucky). The amount of replacement income not coming from Social Security or pension income will come from your personal savings and investments.

The portion of your pre-retirement income that needs to be replaced in retirement is calculated as your "income replacement ratio." Here is an example:

Mary is a 62-year-old married woman from North Carolina.
- Annual earnings: $150,000
- Federal payroll tax: $10,136
- Federal and state income tax: $20,148 (a 16% average tax rate using standard deduction)
- 401(k) contribution: $24,500 (the maximum allowable)
- Net income (earnings minus tax and 401(k) contributions): $95,216

Mary has to replace $95,216 of net income to maintain her current spending. She is planning to retire at 66 with an annual Social Security benefit of $32,460. Therefore, she needs to draw out $62,756 from her savings to replace her income, which represents a 42% income replacement ratio. If her retirement tax rate is not quite zero (due to distributions from her 401(k) or investment income) or Social Security benefits are cut, her income replacement ratio could be higher still.

Your required savings rate is determined by several factors, including your lifetime income stream, how much you earn on your investments, how much you withdraw from your savings and investments in retirement, and how long you live after retirement.

The following guidelines, developed by industry researchers, assume that you began saving at age 25, you retired at age 66, and that your income stream over your working career was similar to a sample of 100,000 U.S. households. The guidelines also assume that your investment portfolio started at age 25 with a mixture of 95% stocks and 5% bonds, and the percentage of stocks in the investment portfolio declined each year according to a formula (120 minus your age) until retirement, when it converts to a safe, retirement income portfolio consisting mostly of bonds. Because the amount you earn on your investments is volatile, savings rates are given in terms of the percent chance of achieving the target income replacement ratio. Here are guideline savings rates for two different income replacement ratios and three different success probabilities.

| | SAVINGS RATE | |
SUCCESS PROBABILITY	40% REPLACEMENT	20% REPLACEMENT
95%	16.8%	8.4%
90%	13.2%	6.6%
50%	5.2%	2.6%

Figure 2

You read the table in Figure 2 like this:

In order to replace 40% of your pre-retirement income from your savings and investments (remember Social Security is replacing some of your income as well), you will need to save about 13% per year from age 25 to age 66 to have a 90% chance of meeting your goal.

If you want to be really sure you will have enough retirement income, you can save about 17% per year to have a 95% chance of meeting your goal.

Notice that if you save only 5%, your chance of replacing 40% of your pre-retirement income from your savings and investments drops to 50%.

At lower income levels, a 20% replacement income might be adequate because Social Security benefits will provide more of your income replacement needs in retirement. At higher income levels, Social Security benefits will provide proportionately less income replacement and the 40% income replacement ratio may not be adequate. However, higher income earners often have greater flexibility to reduce spending in retirement.

The guidelines presented so far assume that you begin saving at age 25 and save consistently to age 66. If you're getting started late, have a steep income trajectory, or haven't been consistent with your savings, you'll need to look at adjustments to your savings rate.

Starting Later

Starting early is important. For example, Figure 3 shows the increases in savings rate required for 40% income replacement rate if you delay starting your savings by five and ten years. If you begin saving at age 35, to have a 90% chance of success you should consider increasing your saving rate from 13% to 19%.

SUCCESS PROBABILITY	START AT 25	START AT 30	START AT 35
95%	16.8%	19.5%	23.8%
90%	13.2%	15.4%	19.2%
50%	5.2%	6.4%	8.7%

Figure 3

Steep Income Trajectory

Steep income trajectories are common in the technology industries. The guidelines from the first savings rate table above may need adjusting if your income climbs quickly over your working career. The path your income takes over your career matters when saving for retirement. If you have a steep income trajectory, you will not have as much income initially and will not be able to save much early in your career relative to your needs at retirement. Late in your career, as your income increases quickly, even saving a larger amount (but at the same rate) won't give you enough time to grow your savings to meet your replacement income needs.

A set of reasonable guidelines for adjusting to a steep income trajectory involves increasing the amount you save as your income increases. For example (see Figure 4 on the next page), as you begin your career earning $50,000 to $60,000 per year, you should consider saving about 9% of your income to achieve a 40% income replacement ratio at retirement with 90% chance of success. As you cross over the $100,000 per year income boundary, your savings rate should be closer to 18%. At over $180,000 per year, you should be saving 26% or more to have a 90% chance of success. Your saving rate should increase with your income if you have a steep income trajectory over your working career.

INCOME RANGE ($, LOW–HIGH)	SUCCESS PROBABILITY		
	95%	90%	50%
≤ 25,000	2.8%	2.2%	0.9%
25,001 – 40,000	5.7%	4.4%	1.7%
40,001 – 50,000	8.5%	6.6%	2.6%
50,001 – 60,000	11.3%	8.8%	3.5%
60,001 – 70,000	14.2%	11.0%	4.4%
70,001 – 85,000	17.0%	13.2%	5.2%
85,001 – 100,000	19.8%	15.4%	6.1%
100,001 – 130,000	22.6%	17.6%	7.0%
130,001 – 180,000	30.6%	23.7%	9.4%
> 180,000	34.0%	26.4%	10.5%

Figure 4

Checking Progress

A useful measure to check your progress with savings is the total net assets you have accumulated divided by your income. Net assets means the value of your savings and investment accounts minus any loans related to those investments. For this calculation, include only savings and investments that will be available to meet your retirement income replacement goal. For example, do not include home equity (value of your home minus your home loan) unless you plan to sell your home and include the sale proceeds in your investment portfolio.

Use Figure 5 below to determine whether you need to consider adjusting your saving rate up or down based on the amount of your accumulated assets. The figure shows adjustments needed to target a 40% income replacement ratio and 90% success probability. For example, a 45-year-old should have net assets equal to 3.75 times his income. If his assets-to-income ratio is only 3.5, he should increase his saving rate by 1% to get back on track. Similarly, if a 55-year-old has accumulated net assets equal to 7.75 times her income, she can reduce her savings rate by 1%.

CHANGE IN SAVING RATE	AGE 35	AGE 45	AGE 55
Increase 1%	0.75	3.50	7.30
On track: no change	1.00	3.75	7.50
Decrease 1%	1.25	3.90	7.75

Figure 5

While the guidelines above are more useful than simple rules of thumb, they are guidelines only. They will not apply to all people in all situations. The most complete and accurate way to determine your individual required saving rate is using detailed financial modeling.

Savings Goals

Now that we've covered how much to save and why it's important, we will look at which accounts to use for saving in what order.

With so many different types of bank, brokerage, and retirement accounts, it can be difficult to understand where to save. Figure 6 provides a list of savings goals and the type of account you can use to save for that goal, listed approximately in the order you would use them for saving. The last column includes a suggestion for the type of investments that are appropriate for that goal and account type.

SAVINGS GOAL	ACCOUNT TYPE	SUGGESTED INVESTMENTS
Emergency	Bank or taxable brokerage	Cash or money market mutual fund
Major purchase	Bank or taxable brokerage	Short-term, high quality bond fund
Retirement	Employer retirement plan (e.g., 401(k), 403(b), 457)	Diversified portfolio of mutual funds
Retirement	IRA, Roth IRA, SEP IRA or other individual retirement account depending on income and other qualifying criteria	Diversified portfolio
Retirement	Taxable brokerage	Diversified portfolio
College	529 educational savings	Diversified portfolio with static or age-based investment allocation
Charity	Donor-advised fund	Diversified portfolio of mutual funds

Figure 6

The order of saving types in the table will work for many people. However, you will want to adjust the order to your particular circumstances. Also, the table suggests filling accounts in order from top to bottom. In reality, you will probably be saving for two or more savings goals at the same time and therefore contributing to two or more types of accounts at the same time.

Briefly, let's review each saving goal and account type in Figure 6.

- **Emergency reserves**. To provide ready cash in the event of emergencies, most financial experts recommend keeping a minimum of three to six months' worth of living expenses in cash. Cash can be held in a bank checking or savings account, or in a taxable brokerage account or money market mutual fund or similar investment. Certificates of Deposit (CDs) are not recommended for emergency reserves because you cannot withdrawal cash before a CD matures without paying early withdrawal penalties.
- **Major purchase**. If you're planning for a major purchase, such as a car or a home, you will want to prioritize this saving after emergency reserves and before retirement saving. You might be saving in this category for months to years. You can save in a bank checking or savings account, or taxable brokerage account. If saving in a taxable brokerage account, a high quality (i.e., with a good credit rating), short-term bond mutual fund can allow you to earn modest interest without taking stock market risk.
- **Retirement**. For people with access to an employer group retirement plan such as 401(k), 403(b) or 457, these types of plans allow employees to make pre-tax

contributions, which can reduce taxes and have larger contribution limits than most other types of retirement accounts. If you do not have access to an employer group retirement plan, you'll save into one of the various types of individual retirement accounts (IRA) depending on your income and other limitations. After maxing out your contributions to an employer retirement plan or IRA, you contribute additional savings to a taxable brokerage account. With group retirement plans, you will have a preselected list of investment options. In an IRA or taxable brokerage account, you will have the option to invest in a wide variety of investments. In either case, building a well-diversified investment portfolio will help you reach your retirement savings goal. Investments are discussed further in Chapter 4.

- **College**. While you're saving for retirement, you might also begin saving for your kids' college education. Section 529 Educational Savings Plans are usually the best vehicle for college savings.

- **Charity**. Donor-advised funds are effective and popular accounts for charitable giving. Donor-advised funds are covered in detail in Chapter 11.

Two other potentially important means of saving are discussed in other places. Employee stock savings plans are described in Chapter 5. Deferred compensation plans, which some companies offer to select highly paid employees, are discussed as a tax deferral technique in Chapter 8.

Saving in 401(k) Accounts

As of March 31, 2018, Americans held $5.3 trillion in 401(k) plans.[12] Except at the newest and smallest startup firms, most employees working for technology companies have access to a 401(k) plan at work. For most people working in technology, their company 401(k) plan will be the most important retirement account for reducing taxes and saving the most money in a tax advantaged account. People sometimes forget that saving to a 401(k) plan counts toward their overall saving goal, so be sure to give yourself credit for saving to this important vehicle. Because most people working in technology industries are eligible for and contribute to a 401(k) plan, this section provides extra detail about using and investing in 401(k) accounts.

401(k) accounts take their confusing name from the code section of the 1978 law that created them: Internal Revenue Code Section 401(k). The rules for using them might seem just as confusing at first.

Pre-tax Contributions and Tax-Deferred Growth

Traditional 401(k) plans allow you to contribute salary or wages into the plan on a pre-tax basis. Your income is reduced by the amount you contribute, and the income tax on your contribution is deferred until you take money out of the plan.

Your contributions to the 401(k) plan then grow tax-deferred, meaning that income tax on earnings in the account is not paid until you withdraw money in retirement. The lack of income tax on investment earnings allows the account value to grow faster than it would if your contributions were invested in a taxable investment account.

Contribution Limits of a 401(k)

There are limits on how much you can contribute to your 401(k) plan. The limits increase periodically for cost-of-living adjustments. For 2018, the annual contribution limit was $18,500 (but not more than 100% of your compensation). If you are 50 or older, you may also make "catch-up" contributions. For 2018, that catch-up limit was $6,000, bringing the total contribution that you can make to $24,500 (and, again, you cannot contribute more than your earnings).

Withdrawals / Distributions from a 401(k)

When you withdraw money from your 401(k) plan, you take a "distribution." Distributions are treated as taxable income to you in the year they are made. For example, if you withdraw $10,000 from your 401(k) account, you add $10,000 to your taxable income in that year.

Distributions are taxed at ordinary income tax rates (not capital gains tax rates), which for many people are lower in retirement than during their career's peak income years. The idea is that by contributing to a 401(k), you defer income until retirement when tax can be paid at lower rates. If you have negative taxable income in retirement—for example, because of mortgage interest and property tax deductions—you may be able to take distributions without paying any income tax at all.

There are two important rules to remember for withdrawals from your 401(k) plan:

1. If you withdraw from your account before you turn 59 and six months, you will pay a penalty equal to 10% of the amount you withdraw, in addition to the income tax on the amount you withdraw. The intent of this rule is to discourage you from using 401(k) funds before you reach retirement age. There are two exceptions to the early withdrawal penalty:

Age 55 Rule, which allows you to take distributions starting at age 55 in certain circumstances.[13] [14]

Rule 72(t), which allows for early distributions if they are part of a series of "substantially equal periodic payments" over your life expectancy and if they begin after you terminate employment.[15]

2. The second rule to remember is that you must begin taking distributions from your account by April 1 of the year following either the calendar year you reach the age of 70 and six months or the year you retire, whichever is later. For example, if you continued working until age 73, your required distributions would start after that, not at age 70 and a half. Once you begin taking required distributions, you must take distributions by December 31 each year thereafter. The so-called "required minimum distribution" (RMD) for the current tax year is determined by dividing your account balance on December 31 of the previous tax year by a number from an Internal Revenue Service (IRS) table that considers life expectancy. The logic behind this rule is to force you to take money out of your account and pay income tax on the withdrawn amounts. The penalties for not taking required minimum distributions are severe. If you fail to withdraw a

RMD, fail to withdraw the full amount of the RMD, or fail to withdraw the RMD by the deadline, the amount not withdrawn is taxed at 50%.

Borrowing from a 401(k)

You may be able to borrow money from your 401(k) plan; however, that is usually not a good idea. IRS rules allow borrowing, but your specific 401(k) may not. The maximum amount you can borrow per IRS rules is (1) the greater of $10,000 or 50% of your account balance, or (2) $50,000, whichever is less. Generally, you may borrow up to half of your account balance up to a maximum of $50,000. Your specific 401(k) plan may not allow you to borrow the maximum amount allowed by the IRS.

One significant problem with borrowing from your 401(k) account is that if you leave the company for any reason, you must pay back your entire 401(k) loan within a short time. The repayment deadline is your tax filing due date, including extensions for the year in which you terminated employment. If you cannot pay back the loan, the amount you borrowed will be treated as a distribution and you will pay income tax on that amount at ordinary income tax rates. You also will pay the 10% early withdrawal penalty if you are not at least 59 and six months old.

401(k) Contributions

Generally, you should contribute the maximum amount to your 401(k) account that your cash flow allows, up to your required savings rate, taking into account your other saving goals. Contributions to a 401(k) plan can significantly reduce your taxable income and save you taxes.

Here is an example:

A middle-aged married couple from California has household taxable income of $200,000 and files a joint tax return.

Taxable income:	$200,000
401(k) contribution:	$18,500 (maximum amount allowed, made by **one** of the couple)
Federal income tax bracket:	24%
California income tax bracket:	9.3%
Taxable income after 401(k) contribution:	**$200,000 - $18,500 = $181,500**
Federal tax saving:	$18,500 x 24% = $4,440
California tax saving:	$18,500 x 9.3% = $1,720
Total tax savings:	**= $6,160**
Net cash 401(k) contribution:	$18,500 - $6,160 **= $12,340**

Because the 401(k) contribution reduces the couple's income tax, the contribution actually "costs" the couple $12,340 instead of $18,500. The couple could save more if the other spouse had also contributed to a 401(k) plan.

The tax saving is an important aspect of 401(k) plans that many people don't consider: the actual cash you must contribute will be less than you think because of tax savings in the current year. This can allow you to contribute and save more than you might otherwise realize you would be able to.

Employer Match Contributions

Whether your employer's 401(k) plan has a matching contribution is also an important consideration in deciding how much to contribute. Some employers offer to match a portion of employee contributions as part of their overall benefits package. If your company offers a match, as a general rule you should contribute at least enough to receive your employer's full matching contribution. The matching contribution is "free" money, and contributing enough to receive the entire match is equivalent to giving yourself a pay raise. The only drawback to this free money is that you won't be able to withdraw it from your 401(k) account without penalty until you reach 59 and six months.

There are many formulas in use to calculate employer matching contributions. One common formula matches an employee's contribution up to a percentage of the employee's compensation. For example, one well-known tech giant's 401(k) plan has a generous match equal to 100% of an employee's contribution up to 6% of compensation.

Matching formulas may even have multiple tiers, which can be confusing. Here's an example of a two-tier matching formula:

Compensation:	$100,000
Employee contribution:	$18,500
Employer matching contribution:	100% on first 3% of employee compensation: 100% x 3% x $100,000 = $3,000 50% on next 2%: 50% x 2% x $100,000 = $1,000 Total employer matching contribution: $4,000
Total employee and employer contribution:	$22,500

As long as this employee contributed 5% of their compensation to their 401(k) plan, they would receive a total match of 4%. This is an example of a "stretch match" formula designed to encourage employees to contribute more to their 401(k) plan. To receive the full $4,000 of "free" money, this employee must contribute $5,000 to their 401(k) plan. Said another way, by contributing enough to earn the matching contribution, this employee earns an 80% return on their contribution each year, risk-free.

Employee contributions to a 401(k) plan are always vested immediately. That means that the money you contribute is yours. Employer contributions that are so-called "safe-harbor" matching contributions are also vested immediately. Certain employer contributions such as discretionary profit-sharing contributions may be subject to a vesting schedule and only become yours over time.

401(k) Investment Options

Your 401(k) plan will provide a set of investments to choose from. The number of investment choices in a typical 401(k) plan is about 20 to 30, which is usually enough to build a well-diversified portfolio without being overwhelming.

The investment options are most often a list of publicly traded mutual funds, which you can research within your 401(k) website or by using publicly available information from financial information providers such as Morningstar.com. You will need to select a number of investments from the list of choices and decide what amount to invest in each. The amounts to invest are usually entered online by specifying a percentage of the total. In addition to publicly traded mutual funds, 401(k) plans can include other types of investment options.

1. Your investment options might also include less well-known collective investment trusts (CITs), which are becoming more prevalent. CITs are private pooled investments and are more difficult to research because they are not publicly traded. Select from among CITs just as you would select among publicly traded mutual funds.

2. Your 401(k) plan's investment options might include a selection of "target date" mutual funds. Target date mutual funds often include a number in their name that represents the year in which you plan to retire. For example, Vanguard's Institutional Target Retirement 2030 Fund (ticker: VTTWX) might be used by people who plan to retire in 2030. Target date funds create a complete portfolio of investments for you within a single mutual fund. The mix of investments inside a target date mutual fund adjusts over time to make it less risky as you get closer to retirement. Even though you are selecting only one mutual fund, you will have a well-diversified portfolio inside of that mutual fund. There is no need to select additional mutual funds to get more diversification.

3. Your 401(k) plan's investment options may also include complete portfolios whose internal investments do not change over time. These options are often referred to as "static risk" options. For example, a model portfolio might be made up 80% of stock mutual funds and 20% of bond mutual funds. It would maintain this split between stocks and bonds over time.

Expense Ratios and Rebalancing 401(k) Investments

No discussion of 401(k) plan investment options is complete without covering expense ratios. The expense ratio of a mutual fund or CIT is an annual fee charged to investors expressed as a percentage of the total assets of the fund. For example, the average expense ratio for stock mutual funds in the U.S. during 2017 was 1.25%.[16] The expense ratio is the percentage of a mutual fund or CIT's assets used to pay for the internal costs of operating the fund, such as interest expense, operating expenses, and management fees. The expense ratio does not include any transaction fees for buying and selling the mutual fund or any initial or deferred sales charges (i.e., "loads").

Expense ratios are a direct subtraction from the return you earn on your mutual fund or CIT investment. For example, if you selected a mutual fund for your 401(k) account that earned a 10% return during the past year and that mutual fund had a 1% expense ratio, then the return you earned was actually only 9%. All else being equal, you should select investments for your 401(k) with the lowest expense ratios.

Once you've selected the percentages of each investment option for your portfolio, you will need to ensure your investments continue to match those percentages over time. You may be offered the option to set a rebalancing frequency. Rebalancing is the process of buying or selling some of each of your investment options to restore them to their original percentage of your account balance. Many 401(k) plan websites offer rebalancing frequencies of annually, semiannually, and quarterly. If there are no transaction costs, selecting the most frequent rebalancing option is preferred. More frequent rebalancing keeps your investments closer to the percentages you have selected. If your 401(k) plan website does not offer an automatic rebalancing option, you will need to rebalance your 401(k) investments manually at least once per year.

401(k) Account Beneficiaries

Your 401(k) plan beneficiaries are the people who will receive your 401(k) account in the event of your death. If you do not select a beneficiary, the 401(k) plan document will determine whether your account will be paid to your estate or to a default beneficiary such as your spouse if your spouse survives you. To ensure that your 401(k) goes to the people you want it to go to in the event of your death, designate a beneficiary or beneficiaries for your account. This is usually done online on the 401(k) plan website or by paper form held on file by the employer. Along with beneficiaries, you often have the option to name contingent beneficiaries in the event the primary designated beneficiaries unexpectedly pass away.

Leaving Your Employer: 401(k) Options

Once you terminate employment with a company where you participated in the 401(k) retirement plan, you have four options available for your old 401(k) account:

- Leave it in the former employer's 401(k) plan
- Roll it over to a new employer's 401(k) plan
- Roll it over to an individual retirement account (IRA)
- Take a distribution

There are pros and cons to each of the four options, depending on your circumstances.

Leave Your 401(k) Account Where It Is

The default option is to leave your money in your former employer's 401(k) plan. If you take no action, your money will remain in your old account, invested in the investment choices you previously selected. You won't be able to make any more contributions to the 401(k) account, but your savings can continue to grow. The primary benefit of this option is that it requires no effort.

Employers incur costs in operating 401(k) plans, and often those costs are passed on to 401(k) plan participants as higher expense ratios on investment choices or fees charged directly to individual participant accounts. Employers decide how much of the cost of operating their 401(k) plan they pay and how much they pass on to participants. If your former employer passes on most of the cost of operating the plan, then the mutual fund expense ratios or account fees in that plan may be high. In that case, you may find it worthwhile to consider other options for your 401(k) account. The amount you pay in fees and costs is disclosed to you in a Participant Disclosure, sometimes also called by its Department of Labor regulation number a 404a-5 disclosure. You can also ask your 401(k) plan administrator about the amount of cost born by the company and employees enrolled in the 401(k) plan.

Another potential downside is that you may simply lose track of the account and fail to pay proper attention to it. If you've lost track of a 401(k) account, call or email your former employer to get your statement delivery restarted or get online access to your account. Even though you are no longer contributing to the account, you need to review the investments at least once a year and preferably two to three times per year.

Rollover to a New 401(k) Plan

A rollover is the process of transferring the balance of your account by carefully following IRS rules that allow the money in your account to maintain tax-deferred status and not inadvertently triggering income tax and early withdrawal penalties on the amount transferred.

Rolling over old accounts to your new employer's 401(k) plan is an effective way to consolidate accounts and keep all of your employer retirement plan money in one place. However, not all plans accept rollover transfers from other 401(k) plans. Confirm with your new employer that their plan accepts rollovers before using this option.

There are reasons you may not want to consolidate accounts, and they relate mostly to the quality of the new plan compared with the old plan. High-quality 401(k) plans offer a full list of investment choices, allowing you to create a portfolio diversified across the major asset classes at low total cost to you. If your new employer's plan is of higher quality, then rolling over old accounts to consolidate them in your new employer's 401(k) plan could be a good option. For example, if the dollar weighted average expense ratio of your investment portfolio is lower in the new plan than in the old plan, then moving to the new plan is worth serious consideration.

Rollover to an IRA

A popular option for old 401(k) accounts is a rollover to an Individual Retirement Account (IRA). As with rollovers to a new employer 401(k) plan, IRA rollovers involve transferring your old 401(k) account balance by carefully following IRS rules to maintain the tax-deferred status of the amount transferred. An IRA can be used to collect and consolidate all of your old 401(k) accounts.

One main advantage of rolling over an old 401(k) to an IRA is the many more investment choices available, particularly for IRAs held at investment brokerage firms such as Fidelity, Charles Schwab, or TD Ameritrade. In an IRA, you can choose from individual stocks, bonds, mutual funds, exchanged-traded funds (ETFs) and others—most of the securities traded on U.S. exchanges—and you are not limited to the 20 to 40 investment choices, typically mutual funds, commonly found in 401(k) plans. The cost of managing your investments in an IRA can often be less than the costs your investments will bear in an employer-sponsored 401(k) plan.

There is an important limitation of IRAs in protection from creditors. Unlike 401(k) accounts, which are protected from creditors under the Employee Retirement Income Security Act (ERISA) of 1974, IRAs may receive only partial protection depending on the state in which you live. In California, for example, IRA assets are protected from creditors only up to the amount needed for your support in retirement considering all of your resources likely to be available as determined by the court. If you work in an occupation that puts you at higher risk of being sued, the creditor protection of a 401(k) account may be an important consideration in deciding whether to roll over your 401(k) to an IRA.[17]

Take a Distribution

A fourth option for your old 401(k) account is withdrawal of funds from your account. This option has clear disadvantages. The distribution is taxable income to you in the year of the distribution (assuming your contributions were pre-tax). This income is taxed at your ordinary income tax rates. Usually, if you are younger than 59 and six months, you will also pay a 10% early withdrawal penalty.

Generally, distributions should be carefully planned and taken only in your retirement years, when you will likely be in a lower income tax bracket than during your working years. Taking a distribution of your entire account balance before retirement is recommended only in the most desperate circumstances.

Saving for College: 529 Plan

The cost of a college education today is truly shocking. The full cost of tuition, room and board, books, fees, and a modest amount of personal expense tops out at about $70,000 per year for the nation's top private colleges and universities. According to the College Board, a moderate budget for in-state residents at four-year public universities for the 2017–18 school year averaged $25,290. In the popular University of California system, full cost for in-state students is about $35,000 for the 2018–2019 school year.

Not only are college costs high, they are growing faster than the prices of most other goods and services in the U.S. economy. Over the last decade, college costs have increased at roughly 5% per year, whereas the general level of price inflation as measured by the Consumer Price Index (CPI) has been well below 2%, and there is no indication that the rate of increase is slowing. Perhaps online education will one day help reign in college costs, but for now the residential model of higher education is still firmly entrenched.

Few families are able to pay the cost of college out of their current income, especially with multiple kids in college at the same time. Most families will need to save for years ahead of time to pay for their kids' college education. Section 529 College Savings Plans are the savings vehicle of choice for most families. A 529 plan allows you to contribute funds after tax, and your money will grow tax free as long as it's used for "qualified educational expenses," which include tuition, room and board, books, and other college costs. There are many online resources with information about 529 college savings plans and how to use them.[18]

Because college is so expensive and financial resources are not unlimited, some families will need to prioritize how much they save for college and how much they save for retirement. Some parents set a limit on the amount they will fund for college and expect their kids to get loans for any balance. Other families make a conscience choice to sacrifice—for example, delaying retirement—in order to fully fund college education for their children. Resolving potential conflict between funding these two important financial goals is highly personal and your decision should be made thoughtfully.

If your family income is well into six figures and your assets are typical for that income level, you probably will not qualify for financial aid. Financial aid formulas used by colleges are complicated and depend on a number of factors including income, assets, number of kids in college, cost of the college, age of the parents, and total family size. While there are no specific income or asset cut-offs for need-based financial aid, a family with income in the $150,000 to $200,000 range, typical assets and one child in college probably will not qualify for need-based financial aid, except perhaps at the most expensive colleges. Even if you don't expect to qualify for need-based financial aid, you should still consider completing the financial aid application forms to get access to student loan programs. Also, some colleges and universities require completion of financial aid forms to be considered for merit scholarships (as opposed to need-based scholarships).

Summary

- Compare your assets-to-income ratio and current savings rate using the guidelines in this chapter for a quick assessment of whether you are on track with your saving.
- Review the recommended order of savings, and accounts types to use, for various goals including emergency fund, major purchase, retirement, college, and charity.
- Contribute the maximum amount your cash flow allows to your employer's 401(k) retirement plan and review your investments at least once per year.
- Consolidate 401(k) plans from former employers to make ongoing management easier.
- Use Section 529 College Savings Plans to save for kids' college education.

Saving is the starting point for accumulating assets to your net worth. The next step in building net worth is to grow your savings. We look at that next in the chapter on investments.

4

Invest for
Financial Success

nvestors today have a bewildering choice of investment options. In the U.S., there are approximately 4,000 companies whose stock trades on major securities exchanges, and outside the U.S., there are approximately 39,000 additional publicly traded companies.[1] In the U.S. bond market, which has a total value about 40% greater than the U.S. stock market, there are over 11,500 different corporate and government bonds that can be bought and sold.[2] Internationally, there are another 9,000 government and corporate bonds. Those are just the individual securities available to investors. At the end of 2017, there were also over 8,500 mutual funds (excluding different share classes) and over 1,800 exchange-traded funds (ETFs) offered by U.S. investment companies.[3]

Given the vast amount of choice, it is nearly impossible to invest successfully to meet your financial goals if you don't have a framework for categorizing, sorting, screening, evaluating, and selecting investment opportunities. There are many approaches to investing, and any number of them might work for you. The approach presented here is used every day by a large number of institutional and professional investment advisors to help families and individuals successfully protect and grow their wealth.

Purpose of Investing

The purpose of investing is not to *create* wealth. Tech start-ups and other risky ventures, building a small business, saving a large portion of your income each year—those are ways you *create* wealth. In contrast, investing is the process of protecting and growing the wealth *you have already created or saved*. However, that doesn't mean the wealth you can generate from investments is not substantial, because it is.

Investing is not a get rich quick scheme. And investing is not the same as speculating. It is not gambling. It is not exciting.

Your investments are not how you plan to grow wealth quickly by making exotic bets. Rather, investing is a mundane process with many detailed steps carried out consistently over decades to keep your money safe and to grow it so that the magic of compounding can do its work.

A disciplined investment process both protects and grows your wealth. For example, incorporating stocks into your investment portfolio allows you to earn higher rates of return than investing in bonds alone, while providing protection against inflation. Investing in a mixture of stocks from many companies, instead of just a few, allows you to earn the high rates of return available to stock without taking the risk of losing a substantial amount of your money if one of the companies you invested in goes bankrupt or has a bad earnings announcement.

To use a sports analogy, grow and protect is like offense and defense—both are required to win a game. Or to use a product development analogy, grow and protect is like adding new features to attract new customers while keeping the existing customer-base happy with product enhancements and bug fixes.

Investing Overview

Exponential Growth and Power of Compounding

One of the most astounding things about investing is how fast money can grow over time. Money grows exponentially, which mathematically means raised to a power. The formula for how fast a lump sum of money can grow is this:

FV=PV × (1+r)ⁿ

FV=Future value
PV=Present value
r=rate of return
n=number of periods

This formula says that the value of an investment in the future equals its value now, multiplied by one plus the investment's rate of return, over the time the money will be invested. For example, if you invest $100,000 at 8% for 30 years, the money grows to $1,006,266. Over 30 years you would earn $906,266 on a $100,000 investment.

The formula for how fast an amount of money *invested regularly* can grow is this:

FV=P[(1+r)ⁿ-1)/r]

FV=Future value
P=Periodic payment
r=rate of return
n=number of periods

For example, if you invest $9,000 (P) per year for 30 years (n) earning 8% per year (r), your investment will grow to $1,019,549 (FV). Over 30 years, you would earn $749,549 on a $270,000 investment.

Rule of 72

Another useful tip for thinking about how fast your money can grow is to use the Rule of 72. This is a quick way to estimate how long it will take for your money to double if you earn a fixed rate of return for the whole period.

To use the Rule of 72, divide the annual rate of return your investment earns into the number 72. The answer is the number of years it takes for your investment to double. For example, if your investment earns an 8% return every year, then it will take 9 years for your investment to double in value (i.e., 72 ÷ 8 = 9). After another 9 years growing at 8% per year, your investment will double again.

The results from the formulas above and the Rule of 72 match what you would expect. The higher the rate of return you earn, the larger the ending balance. The longer you invest, the higher the ending balance. Time and rate of return are the two crucial variables.

Earn Returns by Providing Capital

Your money is a valuable and useful commodity, both to you (to use for paying living expenses) and to corporations and governments that need capital to fund their operations.

When you invest, you provide needed capital to companies in the U.S. and other countries, municipalities, state governments, the U.S. federal government (including its many agencies), and foreign governments. In order to entice investors to provide capital, corporations and governments must pay investors for the use of their money. What you are paid as an investor is the return you earn on your investment.

You might not have thought before about companies and governments having to pay for the use of the money, or capital, they use to fuel their growth and operations. At the most basic level, businesses and other organizations require two inputs to produce their goods and services. One input is labor and the other is capital. Naturally, a company or government must pay its employees to produce its goods and services. Similarly but less obviously, it must pay investors who provide it with capital, whether in the form of loans (bonds) or equity ownership (stock), by providing a rate of return on investors' investment. When you invest, you provide your money to companies and government entities who need capital. In exchange for proving capital they pay you by providing you with a return on your investment—you earn a return by providing capital.

The case of investing in bonds may be the easiest way to understand this. Suppose a corporation needs to borrow money for construction of a new factory. The corporation can sell bonds to investors to raise the cash it needs. The bonds represent a loan from the investors to the corporation. Investors can buy the bonds, paying cash to the corporation to use to build its factory. In exchange, the corporation agrees to pay back the bondholders the amount they paid for the bonds at the maturity date a fixed number of years in the future and to make interest payments on the outstanding bonds (loan) until that maturity date. By purchasing bonds, investors become creditors of the company (people the company owes money to).

Investors will only buy the bonds (i.e., loan the corporation money) if they are compensated for not having the use of their money and for taking risk in lending money, principally the risk that the corporation will not pay back the loan. The interest rate the corporation pays compensates the bondholders. The interest rate bondholders earn on their investment is their rate of return.

In the case of stocks, the linkage isn't as direct as with bonds but the idea is the same. Investors must be compensated for providing equity capital to a company. They must be compensated for not having the use of their money and for taking risk by investing in an enterprise with an uncertain future. When investors buy stock in a company, they pay cash for ownership of a fraction of the company. Ownership confers the right to receive future dividends and vote on company directors and other important matters.

Investors earn their return in the form of dividends paid by the company and in appreciation of its stock price. The company's stock price will appreciate if management makes good use of investor-provided capital to increase the earnings of the company. Increased earnings translate into higher stock price because the value of a company's stock is influenced by its future earnings.[4] An investor's rate of return is calculated using the dividends received and the appreciation in the stock price.

Asset Classes

While stocks, bonds, and cash are three main categories of investments, there are other investment categories and subcategories as well. Professional investors, financial economists, and the financial press call these categories "asset classes."

Asset classes are groups of investments with similar characteristics that behave similarly during changing economic and market conditions. Examples of asset classes are small stocks, large stocks, corporate bonds, government bonds, inflation protected bonds, international stocks, emerging markets stocks, and real estate. Each asset class has its risks and return potential.

Investment Performance Over Time

Reviewing historical investment performance can help you understand the range of investment returns that are possible for different asset classes. This helps keep your expectations about investment returns grounded in reality. An investment's return is the total of its dividends, interest income, realized gain when it is sold, and unrealized gain before it is sold. Investment returns are usually expressed as a percentage per year. For example, if a $1,000 investment returned $100 per year to its investor, it earns a 10% return per year.

Figure 7 below shows the performance of four traditional asset classes, including large stocks, small stocks, government bonds, and Treasury bills over the time period going back to just before the Great Depression. This is a recreation of a classic chart originally from Roger G. Ibbotson and Rex Sinquefield, and now Morningstar, which is updated annually.

Figure 7

Figure 7 shows the growth of a $1 invested in each asset class from January 1, 1926, through December 31, 2017—a period of 92 years. The chart also shows inflation over that period. [5]

Small stocks and large stocks show the greatest growth and have the highest returns. Small stocks earned 12.1% per year, and large stocks earned 10.2% per year over this period. Government bonds and Treasury bills show less growth, earning 5.5% and 3.4% per year respectively over this period.

Stocks achieved much higher growth than the fixed-income investments (government bonds and Treasury bills). However, they did so with much greater volatility, which is represented by the variation of the lines in the graph. Treasury bills are short-term loans made by investors to the U.S. government and are considered by most investors to be the safest investments in the world. There is little to no variation in the line for Treasury bills, demonstrating their low volatility. Government bonds, whose principal and interest are guaranteed by the U.S. government, also are considered safe investments and show minimal volatility. Stocks show the greatest variation indicating they have the most volatility, with smaller, riskier stocks showing the greatest volatility.

Inflation over the period was 2.9% per year. In terms of real purchasing power, subtracting inflation from each of the asset class returns, Treasury bills earned only 0.5% return, government bonds earned 2.6%, large stocks earned 7.3%, and small stocks earned 9.2%. Risky stocks did much better at outrunning inflation than the safer government bonds or Treasury bills.

In reviewing historical investment returns and the performance of your own portfolio, be aware that returns can be dramatically different over different time periods. For example, Figure 8 shows the annual returns, again for the same four asset classes, as of December 31, 2017, for the 92-year period beginning January 1, 1926; the most recent 20-year period beginning December 31, 1997; from October 7, 2007, at the top of the stock market before the Great Recession; and from March 9, 2009, at the bottom of the market during the Great Recession.

START DATE	1/1/1926	12/31/1997	10/7/2007	3/9/2009
Small stocks	12.1%	9.9%	8.4%	20.2%
Large stocks	10.2%	7.3%	7.9%	18.3%
Government bonds	5.5%	6.8%	6.6%	5.7%
Treasury bills	3.4%	1.9%	0.4%	0.2%
Inflation	2.9%	2.1%	1.7%	1.7%

Figure 8

Figure 9 below shows the historical performance for a few more asset classes commonly used to build investment portfolios, including international stocks, real estate, and commodities. Large U.S. stocks are included again for reference over this shorter period from 1980 to 2017.

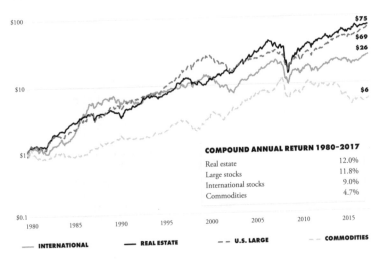

Figure 9

There is not as much historical data available for these asset classes, and the time period of the chart is shorter than for the first chart. Remember, returns can be much different over different time periods.[6]

Risk and Return

The performance charts above illustrate a fundamental concept in investing: risk and return are related. Asset classes with the most variation or volatility also earn higher returns over time. The riskier an investment is, the more investors demand to be compensated to take the risk and make the investment. That is why riskier asset classes are observed to earn higher investment returns on average over time.

For example, would you rather buy the bonds of Microsoft Corporation, one of two remaining companies in the U.S. carrying the highest available rating given by credit rating agencies (AAA), or a local small business whose owner has a bad credit score? Ignoring the size of the respective loans, clearly you would rather lend to Microsoft because you are much more likely to be paid back. If you *were* to lend to the small business, you would demand a higher interest rate to compensate you for the higher risk of not being paid back.

The same is true of investing in company stock. Since 1926, large companies have had an annualized rate of return of about 10.2% per year and small companies have had an annualized rate of return of about 12.1% per year. Investors require a higher rate of return to hold small company stock than large company stock due to the extra risk in investing in smaller companies.

Investment risk can impact your investments at the individual security level, asset class level and overall portfolio level. The volatility seen in investment returns is a result of various market, economic, and business risk factors. Here is a list of common factors you need to keep in mind when investing:

- **Interest-rate risk:** Fluctuations in interest rates may cause investment prices to fluctuate. For example, when interest rates rise, yields on existing bonds become less attractive, causing their market values to decline.
- **Market risk:** The price of a stock, bond, mutual fund or other security may drop in reaction to tangible and intangible events and conditions. This type of risk is caused by external factors independent of a company's particular underlying circumstances. For example, political, economic and social conditions may trigger market events.
- **Inflation risk:** When any type of inflation is present, a dollar today will not buy as much as a dollar next year, because purchasing power is eroding at the rate of inflation.
- **Currency risk:** Foreign investments are subject to fluctuations in the value of the dollar against the currency of the investment's originating country. This is also referred to as exchange rate risk.
- **Reinvestment risk:** This is the risk that future proceeds from investments may have to be reinvested at a potentially lower rate of return (i.e., interest rate). This primarily relates to bonds and other fixed income securities.
- **Business risk:** These risks are associated with a particular industry or company within an industry. For example, a biotechnology company applying for U.S. Food

and Drug Administration approval of a major new drug may not be profitable if the new drug is not approved—the company faces business-specific risk. The risk that online shopping poses to traditional store-based retail companies is an example of industry-specific risk.

- **Liquidity risk**: Liquidity is the ability to readily convert an investment into cash. Generally, assets are more liquid if many buyers are interested in purchasing the asset.

- **Financial risk**: Excessive borrowing to finance a business's operations increases the risk to profitability because the company must meet the terms of its obligations in good times and bad. During periods of financial stress, the inability to meet loan obligations may result in bankruptcy and/or a declining market value.

Asset Allocation

Different asset classes have varying investment performances during different economic and market conditions. For example, small U.S. stocks, real estate, and international bonds can behave differently in response to particular economic shocks, such as a sharp rise in inflation. In addition, asset class performance characteristics (risk and return) change over time. It is impossible to predict the performance of an asset class from year to year.

Figure 10 shows which asset classes had the best and worst performance over the last 15 years. Each box represents an asset class and its annual return for the year. The performance of an asset class can change drastically both in terms of its performance for the year and its performance compared to other asset classes. For example, real estate investment trusts (REITs) were the top performing asset class in 2014 and 2015, but the returns in each of those years were dramatically different at 32.0% and 4.5%, respectively. In 2017, real estate dropped toward the bottom of all asset classes with a return of 3.8% while emerging markets stocks had the best performance with an annual return of 37.3%.

ASSET CLASS RETURNS																
INDEX	ASSET CLASS	2003	2004	2005	2006	2007	2008	2009	2010	2011	2012	2013	2014	2015	2016	2017
S&P 500	U.S. Large	55.8	33.2	34.0	36.0	39.4	11.4	78.5	28.1	9.4	18.2	38.8	32.0	4.5	21.3	37.3
Russell 2000	U.S. Small	47.3	25.6	13.8	32.1	11.2	2.1	31.8	26.9	6.6	17.3	32.4	13.7	1.4	12.0	25.0
MSCI EAFE	International	38.6	20.2	13.5	26.3	8.8	-2.8	28.5	18.9	5.4	17.1	22.8	4.9	1.2	11.2	21.8
MSCI Emerging Markets	Emerging Markets	36.2	18.3	4.9	18.4	5.6	-33.8	27.2	15.1	2.1	16.3	1.2	4.2	0.9	6.7	14.6
DJ U.S. Select REIT	U.S. REIT	28.7	10.9	4.6	15.8	5.5	-37.0	26.5	7.8	0.1	16.0	0.0	2.6	0.0	3.7	3.8
Barclays Capital Treasury Int.	Int. Term Gov't	6.9	4.1	2.9	4.7	4.9	-39.2	15.9	7.8	-4.2	8.1	-0.2	0.0	-0.8	1.1	3.7
Barclays Capital Credit Int.	Int. Term Corps	2.1	2.0	1.6	4.5	-1.6	-43.4	0.2	5.3	-12.1	1.7	-1.3	-2.2	-4.4	1.0	1.1
3-Month Treasury Bill	Cash	1.1	1.1	1.4	3.5	-17.6	-53.3	-1.4	0.1	-18.4	0.1	-2.6	-4.9	-14.9	0.2	0.7

Figure 10

Diversification of Assets

Diversifying your investment portfolio by incorporating multiple asset classes makes your portfolio less susceptible to the wide swings in performance of individual asset classes. Asset classes' individual up-and-down performance will tend to offset each other, reducing your portfolio's overall volatility. The process of combining asset classes in different proportions to create diversified portfolios is called "asset allocation."

Financial professionals who design asset allocations typically begin by selecting the percentage of stocks and bonds in an asset allocation. For example, an asset allocation might include 70% stocks and 30% bonds. The amount of safe bonds compared to the amount of riskier stock is the primary determinant of a portfolio's level of risk and the volatility that someone investing in a portfolio with that asset allocation would expect to experience.

After deciding on the amount of stocks and bonds, asset allocation designers decide how much of the stock portion of the portfolio should be invested in U.S. stock and how much should be invested in international stocks. Within international stocks, asset allocation designers decide how much should be invested in developed countries such as Japan, the United Kingdom, Canada, France, and Germany and how much should be invested in emerging market countries such as China, India, Brazil, and Russia. For U.S. investors, an allocation of 20%–40% of the overall stock portion to international stock is typical.

Within the bond portion of an investment portfolio, the asset allocation can be further broken down to government bonds and corporate bonds, and possibly include inflation-protected bonds or the bonds of international companies or governments.

The asset allocations above include asset classes that are considered traditional asset classes. Asset allocations can also include the following alternative classes:

- Real estate
- Private equity
- Venture capital
- Commodities and managed futures

Real estate in the form of publicly traded REITs is easy for individual investors to include in their investment portfolios. The other alternative asset classes typically are comprised of private securities (non-publicly traded) that have purchase restrictions and are more difficult to include.

Combining asset classes to create an asset allocation is part science and part art. In theory, there is an optimal combination of asset classes, which in correct proportion produces an investment portfolio with the maximum amount of return for a given level of risk, or alternatively the least amount of risk for the return sought. This technique, known as "mean-variance optimization," is the foundation of Modern Portfolio Theory for which Harry Markowitz won the Nobel Prize in Economics in 1952. That's the science part. In practice, using mean-variance optimization requires estimating, from historical data, the future returns and standard deviations for asset classes, and measuring how their performance moves together ("covariance"). The interpretation of that historical data and incorporating it into an asset allocation is the art.

Figure 11 illustrates sample asset allocations produced using the process described above. There are a virtually unlimited number of such asset class combinations. Asset allocations are available from the research departments of brokerage firms and investment product providers, subscription services, qualified investment advisors, and books written by respected experts in this area. While asset allocations are available from internet blogs and articles, as well as print magazines, be careful to use only asset allocations created by reputable organizations and qualified individuals.

ASSET CLASSES	ASSET ALLOCATIONS					
	50/50	60/40	70/30	80/20	90/10	100/0
Large stocks	19.5%	23.4%	27.1%	30.8%	34.5%	38.1%
Small stocks	9.7%	11.7%	13.5%	15.4%	17.2%	19.1%
International stocks	11.3%	13.5%	15.6%	17.8%	19.9%	22.0%
Emerging markets	4.5%	5.4%	6.3%	7.1%	8.0%	8.8%
Real estate	5.0%	6.0%	7.5%	9.0%	10.5%	12.0%
Corporate bonds	25.0%	20.0%	15.0%	10.0%	5.0%	0.0%
Government bonds	25.0%	20.0%	15.0%	10.0%	5.0%	0.0%

Figure 11

Performance of Portfolios

Asset allocation is an important determinant of portfolio performance. The question of how important has been an important debate in the investment management community for decades.[7]

The answer is that it depends on your investment management style.

For portfolios managed using a fixed asset allocation and implemented with index mutual funds or exchange-traded funds, as described and recommend below, asset allocation is the most important factor. For portfolios managed using some form of active management, such as variable asset allocation, security selection, or market timing, the amount of those activities determines their impact on performance.

Figure 12 below shows the performance of five hypothetical portfolios. The portfolios increase in risk as the percentage of stock increases. For example, the portfolio with 75% stocks and 25% bonds ("75/25") is riskier than the portfolio with 50% stocks and 50% bonds ("50/50"). Notice that the return of the portfolios over this time period increases with the portion of stock in the portfolio. For example, the 75/25 portfolio earned 8.5% annual return, while the 50/50 portfolio earned 7.5% annual return. However, during the Great Recession market downturn from 2007 to 2009, the 50/50 portfolio lost only 31% of its value while the 75/25 stock portfolio lost 47% of its value. The relation of risk and return applies to portfolios as well as asset classes. Over a sufficiently long period of time, riskier portfolios holding more stock have historically earned higher returns.

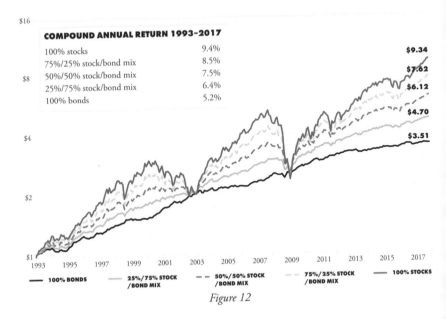

Figure 12

Besides increasing the portion of stock (and decreasing the portion of bonds) held in an investment portfolio to increase its risk and return, including a larger portion small stocks in an investment portfolio will typically increase the portfolio's overall risk and increase the return it can be expected to earn over a long time period. A best practice is to use a judicious combination of small, mid-sized, and large company stock in an investment portfolio.

There is another segmentation of stock investments that tech professionals need to be aware of. Stocks can be separated into two groups: growth stocks and value stocks. Growth stocks are stocks of companies that investors perceive as having a high growth rate. Growth stocks are identified as companies whose shares have a high price-to-earnings ratio and a high price-to-book value ratio. Most tech stocks fall in the growth stock category, and growth stock indices tend to be dominated by technology stocks. For example, the top five companies in the Russell 1000 Growth Index, a group of large U.S. growth stocks, as of 2018 are Apple, Microsoft, Amazon, Facebook, and Alphabet (parent company of Google).

Value stocks are stocks of companies that have a low price compared to their underlying value and are identified as companies whose shares have a low price-to-book value ratio. Value stocks tend to come from industry sectors other than technology such as financial services, energy, utilities, and consumer products. The top five companies in the Russell 1000 Value Index, a group of large U.S. value stocks, as of 2018 are Berkshire Hathaway, JP Morgan Chase, Exxon Mobile, Johnson & Johnson, and Bank of America.

Historically, value stocks have earned higher investment returns than growth stocks both in the U.S. and internationally, and across the company-size spectrum. U.S. large-value stocks have earned an annualized return 2.1% greater than the return for large growth stocks over the time period since 1928.[8] U.S. small value stocks have earned an annualized return 4.5% greater than the return for small growth stocks over the same time period. Similar differences in returns are seen for stocks from developed countries and emerging markets countries. Tilting your asset allocation to include more value stocks may increase your portfolio's return.

The performance of growth and value stocks goes through cycles. During one period of time, growth can be outperforming value; during another period of time, value can be outperforming growth. These cycles can last several years. Because most tech professionals work for growth companies, their equity compensation, bonus, and salary can be closely tied to the economic performance of the tech sector and growth companies. With so much of their income and net worth linked to growth companies, tech professionals may benefit from tilting their investment portfolio toward value companies to diversify away from growth company risk. Adding a value tilt can serve to increase long-term investment return and counterbalance the cyclical growth company risk inherent in having compensation tied to a technology company and industry.

Selecting an Asset Allocation

Selecting an asset allocation for your investment portfolio requires balancing your rate of return requirements with your ability and willingness to bear risk. Ability to take risk relates to the overall strength or your financial situation. Willingness is more subjective and relates to your feelings about investment risk.

Your return requirements are dictated by your spending and savings habits and major long-term financial goals, such as retirement living expenses and kids' college expenses, which determine how hard your investments need to work. You will need to select an asset allocation that can deliver enough investment growth over time to meet your financial goals.

Your ability to take risk is determined by your "time horizon," net worth, and income in relation to your financial goals. For example, if you have a long time horizon (i.e., many years until retirement) and your financial goals are modest in relation to your net worth and income, then you have a greater ability to take risk. The consequences of not meeting your investment return goals are not as severe. However, if you have aggressive financial goals (i.e., excessive spending) relative to your net worth and income, and your time horizon is short, you have less ability to take risk. Your ability to recover from unfavorable investment performance is less and your risk tolerance is reduced.

If the amount of return you need to earn from your investment portfolio must be increased to the point that your portfolio becomes too risky, you may need to adjust your spending, retirement date, or other financial goals. Your financial goals must be realistic given the current size of your investment portfolio and your ability to save and contribute to your portfolio in the future (or limit withdrawals from your portfolio if you're currently retired).

Your ability to take risk and your willingness to take risk may not match. For example, you may feel that you would like to pursue an aggressive investment strategy, taking substantial risk in hopes of earning high returns. However, your time horizon is short and your net worth is low in relation to your retirement spending goals. In this case, your willingness to take risk is greater than your ability to take risk. You will need to respect your lower ability to take risk and select a less aggressive asset allocation. If you have great ability to take risk because of high net worth and modest financial goals, yet you are uncomfortable with financial risk, then you should respect your lower willingness to take risk and invest conservatively.

Generally, the longer your time horizon, the more investment risk you can take. Figure 13 provides suggestions for asset allocations that may be appropriate based on your stage of life. The figure provides a general guideline based primarily on time horizon. It should not be used without considering other factors unique to your individual situation, such as tax constraints, anticipated ongoing or large withdrawals, illiquid investment holdings, or restrictions imposed by trust documents or other legal agreements.

ASSET ALLOCATION SUGGESTIONS				
Life stage	Just starting out	Mid-life accumulating	Nearing retirement	Retired from full-time work
Key facts	In 20s and 30s, with secure job and able to save. Long time horizon allows more risk.	Peak earning years in 40s and 50s. Growing net worth and time horizon allow sustained risk taking.	In 50s and 60s, need to take risk to catch up and shortened time horizon can conflict if net worth is low.	Time horizon may be 20 to 30 years with increased life expectancy. Maintaining purchasing power is key.
Asset allocation	100/0, 90/10, 80/20	80/20, 70/30	80/20, 70/30, 60/40	70/30, 60/40, 50/50

Figure 13

Rebalancing Portfolios

Over time, your investment portfolio may drift from its target asset allocation. Rebalancing is the process for restoring your portfolio to its target asset allocation, which allows you to maintain the proper risk level in your portfolio. Rebalancing during periods of market volatility also may add return.

For example, a hypothetical portfolio holds 70% stocks and 30% bonds. After a period of time, the stocks increase in value to represent 75% of the portfolio and bonds decrease in value to represent 25% of the portfolio. The overall risk of the portfolio has increased because the portfolio is now holding more of the risky stocks. Stocks tend to grow while bonds do not grow (they pay interest instead). To reduce the risk of the portfolio and return the portfolio to the original target asset allocation, the portfolio could be rebalanced by selling stocks and buying bonds until the portfolio is again comprised of 70% stocks and 30% bonds. In a full portfolio rebalance, all asset classes are restored to their target values.

Rebalancing can be performed according to a schedule—for example, annually or quarterly—or can be triggered when asset class percentages exceed a range around their target percentage values. When using a range around asset class allocation percentages, the size of the range is important. Too large a range will cause the portfolio to not be rebalanced, while too tight a range will generate excessive trades. Regardless of rebalancing method, a best practice is to rebalance at least annually.

Asset Location

"Asset location" sounds like asset allocation but it is a different topic. Asset location involves the preference for placing particular asset class investments in certain types of investment accounts to reduce taxes. It matters what types of investments are held in what types of accounts.

For example, corporate bonds pay interest, which is taxable at ordinary income tax rates. By locating corporate bonds in a tax deferred account such as an Individual Retirement Account (IRA), the interest income on the bonds is shielded from current taxation, which increases portfolio net return. A series of studies indicate that proper asset location can result in an additional 5% to 15% net worth over an investment lifetime.[9]

While conceptually simple, proper asset location can be difficult to achieve in practice, particularly when rebalancing across multiple accounts. Institutional investors and investment advisors have access to software systems to help them implement asset location in their clients' portfolios.

You can apply asset location principles in your portfolio without software by following this guideline: When deciding which asset classes to hold in your tax-deferred and taxable accounts, "fill up" your tax-deferred accounts first with asset classes in order of least tax efficient to most tax efficient.

The list on the opposite page organizes asset classes in rough order of tax inefficiency, with least tax-efficient asset classes first. Once your tax-deferred accounts are "full," locate the remainder of your investments in your taxable accounts. After this exercise, if any taxable bonds are left in your taxable accounts, consider replacing them with more tax-efficient municipal bonds.

The order in which to "locate" asset classes in tax-deferred accounts is:

High-yield corporate bonds

Corporate bonds

Government bonds

Real estate (REITs)

Commodities

Emerging market stocks

International stocks

U.S. small stocks

U.S. large stocks

Proper asset location also reduces transaction costs by not copying the same asset allocation in all of your accounts. Instead, asset classes are distributed among the various accounts, resulting in fewer initial trades and fewer ongoing trades during rebalancing. Lower transaction costs increase net return, which compounds over time to increase your net worth.

Liquid Investment Portfolio

After selecting an asset allocation, the next step in creating an investment portfolio is to select investments for each asset class. An asset allocation can be implemented in a portfolio of investments using individual stocks and bonds, mutual funds, exchange-traded funds, or any combination of these.

Individual Stocks and Bonds

Most individual investors will not have sufficient time or expertise to research and monitor the large number of individual securities required to build an investment portfolio consisting of individual securities. Research says that about 30 individual stocks are required per asset class to diversify away most of the company-specific risk and leave only the risk and return characteristics of the asset class. If your asset allocation includes 8 asset classes, then you need to select and monitor 240 individual securities in your investment portfolio to achieve minimum diversification. If your asset allocation has 12 asset classes, that's 360 individual stocks and bonds you need to research and monitor. That level of effort is not practical for most people.

Even if you have industry expertise in an area, for example social media or biotech stocks, and can make informed and timely investment decisions, that area makes up only a fraction of one or two asset classes, leaving you struggling to research stocks and bonds in the other asset classes. While some asset classes may be familiar, such as small and large U.S. stocks, some asset classes are obscure. Not many individual investors have a working knowledge of corporate bonds, real estate investment trusts or commodities.

Mutual Funds and Exchange-Traded Funds

For most individual investors, using "pre-packaged" groups of securities will make the most sense in building out an investment portfolio. Mutual funds and exchange-traded funds (ETFs) are investment products that contain a pool or basket of individual stocks, bonds or both, chosen by the mutual fund or ETF's investment management team.

Modern mutual funds have been around since the 1950s, while ETFs originated in 1998. Today, there are both mutual funds and ETFs that hold securities representing all traditional asset classes, and newer alternative asset classes, like real estate and commodities. Using mutual funds and ETFs, investors can select one or a few mutual funds for each asset class, greatly reducing the number of individual securities to select and monitor, while providing broad diversification through the collection of up to hundreds or more individual stocks or bonds in a mutual fund or ETF.

In addition to mutual funds and ETFs, which track asset class performance, there are mutual funds and ETFs that apply a wide variety of investment styles and focuses. Some allow investing by sector or industry, such as technology, pharmaceuticals, healthcare, or consumer products. Some allow tracking an investment style, such as value or growth companies or a market capitalization (company size) focus on small or large company stocks. Others track the performance of particular countries or regions of the world.

While mutual funds and ETFs are similar in that they each consist of a collection of individual stocks or bonds, they are different in important ways.

1. Buying, Selling, and Tax Efficiency

- With mutual funds, the price is set and all purchase and sale transactions occur at the close of trading each day. When investors sell mutual fund shares, they sell to the mutual fund company itself, and the fund's manager sells underlying investments in the mutual fund to raise cash to pay them—a process called "redemption." When the fund manager sells stocks or bonds in the mutual fund for redemptions, it can create taxable capital gains, which are passed on to all shareholders.

- ETFs are bought and sold like stock and their price fluctuates throughout the trading day when stock exchanges are open. In contrast to mutual funds, when you sell ETF shares, you sell them to another investor on an exchange. None of the underlying securities are sold, and no taxable capital gains are created on sales of the underlying securities (though you still may have taxable capital gain on your shares if they appreciated while you held them). Because of the difference in the way mutual fund shares and ETF shares are sold, ETFs may be more tax efficient.

2. Expenses

- Mutual funds have expenses including commissions, transaction fees, redemption fees and operating expenses. Commissions, also known as "loads," are payments by the mutual fund company to people who sell their product. They can range from 1% to 5% of the value of the mutual fund and can be applied on purchase or sale. You can avoid paying commissions by buying only "no-load" versions of mutual funds, which are typically the same as the "load" versions minus the commissions.
- Brokerage firms may charge a transaction fee to purchase or sell some mutual funds. Redemption fees are charged by some but not all mutual funds

to discourage active buying and selling of the
mutual fund. If a mutual fund with a redemption
fee is sold before a certain period of time, typically
30 to 60 days and up to one year, then a redemption fee is charged.

ETFs do not have loads (sales commissions) or redemption fees
like mutual funds do. When you buy or sell an ETF, you will pay a
brokerage commission just like you would pay for a stock transaction.

Operating expenses are the business costs of operating a mutual
fund or ETF, including paying investment management staff. Operating expenses are usually calculated as a percentage of a mutual
fund or ETF's total assets and reported as an expense ratio. Operating expenses reduce your investment return. With all other
factors equal, a mutual fund or ETF with lower expense ratio is
preferred over a mutual fund or ETF with a higher expense ratio
because lower expenses result in a higher rate of return. Due to
their unique internal structure, ETFs generally have lower expense
ratios than mutual funds.

Active vs. Passive Management

Mutual funds and ETFs can also be differentiated based on whether their investment managers use active or passive investment strategies.

In active management, mutual fund or ETF fund managers
attempt to earn more than the market rate of return and "beat the
market" using strategies such as market timing and security selection
(i.e., stock picking).

In passive management, fund managers create a portfolio that
mimics a market index to earn the rate of return for that market.

Mutual funds or ETFs that mirror a market index are known as "index funds." Figure 14 lists popular market indices and which asset class they represent.

MARKET INDEX	ASSET CLASS REPRESENTED	DESCRIPTION
Standard & Poor's 500 (S&P 500)	U.S. large stocks	500 largest U.S. companies by market capitalization.
Russell 2000	U.S. small stocks	2,000 of the smallest U.S. companies by market capitalization.
MSCI EAFE	International developed countries	Morgan Stanley Capital International Europe, Australasia and Far East. Covers 21 developed country markets excluding U.S. and Canada.
MSCI Emerging Markets	Emerging markets	Morgan Stanley Capital International Emerging Markets. Covers 24 emerging market countries including China, Korea (South), Taiwan, India, Brazil and South Africa in descending order.
Dow Jones U.S. Select REIT Index	Real estate	A collection of real estate investment trusts (REITs).
Bloomberg Barclays U.S. 5–10 Year Corporate Bond Index	Corporate bonds	Intermediate term corporate bonds.
Bloomberg Barclays U.S. 5–10 Year Treasury Bond Index	U.S. government bonds	Intermediate term U.S. Treasury bonds and bonds from agencies such as Fannie Mae and Small Business Administration.

Figure 14

Most major financial markets are highly efficient, which means that prices of stocks and bonds in those markets reflect all available information.[10] As a result, it is exceedingly difficult and costly to beat the market through stock picking and other active management techniques. In fact, index funds historically have outperformed the majority of their actively managed counterparts. While some actively managed funds do earn higher returns than index funds in a given year or short sequence of years, they rarely repeat that outperformance. No reliable method is available to determine which active managers will outperform their comparative index in a given year or sequence of years.

The lure of past performance is strong. It is easy to imagine that an active manager with a three- to five-year track record of outperformance will repeat that performance. However, there is a great deal of randomness in investing. The data is noisy. Some active managers will outperform in any given year by sheer luck or for several years by random chance. Statistically, outperformance will happen. The difficult task for investors is determining whether multi-year outperformance is the result of a manager's skill or just plain old luck. In many cases, the answer is luck.

For most people, implementing your asset allocation with passively-managed index mutual funds and ETFs from Vanguard, Dimensional Fund Advisors, and iShares (or similar) will give the best results. If you want to earn higher returns, the most reliable way to do that is to adjust your asset allocation to take more risk (e.g., include more stock and less bonds), rather than trying to select active investment managers with the "hot hand."

Return Boosters for High Net Worth Investors

High net worth investors with larger portfolios who seek additional sources of return and diversification for their portfolios can consider alternative asset classes such as private equity, venture capital, hedge funds, real estate, managed futures, and commodities. Incorporating many of these asset classes into your portfolio requires investing in private, illiquid, and often complicated securities.

One convenient way to group alternative asset classes is by investment objective. Investors use private equity and venture capital in their portfolios primarily to increase the return of the investment portfolio with the higher returns that can be earned with these asset classes. Managed futures and commodities tend to be used by investors to add diversification to their portfolios—these asset classes often have returns which move independently of stock and bond markets. Real estate often provides both an extra source of return and a diversification benefit. An investor's goal with hedge funds depends on the hedge fund's specific strategy.

Risk and return are related, and there is no free lunch in investing. To earn higher returns, you have to expose your portfolio to higher risk. One important source of extra risk in alternative investments is the fact that they are often private investments in which your money is tied up for many years. For example, investments in private equity and venture capital are typically in the form of a limited partnership with an expected life of eight to ten years.

Private Equity

Private equity is ownership in companies whose stock does not trade on public stock exchanges. By definition, private equity requires investing in private, non-publicly traded securities. Most authorities agree that private equity is a true, distinct asset class. Subcategories of private equity include leveraged buy-out, growth equity, private real estate, private debt, and venture capital.

Historically, private equity (buy-out) has provided a return of about 3% to 4% more than public equity. In addition to that, top quartile private equity managers have earned a return approximately double that of bottom quartile managers.[11] The variability in returns ("dispersion") earned by private equity fund managers is high. In private equity investments, manager selection is key.

The cash flow associated with private equity investments exhibits a pattern known as the "J-curve," which gets its name from the pattern of cash in and cash out that resembles a stretched out letter J. In the early years, investors contribute money to private equity funds to make new investments and grow existing companies. In later years, as companies within a private equity fund are sold or go public, cash is returned to investors. Some investments reach maturity earlier than others and have a quick exit. Other companies take longer to reach maturity and return cash to investors later.

While the typical life of a private equity fund is eight to ten years, the cash flow weighted average time of investment is about five years, which means you usually have most of your money back within five years. Returns of private equity funds are often tracked according to their vintage year, i.e., the year investors first contribute cash to the fund. Depending on general economic conditions, private equity returns can vary by vintage year. Ideally, your private equity investments should be diversified across vintage years in addition to factors such as managers, company size, industries, etc.

There are several ways to invest in private equity. Investors can buy stock in individual private companies to fill out their private equity allocation. This requires taking on a role as active investor performing due diligence on individual companies and monitoring them, even getting involved with day-to-day operations. This is time consuming work.

Another and more common way to invest in private equity is to invest in one or more private equity funds managed by professional investment managers, such as well-known private equity firms Blackstone, Carlyle Group, Kohlberg Kravis & Roberts, and technology-focused Silver Lake. Private equity firms add significant value to the companies they invest in, providing not just capital but management consulting services and a variety of resources through their networks of companies. Private equity funds typically operate in a limited partnership structure with minimum investment amounts of $1 million to $5 million for the largest funds run by top private equity firms. Smaller funds may have minimums below $1 million.

In the past, private equity has been appropriate only for the largest investment portfolios because of high investment minimums. For example, if an asset allocation called for 10% private equity, an investor would need a total portfolio value of $10 million to hold two $500,000 private equity fund investments. However, recent developments within private equity have made it more accessible.

New investment vehicles known as "access funds" have emerged that allow investors to pool their investment dollars and invest in private equity funds that have high minimum investment requirements. Access funds are offered by investment advisory firms, brokerage firms, and technology firms creating alternative investment platforms. Access funds typically are structured as limited partnerships or limited liability companies (LLCs) to invest in one or more new (primary) private equity fund offerings. Access funds have lower investment minimums, often $250,000 and even as low as $100,000. A drawback of access funds is that investors pay management fees to both underlying private equity fund and the organizers of the access fund.

Another new way to access private equity is through "secondary funds." In a secondary fund, investment firms purchase limited partnership interests from the original investors who need to sell some or all of their position, often as a result of rebalancing. Secondary funds buy the limited partnership interests at a discount and offer a portfolio of private equity investments in a single fund. Because they typically hold investments from several private equity managers, and those investments are from different vintage years, secondary funds can provide diversification across both managers and vintage years at a lower minimum investment amount, as little as $25,000 to $50,000.

Venture Capital

Venture capital is well-known in the technology industry as a source of capital for startup companies. If you're working at a startup, chances are your company is funded with venture capital. Technically a subcategory of private equity, venture capital is usually considered a separate asset class due to its distinct return and risk profile, and the unique way investment return is created within startup company investments.

The limited partners of venture capital funds are typically institutional investors, such as university endowments, pension plans, and insurance companies. There is little to no access for individual investors to venture capital funds by first-tier venture capital firms, such as Kleiner Perkins Caufield & Byers, Mohr Davidow Ventures, and Sequoia Capital. Some top venture capital funds may offer executives and founders of their portfolio companies the ability to invest in their funds. Less established venture capital firms also may offer access to individual high net worth investors. Generally, investment opportunities in venture capital funds, even for high net worth investors, are limited.

While most venture capital is invested using a limited partnership structure, individual high net worth investors can invest directly into startup companies. These "angel investors" are typically successful executives with extensive operational experience whose net worth resulted from initial public offerings (IPOs) or acquisitions of one or more companies they worked for. Angel investors are often actively involved with the companies they invest in, contributing capital along with expertise, connections, and labor.

Hedge Funds

Hedge funds are private investment funds typically organized as limited partnerships. The distinguishing characteristic of hedge funds is that their managers are unconstrained—hedge fund managers are allowed to invest in any way they see fit as long as their approach is disclosed to investors. Hedge funds typically have a minimum investment of $500,000 to $1 million. The standard hedge fund fee has two components: a 2% annual management fee and a performance-based fee, which is equal to 20% of any gain in the fund's value, the so-called 2-and-20 fee.

Economists and investors debate whether hedge funds are a true and distinct asset class that can provide additional return or diversification benefits to traditional asset classes. Some believe (the author included) that hedge funds are not a separate asset class but just a different way to invest. If that's the case, it may be better to consider hedge funds as a portion of a portfolio's equity allocation and not part of alternative investments.

Diversification Enhancers

Real Estate

Real estate can provide solid returns and good diversification to traditional asset classes. Historically, real estate has increased in value during periods of inflation and provides protection against inflation in investment portfolios.

There are many ways to invest in real estate, including direct ownership in properties or through a pooled investment vehicle. If holding real estate directly, investors may buy property in their name (or trust's name) or buy it with other investors through a "tenant in common" structure, also known as a TIC. Groups of investors may also create a limited liability corporation or limited partnership to own real estate together. Investment companies offer pooled real estate investments using these structures as well.

The largest real estate vehicles are real estate investment trusts (REITs). A REIT can be private or publicly traded. There are mutual funds and ETFs which hold multiple individual REITs to provide diversification and exposure to the real estate asset class. REITs originated in the U.S. and are now available in many countries around the world. Publicly traded U.S. and global REITs provide good exposure to the real estate asset class with high liquidity and low cost.

Real estate investing can involve many types of properties and projects, but as an asset class, it typically does not include single family homes. Professionally managed real estate investment funds, such as REITs and limited partnerships, invest in office buildings, shopping centers, public storage facilities, industrial parks, and other types of commercial real estate. They also invest in multi-tenant residential real estate, usually medium to large apartment complexes.

Real estate funds can be focused on a particular geography, type of property (e.g., shopping centers), or even stage of development, from raw land, through permitted project to operating property. Some investors and funds focus on rehabilitating or improving existing real estate using investor capital to improve its cash flow or increase its value.

Commodities

Commodities may provide diversification and protection against inflation in investment portfolios. Investing in physical commodities directly is difficult. Most individual investors hold commodities though a private limited partnership, mutual fund, or ETF, which gain exposure to physical commodities through the future markets. Commodity investments provide exposure to the major commodity groups, including energy, precious metals, industrial metals, livestock, grains, and other agricultural commodities such as cocoa, coffee, cotton, and sugar.

Managed Futures

Trend-following in the futures markets has a history going back over 200 years and takes advantage of a behavioral bias of investors in underreacting to news initially and then overshooting in response. Managed futures have their highest returns during periods of volatility (up and down), which may make them a good diversifier.

In the past, managed futures investments were available only as private limited partnerships for high net worth investors and institutions. Recently, managed futures have become available in publicly traded mutual fund format. With manage futures, investment managers buy and sell futures contracts on behalf of their investors in a wide variety of markets, including the commodity futures markets and currencies, and also financial futures such as S&P 500 index futures. Fund managers use sophisticated computer models and quantitative techniques to make their investments. Many managed futures fund managers use a trend-following strategy with different managers having expertise over different timeframes, for example days, weeks, or months.

Accredited Investors & Qualified Purchasers

Investing in many categories of alternative investments such as private equity, venture capital, hedge funds, and managed futures all require buying private securities that are not registered with the U.S. Securities and Exchange Commission (SEC) and not traded in public markets. Federal securities law and regulation restrict who can buy these private securities. Before investing in these areas you will need to become familiar with the qualifying requirements.

Accredited Investors

The Securities Act of 1933 ("1933 Act") requires that offers and sales of securities be registered with the SEC. For example, when a startup company prepares to sell its stock to the public for the first time in an initial public offering (IPO), i.e., "goes public," it files a registration statement with the SEC, registering its shares. Registration with the SEC is intended to ensure investors have full and fair disclosure of important information to make informed investment decisions.

The 1933 Act contains a number of exemptions that companies and investment funds can use to avoid having to register their securities with the SEC. The most important exemptions are found in Regulation D of the 1933 Act. The amount of capital companies and private investment funds raise using those exemptions is substantial. In 2014, together they raised over $1.3 trillion, an amount comparable to registered offerings (i.e., public stock and bond offerings).[12]

A commonly used exemption under Regulation D of the 1933 Act requires that companies and private investment funds must offer and sell their unregistered (i.e., private) securities only to investors who qualify as accredited investors. Individuals are accredited investors if they meet *either* of the following criteria:

1. Earned individual income in excess of $200,000 in each of the two most recent years or joint income with their spouse in excess of $300,000 in each of those years and has a reasonable expectation of reaching the same income level in the current year.[13]

2. Have individual net worth, or joint net worth with their spouse, of $1 million, excluding the value of their primary residence.[14]

For the income test, you must meet the same test for the entire three year period (prior two years and current year). For example, you must have individual income of $200,000 or more for three years or you must have joint income with your spouse of $300,000 for three years.

For the net worth test, the equity in your primary residence is *not* included in your net worth. Be aware there is a 60-day "look-back period," which requires any loan taken against your home within 60 days of buying securities is included as a liability in your net worth. This rule is intended to prevent investors from artificially inflating their net worth by borrowing against their home equity and converting their home equity into cash or other assets that would be included in the net worth calculation.

For the net worth test, your net worth is defined simply as assets minus liabilities. The value of vested employee stock options is included in net worth. [15] You are allowed to combine the property you and your spouse own, even if the property is not held jointly. [16] You are not required to buy securities jointly with your spouse to qualify as an accredited investor under the joint net worth test.

The accredited investor definition is intended to "encompass those persons whose financial sophistication and ability to sustain the risk of loss of investment or ability to fend for themselves render the protections of the Securities Act's registration process unnecessary." [17] In other words, the purpose of the accredited investor definition is to identify investors who have the ability to understand the unique risks of these often complicated investments and who can bear the economic risk of investing in them. Companies and private funds raising capital through non-registered private offerings, sometimes referred to as private placements, are not required to make the same comprehensive disclosures to accredited investors that issuers of registered, publicly traded securities are required to make to public market investors.

Trusts as Accredited Investors

Individual investors often hold their investment accounts and other assets in a "revocable" or "irrevocable trust" for estate planning purposes.

Revocable trusts meet the definition of accredited investor, provided that all of the owners of the trust are themselves accredited investors.[18] If you are the grantor of your revocable trust (i.e., you created it) and you have the power to amend or revoke it at any time, and you are an accredited investor under the two-part income or net worth test above, then your revocable trust, which will hold your investment, is also considered an accredited investor.

For an irrevocable trust, separate trust rules apply. Irrevocable trusts cannot be amended or revoked (canceled). Generally, an irrevocable trust meets the definition of accredited investor if it has total assets in excess of $5 million, was not formed for the specific purpose of investing in the securities being considered for purchase, and is being directed by a *sophisticated person*.[19] A sophisticated investor is someone who either alone, or with their financial advisor, has enough knowledge and experience in financial and business matters to be capable of evaluating the merits and risks of the prospective investment.[20] Similar to revocable trusts, an irrevocable trust might qualify as an accredited investor if all of the grantors (creators) are accredited investors and each grantor is considered an owner due to the specific features of the trust.[21]

Qualified Purchasers

As an investor in private securities, you will most commonly need to meet the accredited investor qualification criterion. However, there are investments that require you meet a more stringent standard.

A private investment fund is exempt from the Investment Company of 1940 ("1940 Act"), and can avoid its tough regulatory requirements, if the private fund 1) does not offer its securities publicly, and 2) does not have more than 100 investors.[22] A private investment fund can meet the requirements by offering and selling securities only to accredited investors and by limiting the number of investors to 100 or less.

Alternatively, a private investment fund is exempt from 1940 Act regulation if the private fund 1) does not offer its securities publicly, and 2) all of its investors are *qualified purchasers*.[23] Individuals and trusts generally qualify as *qualified purchasers* if they own $5 million or more of investments.[24] Some private investment funds will require that you meet the qualified purchaser criterion in order to invest.

Meeting the Criteria

If you have questions about whether you meet the definition of accredited investor or qualified purchaser, a good place to start is with the company or private fund that is offering the securities you are considering buying. Companies and private funds have staff whose responsibilities include ensuring that investors buying their securities are qualified under the SEC's rules. Their compliance teams typically include in-house or outside securities attorneys who can help analyze the facts and circumstances of your particular situation.

Summary

- Review historical investment performance to become familiar with what is possible to earn and to properly set your expectations for your investment performance.
- Select or develop an asset allocation for your investment portfolio that is appropriate to your stage of life and that suits your willingness, ability and need to take risk.
- Rebalance your portfolio at least annually to maintain proper risk level.
- Use asset location across your accounts to reduce the tax drag on your investments.
- As a starting place, build your investment portfolio with traditional stock and bond asset classes using low expense, tax efficient index mutual funds or exchange-traded funds.
- For more diversification, look to alternative asset classes, such as real estate, commodities, and managed futures.
- If you are a high net worth investor, consider adding private equity, venture capital, or hedge funds to your portfolio to increase return.
- If you will be investing in private securities, such as private company stock or venture capital partnerships, learn the federal and state requirements for accredited investors and qualified purchasers.

Next up, equity compensation. The following chapter includes lots of information on restricted stock units, stock options, employee stock purchase plans, and special topics on early exercise election and insider trading.

5

Taking Stock: Equity Compensation

From a personal finance perspective, "equity compensation" is what distinguishes technology industries from most other industries. Technology companies often offer broad-based equity compensation programs through which a large number of employees acquire company stock and become part owners of the companies they work for.

Stock ownership aligns employee interests with shareholder interests that, in the case of tech companies, are high growth rates and remaining innovative in an ultra-competitive field. These stock-based compensation programs also help tech companies attract and retain top talent they need to power their growth.

For tech professionals, equity compensation means the potential to earn more (sometimes a lot more) if the company is successful. Stock ownership can add a meaningful amount of extra take-home pay or earn the employee a life-changing sum of money. However, potentially valuable stock-based compensation programs each have their own characteristics and limitations, which can be difficult to understand.

This chapter reviews employee stock-purchase plans, restricted stock, restricted stock units, non-qualified stock options, and incentive stock options, providing a description of their main features and recommendations for how they can contribute to effective financial planning.

Employee Stock Purchase Plan

Publicly traded companies may offer an Employee Stock Purchase Plan (ESPP) that allows you to buy your employer's stock over a period of time at a discount of up to 15% or more from its current market value. You can then sell your ESPP shares to capture the built-in investment gain.

Companies offer ESPPs to give their employees an opportunity to earn more and contribute to the company's success, and to ensure employees' interests align with the company and other shareholders' interests.

How They Work

When enrolled in an ESPP, you buy shares of your company's stock over time via regular deductions from your paycheck. Your payroll deductions are collected during a period of time called the "offering period," which usually varies in length from 6 months to 24 months depending on the features of your company's ESPP.

The structuring of offering periods varies from plan to plan and company to company. Some companies run ESPP offering periods one after another (a new offering period begins at the end of the last offering period). Other companies run ESPPs with overlapping offering periods (several offering periods, each with a different start date, are open at the same time). To contribute to your ESPP, you must wait until the start of the next offering period.

Some ESPPs buy shares several times within the offering period at intervals called "purchase periods." For example, if the offering period is 24 months, the ESPP may have four purchase periods. The purchase periods may end at 6 months, 12 months, 18 months, and 24 months. Other ESPPs may purchase shares only at the end of the offering period. Purchase periods within the offering period allow you to sell your investment sooner.

At the end of the offering period or a purchase period, your company's ESPP administrator buys shares of the company stock for you with your collected funds and deposits the shares to your account. The number of shares purchased is determined by the total money collected from your paycheck deductions during the offering period divided by the purchase price on that date.

You sell your shares by placing "sell orders" within the account your employer created for you. Typically, you have online access to your account, so you can sell with a few clicks of your mouse. Your shares are sold to other investors on public stock exchanges.

Purchase-Price Discount

An important benefit of ESPPs is they can allow you to buy company stock at a discount to its current market value. If your company's ESPP is a "tax-qualified plan" or "Section 423 plan" designed to comply with certain tax rules, then you may be able to purchase shares at a discount.[1] The price you pay to buy shares depends on your specific ESPP features and can range from market price on the purchase date to as low as 85% of market price for tax-qualified plans.[2]

Lookback Pricing

Some tax-qualified plans also have a special feature called "look-back pricing," which allows you to buy shares at a discount from the price at the beginning of the offering period or on the actual purchase date, whichever is lower (in-between days don't matter).[3] Lookback pricing enables you to buy shares at a greater discount if the company's stock price appreciates during the offering period.

ESPPs with features including the maximum 15% discount, lookback pricing, and long offering periods are particularly valuable when the company's stock price is appreciating and can result in purchase price discounts well above 15%. ESPPs with maximum

15% discount and lookback pricing are common among companies in technology industries.

Example: 15% Discount and Lookback Pricing

In this example, the company stock price was $100 per share on the first day of the offering period but increases to $120 on the last day (the purchase date) of a 24-month offering period.

With lookback pricing, the 15% discount applies to the lower number. Therefore, because the market price of the stock was lower on the first day of the offering period, the price you pay would be 85% of $100, or $85 per share. This represents a discount of 29% from a market value of $120 (the price on the purchase date).

Instead, if the company's stock price dropped to $80 per share by the purchase date, your buy price would be 85% of $80, or $68. What you pay would then represent a discount of 15% from the market value. This demonstrates an important point: Even if the company's stock price declines, the smallest possible discount on your share purchases would be 15% (for ESPPs that allow the maximum 15% discount).

The investment gain on your shares in this case is greater than the 15% discount from purchase price that your company plan allows employees. Your investment gain is 17.6% ($80 minus $68, divided by $68). If you sell your shares immediately when you receive them, you will earn a 17.6% return on your investment, with little or no risk. This is the smallest investment return you can earn (again, for ESPPs that allow the maximum 15% discount).

Your investment gain will be even greater if your company's stock price increases during the offering period. The combined effect of buying at a 15% discount, lookback pricing, and rising stock price lead to a big gain in this example. With the stock price appreciating to $120, the investment gain on your shares is 41.2% ($120 minus $85, divided by $85).

ESPP Taxation

It is important to note that the money taken out of your paycheck to purchase company stock does not reduce your taxable income—these payroll deductions are "after-tax" deductions, meaning that you pay tax on the total income in your paycheck and the money taken out for ESPP is from what is left after taxes have been withheld.

If your company's ESPP is a tax-qualified plan, your tax treatment may be better if you hold your shares. With a tax-qualified plan, you have no income for tax purposes when shares are purchased in your account, only when you later sell the shares. The amount and type of income you earn depends on how long you hold your shares. The income you earn will either be classified "ordinary income" or "capital gain."

To receive favorable tax treatment, you must hold your shares for two years from the first day of the offering period and one year after you receive purchased shares in your account. If you meet this "holding period rule," more of your income will be classified as capital gain, which is taxed at lower capital gains tax rates, and less of your income will be classified as ordinary income, which is taxed at higher ordinary income tax rates.

The amount of income that will be classified as ordinary income if you meet the holding period rule is the lower of the amounts calculated by either:

A. The difference between the stock price on the date you sold your shares and the amount you paid to buy them, *or*

B. The difference between the market value of the shares on the first day of the offering period and the price you would have paid (including discount) if you had bought shares that day.[4]

The remaining increase in value when you sell the shares (if any) is classified as capital gain income.

Part (B) of the above ordinary income calculation is what can allow you to pay less tax by meeting the holding-period rule. When the stock price is appreciating, the amount of discount you received on your share purchase (which is taxed as ordinary income) will be lower when measured on the first day of the offering period rather than on the sale date after the stock price has risen, resulting in lower taxable income.

For example, assume your ESPP includes a 15% purchase-price discount and allows lookback pricing. Also assume the company stock price is $40 per share at the beginning of a 6-month offering period, $44 per share at the end of the offering period when shares are purchased and $50 per share after 18 months and 24 months from the beginning of the offering period. In this case, the company will purchase shares at 85% of $40 (the lesser of $44 or $40 using lookback pricing), or $34 per share. If you sell the shares at 24 months from the beginning of the offering period for $50 per share, you will have met the holding period requirement. You will have ordinary income equal to the lesser of A) sale price of $50 per share minus purchase price of $34 per share = $16 per share or B) market value of $40 per share minus purchase price of $34 per share = $6 per share. Using the lower amount, you have $6 per share of ordinary income. You also have $50 per share minus $40 per share = $10 per share of capital gain taxed at the lower long-term capital gains tax rates.

If you do not meet the holding-period rule, your ordinary income is equal to difference between the stock price on the purchase date and the amount you paid for the shares. Continuing the example, if you sold your ESPP shares 18 months after the beginning of the offering period for $50 per share you would not have met the holding period requirement. You would have ordinary income of $44 per share minus $34 per share = $10 per share. You would also have capital gain of $50 per share minus $44 per share = $6 per share. In this case, more of the income is classified as the higher taxed ordinary income and less is classified as the lower taxed capital gain, increasing your overall tax bill, as compared to the case where you met the holding period requirement.

If your company's ESPP is not a tax-qualified plan, all of your income is classified as ordinary income. Your income is equal to the difference between the market value of the shares on the date shares are purchased and the amount you paid for them.

Tax law limits your annual contributions to your company's ESPP. The maximum annual contribution is $25,000 worth of stock, based on market value on the first day of the offering period.[5] Therefore, if you buy your shares at a discount, you will not be able to contribute the full $25,000. Your contribution in dollars will be less. For example, if the market value of the company's stock is $25 on the first day of the offering period and you purchase shares at a 15% discount on that day, you are able to buy 1,000 shares worth $25,000 for $21,250 (0.85 x $25 x 1,000 = $21,250). Your actual cash contribution of $21,250 is less than the $25,000 market value of the stock purchased.

ESPPs also often have limits on the amount you can contribute as a percentage of your pay. A common limit is 10% of your annual compensation.

Employers are not required to withhold income tax or payroll tax (for Social Security and Medicare programs) on transactions within tax-qualified ESPPs, which are the most common within the tech industry.

Planning for ESPP

Your company's ESPP can be a great benefit for you. Here are a few points to consider about participating in the ESPP.

1. Sell your ESPP shares when you receive them.

By selling your shares immediately, you secure your built-in investment gain. At the same time, you remove any possibility that your investment can lose value if the stock price falls. Through the ESPP, you bought stock at a discount, allowing your investment to step up in value without market risk (I call this "free money"). If you hold your shares beyond the purchase date, you expose your investment to much more risk, with no way to earn additional built-in gain.

When you sell your shares, you get your cash back, which is then available to invest again in your company's ESPP. By recirculating funds and reinvesting, you earn the built-in rate of return non-stop.

You may consider holding your shares to receive better tax treatment. However, tax benefits for holding are difficult to calculate and also risky. The best option to choose (hold or sell) depends on the company's stock price on the first day of the offering period, the purchase date, and the date you sell your shares. If you are holding shares, your sell date will be in the future. You cannot know ahead of time what your sell price will be; therefore, until then, you will not know whether or not it would have been better to sell before the end of the holding period. By holding, you risk your shares losing value in exchange for uncertain tax benefits.

2. Find out when the trading window is open.

Many companies impose "blackout" periods or "trading windows" surrounding earnings announcements and corporate transactions. During a blackout period or when the trading window is "closed," employees may not sell or buy the company's stock. Companies enforce blackout periods and trading windows to prevent insider trading, whether deliberate or inadvertent, by employees with inside information. You cannot sell your ESPP shares during blackout periods, which usually last a few days or weeks. Holding shares during a trading window or blackout period exposes your investment to market risk until you can sell them. Your company's trading window practices should be a factor in your decision to enroll in the ESPP.

3. Contribute the maximum amount possible to your ESPP.

Saving and investing in an ESPP can strain your cash flow when you begin contributing because you divert money you're using for other purposes to the ESPP. But once your first offering (or purchase period) ends, you can sell your shares and get your money back. Your sale proceeds include built-in gain and will be more than your contributions. You will then have cash from your original contribution to reinvest in the ESPP, and you can also add the funds from built-in gain to your long-term investment portfolio. Alternatively, you can use these funds as extra income to meet living expenses.

Most ESPPs will automatically enroll you in the next offering period unless you opt out, so you can continue taking advantage of this great benefit with little effort. Your total cash commitment is one offering period (or purchase period) of contributions. Some companies allow you to withdraw funds during the offering period if you need cash for an emergency.

The Silicon Valley chapter of the National Association of Stock Plan Professionals found that ESPP participation in northern California is the highest in the nation. Well over half of companies in northern California report employee ESPP participation rates ranging from 60% to 90%. In the rest of the country, only 20% of companies report participation rates this high. They attribute this difference to generous features including lookback pricing and 24-month offering periods.[6] If your company's ESPP has great features like these, as well as the maximum 15% purchase discount, consider enrolling and contributing as much as you can.

Restricted Stock & Restricted Stock Units

Publicly traded technology companies are increasingly using "restricted stock" and "restricted stock units" (RSUs) to give employees ownership in the company.[7] Many technology companies offer RSUs to a large percentage of their employees, including executives, managers, and professional staff. Apple made news in October 2015 by giving RSUs to all employees, including those working in Apple retail stores. If you work for a publicly traded technology company, there's a good chance RSUs are part of your compensation package.

Large private companies that expect to go public within a few years have also started using RSUs. Facebook innovated this practice, and began issuing RSUs instead of stock options in 2007, five years before its initial public offering (IPO) in 2012, in order to work around securities laws requiring companies to go public once they have more than 500 shareholders.[8] The value of Facebook stock (even then as a private company) was high, which potentially left little upside for employees if they were given stock options.

Small private companies typically do not offer restricted stock or RSUs as equity compensation because of the way they are taxed to employees (as described below).

Restricted Stock and RSUs: Basics

Restricted stock and restricted stock units are two of the simplest forms of equity compensation. Their relative simplicity is part of the reason for their increased popularity with companies and their employees.

Restricted stock is company stock your employer gives to you as part of your total compensation package that you cannot sell or transfer until certain conditions have been met. Typically, your ownership in the stock "vests," meaning its restrictions are removed over time, or as company or individual performance goals are met. If you leave the company, you "forfeit" or lose your unvested restricted shares. Once your restricted stock is vested (and its restrictions are removed), you own the shares and may sell or transfer them.

Somewhat differently, an RSU is a *promise* by your employer to transfer shares of company stock to you when certain conditions have been met. As with restricted stock, your RSUs vest over time or when company or individual performance goals have been met. If you leave the company, you lose your unvested units and they cannot be exchanged for company stock. Once your RSUs vest and the company exchanges your units for actual shares of company stock (usually at a 1:1 ratio), you own the shares and can sell them or transfer them. Some RSUs are settled in cash, and some offer the option of receiving shares or cash.

The main difference between restricted stock and restricted stock units is that with restricted stock you receive shares of stock up front, whereas with restricted stock units, the company pledges to transfer shares of stock to you in the future. For employees, the difference between receiving restricted stock and RSUs is negligible—in both cases an employee owns company stock after a vesting period. Public companies prefer RSUs over restricted stock because granting RSUs doesn't require actual share transfers with its associated cost and administrative burden. RSU grants also don't increase the number of shares outstanding until units are converted to shares.

Restricted shares typically have voting rights and are entitled to receive dividends. RSUs are not actual shares, so employees do not have voting rights and are not entitled to receive dividends. Some companies pay RSU holders an amount equal to the dividends they would have received if they held actual shares.

Your company's stock plan administrator makes your restricted stock and RSU information available to you online through a stock plan services partner that manages accounts for all the company employees participating. Stock plan servicing firms are usually large brokerage firms, such as E*Trade, Fidelity Investments, Charles

Schwab, and Morgan Stanley. Your online account typically includes information about all of the equity compensation programs you are participating in, including ESPP, restricted stock, RSU, and stock options.

The day on which your company gives you restricted stock or RSUs is the "award date" or the "grant date." The two terms are used interchangeably.

Your company will ask and may require that you "accept" your restricted stock or RSU grant, typically online at the website operated by your company's stock plan servicing partner. By accepting your grant, you instruct the company how you would like to have taxes withheld so that the company can meet its legal obligations to properly withhold tax when you receive shares in your account after vesting.

Vesting

Vesting is designed to encourage employees to stay with the company. When you are deciding whether to leave a company before your restricted stock or RSUs has completely vested, you are also making the sometimes difficult decision about how much unvested stock or units to "leave on the table."

Restricted stock and RSUs typically vest either monthly or quarterly for three to five years with a one-year "cliff." A one-year cliff means that either 12 months or four quarters of vesting complete all at once at the end of the first year. Cliff vesting is used to make sure new employees will be a good fit with the company before they become owners and to encourage existing employees who are issued new restricted stock or RSU grants to remain with the company for at least one year. For example, an RSU vesting quarterly over three years with a one-year cliff will be one-third vested at the end of one year. After the first year, one-eighth of the remaining amount will vest each quarter over the next two years.

Once you receive shares of stock, either as a result of restrictions being removed from restricted stock after vesting or upon conversion of restricted stock units to actual shares after vesting, you have the following options:

- You can continue to hold the shares.
- Transfer the shares to another brokerage account (and continue to hold them or sell them).
- Sell the shares, and transfer the cash proceeds to a bank or brokerage account.

As an aside, since 2014, brokerage firms have been required to track and transfer the cost basis of the shares to any brokerage firm you transfer your shares to. This makes tracking cost basis and correctly calculating gain on ultimate sales of your shares much easier than it was just a few years ago, meaning fewer things for you to worry about.

What Is It Worth?

The value of your restricted stock or RSUs is easy to calculate. Multiply the number of shares or units (assuming a 1:1 conversion ratio units to shares) by the current stock price of the company. The result is the total value of your restricted stock or RSU. Nearly all online accounts will show you separately the value of the vested portion of your restricted stock or RSUs and the value of the unvested portion of your restricted stock or RSUs. Most stock plan websites also provide information about the vesting schedule of your grants.

Restricted Stock & RSU Taxation

Restricted stock is not taxable to you when you receive it. The stock becomes taxable to you as it vests, and your shares are no longer subject to restrictions on sale or transfer. The market value of the shares you receive is taxable to you as ordinary income and is reported on your paystub along with your regular pay amounts. For example, if you became vested in 250 shares of your company's stock and the stock was trading at $20 per share on the day your shares vested, you would have $5,000 of ordinary income from those shares. Any dividends you receive also are taxed as ordinary income, not dividend income.

Taxation of RSUs works similarly. When your RSUs vest, your company's stock plan administrator exchanges your vested restricted stock units for actual shares of your company's stock and places those shares in your account. The market value of the shares you receive is taxable to you as ordinary income.

Income from restricted stock and RSUs shows up on your paystub along with your normal salary and bonus income. And just like with regular wage income, your employer is required to withhold taxes on the income you receive in the form of shares. However, because you receive income in the form of shares and not cash, there is no cash available to withhold for taxes. Your company may give you the option to pay the taxes with cash from other sources, for example your stock plan account. More commonly, your company will either withhold some of your shares to pay taxes or automatically sell some of your shares to pay taxes.

The amount of withholding for taxes on income from stock is not the same as the amount of withholding from your wage and salary income as determined by the number of allowances you selected on Form W-4. Taxes on stock income are withheld at different rates. For income received in the form of company stock, your company will follow IRS rules for withholding federal income tax according to the supplemental wage withholding rules.[9] Supplemental wages include wage payments that are reported separately on your paystub from your regular wages and include bonuses, commissions, severance, accumulated sick leave, back pay, awards, restricted stock, and RSUs. Those rules state that on supplemental wages above $1 million, income tax is withheld at a rate of 37% (decreased from 39.6% in 2017). On supplemental wages of $1 million or less, income tax is withheld either at a flat rate of 22% (decreased from 25% in 2017) or supplemental income is added to regular income, and the regular wage withholding rate for the combined income is used.

For tech-industry states with a state-income tax, most require withholding on supplemental wage income at rates ranging from 3% to 6%. California and New York are standouts with higher withholding rates of 10.23% and 9.62%, respectively.

The key issue here is that withholding rates on your restricted stock and RSU income may not be the same as those for your regular income. The amount of tax withheld for you overall, for both types of income, may be more or less than you will be required to pay in taxes when you file your tax returns. You could be in for a surprise in April if you are not aware of the supplemental wage withholding rules.

Your restricted stock and RSU income are subject to payroll taxes in addition to federal and state income tax. Payroll taxes include federal Social Security and Medicare taxes and potentially additional state and local taxes, depending on where you live.

Unlike incentive stock options, there are no direct Alternative Minimum Tax (AMT) considerations for restricted stock and RSUs. Only regular tax rules apply.

After you receive actual shares, your cost basis in those shares is their market value on the day you receive them. Taxation after you receive your shares follows the normal rules for gains and losses on investments. If you hold your shares for one year or more and then sell them, you will be taxed at the favorable long-term capital gains tax rates. If you hold your shares for less than one year and then sell them, any gain will be taxed at short-term capital gains rates, which are your ordinary income tax rates. If your shares lose value and you sell them, you are limited in the amount of capital loss you can deduct from your income on your federal tax return to $3,000 per year. Unused losses carry forward to future years.

Planning for Restricted Stock & RSUs

Restricted stock and RSUs are easy to understand and use. However, there are a few planning points to keep in mind in working with your restricted stock and RSUs.

1. Don't forget to include the gain from stock sales in your income tax planning.

Because restricted stock and RSUs are taxed as ordinary income when they vest with both income and tax withholdings reported on your paystub, it's easy to forget about potential income (or loss) on shares you hold and sell later. Remember that any increase in value is capital gain and is taxable at capital gain tax rates.

The trade confirmation statement from the brokerage firm that executed your sell trades will show you the price at which you sold and may show your cost basis. Your taxable gain is equal to the difference between the selling price and your cost basis per share, multiplied times the number of shares you sold. The brokerage firm will not withhold tax from the proceeds, unlike when you receive your vested shares. Be sure to include this amount in your income tax projection during the year. You may need to make estimated tax payments to cover capital gain from these sales.

2. Avoid becoming dependent on the restricted stock or RSU income subsidy.

If your current employer is generous with stock grants and your next employer is less generous, you may find yourself having to make a harsh adjustment in lifestyle when you change jobs. You may become accustomed to receiving extra income from restricted stock or RSUs above your salary or wage income. Without realizing it, you may be subsidizing your lifestyle expenditures with restricted stock or RSU income, which is above your regular compensation.

A best practice is to live on your regular compensation (potentially including bonuses or other incentive compensation) and treat your restricted stock or RSU income as extra income to be saved. That approach will keep your lifestyle expenditures in line with your core long-term income producing ability.

3. Sell your shares as they vest.

Your cost basis in your shares is the price per share when you received them. The regular capital gains tax rules apply going forward. There is no tax advantage to holding your shares because there is no taxable gain on the day you receive them. Selling your shares allows you to diversify away some of the concentrated risk you have as a result of being employed by and holding stock of the same company. If you have a large amount of unvested RSUs or restricted stock, you have plenty remaining investment in your company's stock and selling vested shares to diversify—as opposed to holding vested shares—often makes the most sense.

Stock Options

Stock options are often given to executives, managers, and employees of technology startup companies to incent them to help rapidly grow the company. Stock options have the potential to rapidly grow your personal net worth.

A stock option gives you the right to buy a specific number of shares of your company's stock at a specific price—known as either the exercise, grant, or strike price—for a specific amount of time. The exercise price is usually equal to the value of the stock on the day you received the option. For example, an early-stage venture capital-backed startup might grant stock options with an exercise price of $0.10 per share.[10]

To use your option, you inform the company you wish to exercise your option to buy shares and then you pay the exercise price for the number of shares you want to purchase.

The value of your stock option at any point in time is equal to:

1. The current value of the company's stock, minus the exercise price if the current value of the company's stock price is greater than the exercise price, *or*

2. Zero if the current value of the company's stock price is equal to or less than the exercise price.

For example, if your company's stock is worth $10.00 per share, and the strike price of your option is $0.10 per share, the value of your option is $9.90 per share. If you were granted an option to purchase 20,000 shares, the total value of your option is $198,000. However, if the value of the company's stock is $0.05 per share, the value of your option per share is $0.00 and the total value of your option to buy 20,000 shares is $0.

Exercising Options

You are not required to exercise your option. The option gives you the right but not the obligation to purchase your company's stock. Said another way, you can buy shares of your company's stock if you decide to, but you don't have to. There is a cost to exercising your option.

In exercising your option you must pay the exercise price to buy your shares. Continuing our example, if you decided to exercise your option and purchase shares of your company stock, you would pay $0.10 per share to buy the stock. You can exercise your option on part or all of the number of shares granted to you. If you exercised half of your shares, you would pay $0.10 per share for 10,000 shares for a total of $1,000. If you exercised all your shares, you would pay a total of $2,000 to own them.

Vesting

Stock options are normally subject to vesting, which means you may exercise your option only after you have worked for your employer for the required time. Stock options commonly vest monthly over four years and include a one-year "cliff," which means 12 months of vesting completes at the end of the first year. That is, you cannot exercise your option any time before you have worked for your employer for 12 months. For example, a stock option vesting monthly over four years with a one year cliff will be one-fourth vested at the end of one year and will then vest 1/36th of the remaining amount each month over the next three years.

Stock options include vesting provisions to discourage employees from leaving the company. The value of your stock option may grow to substantial value as the company grows, but you will need to remain with the company as your option vests to realize its full value. This aspect of stock options is sometimes referred to as "golden handcuffs." The one-year cliff in the vesting schedule is designed to ensure employees will be long-term contributors before allowing them to become owners in the company.

Option Agreement

Your stock option is a legal agreement between you and the company, specifying the terms under which the company is willing to sell its stock to you. Your option grant document lists the specific number of shares you will receive, exercise price, date of grant, and other terms that are specific to your grant.

Other general terms of your option agreement are detailed in the company's stock plan, which is a separate document. It is important that you understand the terms of your option agreement included in both the grant document and the stock plan document. There are decisions you will need to make and actions you will need to take at various points in time to realize the value in your stock options.

For example, your option ends and loses its value when you leave the company or it expires.

Your stock option may have a limited period after you terminate employment, during which you can exercise your option. A typical time period is 90 days.[11] It is imperative that you know whether your option agreement contains a grace period and how long that grace period lasts if you are terminating employment.

Also stock option agreements commonly have a 10-year term.[12] After 10 years, the option agreement expires and you lose your right to buy the company's stock at the specified price. Not being aware of the term could cause you to lose the value of your vested options. If you are within one year of option expiration, or you have just terminated employment and entered a grace period, you may want to add the exercise-by date to your calendar.

Magic of Options

Two aspects of stock options make them valuable to their owners. First, companies using stock options as part of their equity compensation program for employees are often generous with the amount of stock awarded. This is particularly true for key contributors in technology startup companies.[13] For example, an option to purchase 40,000 shares at $0.10 would be worth $400,000 if the company's stock price grew to $10 per share above the exercise price and $1.2 million if the stock price grew to $30 per share above exercise price. Stock price growth rates like this are possible for technology companies; indeed, obtaining high growth rates for the company is the reason investors incent key contributors with stock options.

The second aspect of stock options that makes them valuable is the structure of a stock option itself. Due to the fixed exercise price, the value of an option increases more in percentage terms than the value of the company stock as the stock price increases.

Here's an example:

Let's assume you own 1,000 shares of your company's stock.

The current stock price is $10 per share, so
the value of your stock is $10,000.

If the stock price increases to $13 per share,
your shares become worth $13,000.

Therefore, they have increased in value by $3,000 or 30%.

Instead, let's assume you have an option to purchase 1,000
shares of your company's stock at $2.00 per share.

If the stock price is $10 per share, the
value of your option is $8,000.

If the stock price increases to $13 per share,
your option becomes worth $11,000.

Therefore, the value of your option has grown
$3,000 or 37.5% ($3,000 divided by $8,000).

Even though both the stock and option increased in value by $3,000, the option increased more in value in percentage terms because the increase was from a lower starting value.

Non-qualified Stock Options (NSOs)

There are two main types of stock option: "non-qualified stock options" (NSO or NQSO) and "incentive stock options" (ISO). It is important for you to know which types of stock option you have been granted because the taxation of these two types of options is significantly different. You may have both types of options.

(ISOs are "qualified," which in taxation parlance means they meet the legal requirements to receive special tax treatment.[14] Non-qualified stock options don't receive special tax treatment.)

There are no tax costs when you receive your NSO or as it vests. However, once your NSO has vested and you exercise your stock option (fully or partially), the difference between the stock price and strike price is taxed as ordinary income. Your company will report the income to you on your paystub during the pay period you exercise your option and on your annual Form W-2.

After you exercise your option and receive shares, your cost basis in those shares is the market value of the stock at the time you exercised. Taxation after you receive your shares follows the normal rules for gains and losses on investments. If you hold your shares for one year or more and then sell them, you will be taxed at the favorable long-term capital gains tax rates. If you hold your shares for less than one year and then sell them, any gain will be taxed at short-term capital gains rates, which are your ordinary income tax rates. Your holding period for long-term capital gains treatment begins on the day you exercised.

Technology stocks are volatile and price declines are not un-common. So, be aware that if your company stock price drops after you exercise your NSO option, the amount of ordinary income you report as a result of exercising your option is not reduced. You can think about the income from your option in two parts: the first part is the gain on your option at the time you exercise, which is taxed as ordinary income and reported on your paystub and W-2. The second part is any capital gain or loss on the later sale of shares, which is taxed according the regular rules for investments.

There are no direct alternative minimum tax (AMT) costs with NSOs, as there are with ISOs. Only regular income tax rules apply. Income on NSOs is subject to federal payroll taxes and potentially state and local payroll taxes as well.

Incentive Stock Options (ISOs)

While otherwise similar, an ISO has potentially tax-saving features that a NSOs does not have. For one thing, no payroll taxes apply to ISOs.

Regular Tax

Under the regular tax rules, when you exercise an ISO, any increase in its value from the grant date is not taxed. The increase in value is taxed when you sell the shares.

ISOs receive special tax treatment under regular tax rules if you meet the required holding period rules. If you hold the shares for two years from the date you received your option and one year after you exercised your option, then any gain will be taxed at long-term capital gain tax rates instead of the higher ordinary income tax rates.

If you sell your shares before meeting the holding period rule, then you will not receive special tax treatment. Any gain on the option at exercise (market value at exercise minus exercise price) will be taxed as ordinary income and any gain above that (market value at sale minus market value at exercise) will be taxed as capital gain.

ISOs & AMT

The alternative minimum tax (AMT) system and treatment of ISOs under it are complicated. A detailed description of them is beyond the scope of this book.[15] However, a brief description of the essential elements is included here.

The AMT system is a second tax system in addition to the regular tax system. When filing your federal tax return, you must calculate your tax owed under both systems and pay the higher of the tax calculated. If your calculated tax is higher under the AMT system, then you include the extra AMT tax on your regular tax return as AMT. This is what most people refer to as having to pay AMT. It's really the difference between the tax you owe under the AMT system and the regular tax system.

Under AMT rules, any gain in the value of your ISO shares is taxed when you *exercise* your option, *not* when you sell your shares (as is the case under the regular tax system). There are no tax costs under AMT rules when you receive options.

AMT tax treatment of your ISO shares further depends on when you sell them. If you sell your ISO shares within the calendar year you exercised your option, the AMT tax treatment is the same as under the regular tax system. But, if you sell your ISO shares after the calendar year in which you exercised your option, the AMT tax treatment is the same as for a non-qualified stock option under the regular tax system.[16] This is generally the case if you were holding your shares to receive special long-term capital gains treatment under the regular tax system. Depending on your individual circumstances, this AMT tax treatment of your ISO shares as NSO shares may erase some of the regular tax savings from meeting the holding period rule. However, with the favorable changes to AMT in the 2018 tax law, which allow more income without incurring

AMT, you should re-analyze your ISO stock option strategies to determine whether exercising and holding for long-term capital gain treatment under the regular tax system will provide increased tax savings going forward.

If you have worked in the technology industry for any length of time, you have probably heard a story or two about someone who exercised stock options and got into trouble with AMT. That story most likely involved ISOs and a drop in the company's stock price after the person exercised their option. If you exercise an ISO with the intent of holding your shares to get long-term capital gain treatment under the regular tax system, your gain becomes taxable under the AMT system on exercise, and you will owe tax under the AMT system. If the stock price drops before you sell your shares, you still owe the same amount of tax under AMT. The value of your holdings might even fall below the amount of tax you owe under the AMT system, and you will be required to pay the tax from other assets.

Planning with ISOs & NSOs

Consider these tax tips when planning exercise and sale strategies with your incentive and non-qualified stock options.

1. Sell enough ISO shares on exercise to cover taxes.

Consider selling enough shares to cover the AMT obligation when exercising an incentive stock option. Set those funds aside to pay the tax owed so that you will have it even if the stock price declines after you exercise.

2. Run tax projections to determine whether an exercise-and-hold ISO tax strategy is beneficial.

While the exercise-and-hold tax strategy for ISOs can lower your tax under the regular tax system, AMT treatment of incentive stock options offsets much of the reduction in many cases. Preparing tax projections under both the regular and alternative minimum tax systems under various holding period assumptions can help you determine whether the tax benefits of holding are worth the risk of a stock price drop.

3. Run multi-year tax projections for NSO exercise and sale.

Consider spreading the exercise and sale of NSOs over several years to spread the extra income over two, three, four, or more years. Spreading income reduces gross income, which can allow you to pay tax at a lower rate.

Two Special Topics

There are two special topics that you should be aware of in regards to equity compensation that are outlined in this section: Section 83(b) election, which can greatly reduce your income tax on certain types of equity compensation in certain circumstances, and the SEC Rule 10b5-1 trading plan, which can help protect you against charges of insider trading when buying or selling your company's stock.

83(b) Election

When you receive stock from your company that is subject to vesting, the stock becomes taxable to you as the shares vest. Using an 83(b) election, you can elect to have income from the restricted shares taxed to you in the year you received the shares instead of the year in which they vest.[17] However, if you receive shares that are not subject to vesting, they will be taxable to you when you receive them and an 83(b) election will not be available.

Suppose you received 10,000 shares at $0.01 per share in a company that are subject to a four-year vesting schedule with one-quarter of the shares vesting each year. Compare the following scenarios.

83(b) election

With an election on all of the shares, you will be taxed on the value of those shares in the year you received them (10,000 x $0.01). You will, therefore, owe tax on ordinary income of $100 (fair market value of the shares less what you paid for them ($0)). You have also started the one-year counter on long-term capital gain holding treatment. If you sell the shares after one-year, the gain on the shares will be taxed as long-term capital gain.

No 83(b) election

You will owe tax on ordinary income equal to the value of the shares vested in each subsequent year. Therefore, if the shares are worth $1.00 per share at the end of the first year, you would owe tax on ordinary income of $2,500. If the shares are worth $5.00 at the end of the second year, you would owe tax in that year on ordinary income of $12,500.

That process continues until all of the shares are vested. Each year, as the shares vest, the long-term capital gains counter starts for the portion of shares vested that year. Notice that the amount of tax paid at ordinary income rates is greater if no 83(b) election is made. Notice also that tax is paid in each subsequent year. If the company remains privately held, you will not be able to sell shares to raise cash to pay the taxes. You will have to pay the tax from other assets.

RSUs

Unfortunately, 83(b) elections do not work for restricted stock units (RSUs) because the company does not actually transfer shares to you until vesting is complete. Since no shares have transferred until vesting, you cannot elect to be taxed early because transfer and vesting happen at the same time. In contrast, with restricted stock, the shares are transferred up front subject to a vesting schedule.

Stock Options

The election also does not apply to stock options with one exception. With stock options you have a right to purchase shares in the future after vesting, but no shares are transferred to you when you receive your option. In order to make an 83(b) election, shares must be transferred to you. Once the option vests, the price of the stock may have already appreciated, thereby defeating the objective of an 83(b) election. But, some stock option plans allow early exercising of stock options before they vest. With stock options that allow early exercise, you can take advantage of an 83(b) election.

1. Early-exercise NSOs: In this case, you would exercise your shares, make an 83(b) election, and owe tax at ordinary income tax rates on the difference between the fair market of the shares when you exercised and the price you paid for the shares. There is an investment risk in owning the shares because there is no way to get your money back if the company fails and the shares wind up being worth nothing.

2. Early-exercise ISOs: Because you don't owe any regular tax when you exercise your option, there is no benefit to making an 83(b) election for regular tax purposes. However, you may owe AMT on the gain in the options when you exercise, and an 83(b) election allows you to pay AMT now before the options have a chance to appreciate. Again there is an investment component to this decision. Before you exercise early to buy company stock, and before you pay tax now in the hope it will be less than the amount of tax you will pay later, be sure you are confident in the company's prospects.

Section 83(b) elections must be made **within 30 calendar days** of your receipt of the shares of stock subject to the election. There are no exceptions to IRS's strict deadline. For this reason, it is extremely important that you have proof that you filed your election on time with the IRS. You must also attach a copy of the election to your tax return.

Rather than providing a special 83(b) election form, the IRS has provided a sample list of information that it says satisfies the requirements of a proper 83(b) election.[18] You or your tax advisor will need to create an election form that includes the information required by IRS and follow IRS instructions for proper filing.

The opportunities and restrictions surrounding 83(b) elections are complex and can be confusing. If you are not confident in your understanding in this area, seek the advice and counsel of a qualified tax adviser.

10b5-1 Plans

Please note: What follows is NOT legal advice or even a complete treatment of this area or related areas such as insider transaction reporting. This is a complicated area of securities law that has evolved from court cases over many years. How it applies to you depends on your unique facts and circumstances.

Selling or buying a company's stock (or other securities) when you are aware of "material nonpublic information" about the company is called insider trading and it is illegal.[19] If found guilty of insider trading, you may face civil penalties of up to three times the profit you made or losses you avoided.[20] You may also face criminal charges with maximum penalties of 20 years' jail time or $5 million in fines, or both.[21] The same applies to your friends and family if you tip them off about material nonpublic information.

There are two parts to the definition of material nonpublic information:

1. Nonpublic information is information about a company that has not been communicated to the general public and securities markets. Information is public if it has been widely disseminated, for example through a prospectus, company press release, earnings announce-

ment, Securities and Exchange Commission (SEC) filing, *Wall Street Journal* article, or data service such as Bloomberg or Morningstar.

2. Material information is information that an average prudent investor would consider important in making a decision whether to buy or sell a particular stock (or other security) or that would affect the price of the stock. In short, material nonpublic information is important information that would probably affect a company's stock price if it were known to the public.

The management team, officers, and directors of publicly traded companies are often in possession of material nonpublic information. Other employees might be aware of material nonpublic information from time to time as well; for example, members of a sales team who just won a large order or scientists running a clinical trial for a new drug who see positive or negative results. In fact, many employees, particularly in smaller, publicly traded technology and biotechnology companies are regularly aware of inside information.[22] If you are regularly in possession of material nonpublic information and want to trade your company's stock, consider protecting yourself from insider trading charges by:

1. Becoming familiar with your company's policies regarding insider trading;

2. Consulting with your company's attorneys and any brokerage firm your company works regarding 10b5-1 trading plans;

3. Discussing your situation with an outside attorney who specializes in securities law.

How can employees, managers, executives, officers, and directors who may become aware of material nonpublic information exercise stock options and sell or buy stock in their company without committing insider trading? One popular approach is to use an SEC Rule 10b5-1 "trading plan," which provides an affirmative defense to insider trading charges.

A trading plan is a written plan to buy or sell company stock (or other securities) put in place when the employee or director is not aware of any material nonpublic information. The 10b5-1 trading plan is for a fixed period of time and usually takes the form of an agreement with the brokerage firm that will execute transactions called for in the plan. Per SEC Rule 10b5-1, the trading plan must do the following:

- Specify the amount, price (possibly including a limit price) and dates for purchases and sales;
- Include a written formula or algorithm, or computer program, for determining amount, price and dates; or
- Give full discretion to the brokerage firm to determine how, when or whether to make purchases or sales, provided that the brokerage firm is not aware of any material nonpublic information when it executes trades.

A simple example of a 10b5-1 trading plan might be to exercise and sell 1,000 shares under a stock option agreement each month for next 12 months. Another example might be to sell $125,000 worth of stock each quarter for the next eight quarters. Another example might be to liquidate 2% of stock holdings each month for 15 months.

The 10b5-1 trading plan must be followed in order for it to be an effective affirmative defense to insider trading charges.[23] The person entering the 10b5-1 trading plan must not attempt to influence transactions made according to the plan once the plan is in place. No hedging transactions outside of the plan are allowed which would have the effect of altering or negating the trading plan. The plan must be entered into in good faith and not as part of a scheme to evade insider trading rules.[24] While not specifically required by 10b5-1, many attorneys recommend a waiting period after a trading plan is in place before transactions can occur.

Summary

- Become familiar with the features and tax treatment of major types of equity compensation available to you including non-qualified and incentive stock options, restricted stock, restricted stock units and employee stock purchase plans.
- If your employer's ESPP has favorable features, earn the nearly risk free, built-in investment gain by enrolling in the plan, maxing out your contribution, and selling your shares when you receive them.
- With restricted stock and RSUs, there is no tax benefit to holding shares so generally it's best to sell your shares as they vest to diversify your investments.

- Avoid becoming dependent on an equity compensation subsidy to your income.
- Be sure to include any gain from the sale of ESPP, restricted stock and RSU shares in your income tax planning.
- For ISOs, run tax projections to determine whether an exercise-and-hold strategy is beneficial under regular and AMT tax systems, and consider selling some shares upon exercise to pay taxes.
- For NSOs, run multi-year tax projections to determine whether spreading income over several years can reduce your tax liability by paying tax in lower rate brackets.
- Keep in mind that technology stocks are often risky and volatile. Balance tax considerations with investment considerations: the risk of holding technology stock and suffering a large price decline may outweigh any benefit from a particular tax strategy.
- Be aware when your company's trading window is open for sales of shares from exercised stock options, restricted stock, RSUs, and ESPP.
- With restricted stock subject to vesting and early-exercise eligible stock options, consider making an 83(b) tax election.
- If you are regularly in possession of "material nonpublic" information and want to sell or buy your employer's publicly traded stock, a 10b5-1 trading plan can provide protection against insider trading charges.

The previous two chapters are related in a way you may not have thought about before. In its simplest form, your personal wealth is the sum of your investment capital and your human capital. Your investment capital is the value of your current investments. Your human capital is the total value of all your future earnings. The chapter before this one covered how to manage your investment capital. This chapter covered an important part of the average tech professional's human capital: their stock-based compensation.

Early in our careers, almost all of our wealth is in the form of human capital as we have only just begun to save and accumulate financial assets. Over time, the value of our human capital declines with fewer years left to work and our investment capital grows as we save and invest.

Building personal wealth involves maximizing your human capital and simultaneously converting as much of it as possible to investment capital over time.

You monetize your human capital by taking full advantage of features in your compensation package, including and particularly your equity compensation. Making yourself more valuable to your employer or investors, and asking for a raise every now and then can be a great idea, too.

The next chapter covers what is, for many tech professionals, the largest and most expensive single asset: a home. Because of the high cost of housing generally and the extra high cost of housing in many tech cities, this area of your personal finances gets special attention.

Home Truths About Real Estate

magine two homes. One is an attractive 1980s two-story custom-built home: four bedrooms, four bathrooms, 2,600 square feet on an 8,000 square-foot lot in a desirable, family-friendly neighborhood with tree-lined streets and good schools.

The second is a two-story home built in the mid-1970s as part of a suburban housing development. It's located in a quiet neighborhood with wide streets, mature trees, and a good school district. It is 2,200 square feet, has four bedrooms, three bathrooms, a two-car garage, and sits on an 8,000 square-foot lot.

Not much to choose between these two homes, from the description. Both homes were for sale recently. How much would you expect to pay for each? The first home is slightly newer, slightly larger and probably has slightly better curb appeal for most people. You might think the first home is worth more.

However, that home is located in the upscale western suburbs of Des Moines, Iowa, a city ranked #4 on U.S. News and World Report's 100 Best Places to Live in the USA ranking.[1] The asking price on this home was $349,900. The second home is located in Santa Clara, California, in the middle of Silicon Valley. The asking price on this home was $1,990,000—more than five times the price of the first home.

The goal-crushing cost of housing in Silicon Valley, and now increasingly in other tech-industry cities, can be an obstacle to building net worth and meeting your financial objectives.

For many families, their home is one of their biggest investments—if not their single largest asset. Because your home may represent a significant portion of your net worth, decisions surrounding your home require special attention. Some of the important questions that come up frequently are covered in this chapter:

- Should you consider your home an investment?
- Should you pay off your mortgage (or pay it down faster)?
- Should you refinance your home loan?
- What is the impact of property tax?
- Should you rent or buy?
- Should you own rental real estate?
- How does property tax affect decisions about private school?

Housing Costs

Silicon Valley

Silicon Valley is spread across a wide geographic area, spanning Santa Clara County in the south and running up the San Francisco peninsula, through San Mateo County to the city of San Francisco in the north. Santa Clara County is home to the original Silicon Valley iconic companies: Hewlett-Packard, Fairchild Semiconductor, Intel, and Cisco Systems. Apple, Facebook, Google, and Netflix are now headquartered in Santa Clara County, along with hundreds of other established and startup technology and biotechnology companies. People crowd to Silicon Valley from all over the world to work, drawn by its possibilities, and turning the region into a truly global cultural hub. It is also a really expensive place to live.

In May 2018, the median selling price of a single family home in Santa Clara County reached $1.4 million, over five times the median home price in the United States.[2] In San Mateo County and San Francisco County, the next two counties further to the north, the median selling price was even higher at $1.6 million, the highest of all Californian counties.

Purchasing a home in Santa Clara County at the median price of $1.4 million requires a minimum $280,000 down payment (20%) and a mortgage of $1,120,000 (80%). In 2018, in Santa Clara and San Mateo counties, mortgages over $679,650 are categorized as "jumbo" mortgages by the Federal Housing Finance Agency (FHFA), and they carry a higher interest rate than conventional loans. Jumbo loan limits vary by county within the U.S. With a 4.5% annual interest rate on a 30-year fixed-rate mortgage, your annual mortgage payments would total over $68,000. Add property tax (including municipal add-ons) of 1.25%, or about another $17,500 per year. Home insurance is required by lenders and may add another $2,000 per year, depending on the home's age, type of construction, location, and other factors. Together, loan payments, property tax, and insurance for the median-priced home in Santa Clara County total over $87,000 per year.

Other Tech Cities

Figure 15 shows housing affordability in the 15 cities with the largest tech-industry employment in the United States. California's tech cities top the list, having the least affordable housing. Based on affordability index, California is more than twice as expensive as the U.S. as a whole and much higher than other tech cities. Affordability is measured by dividing the median price of a single family home by the median household income in a region. A higher affordability ratio means the city is less affordable. Most major tech cities are worse than the U.S. average for affordability.

	AFFORDABILITY RATIO		
	2015	**2016**	**2017**
San Jose-Sunnyvale-Santa Clara, CA	9.2	9.3	10.0
Los Angeles-Long Beach-Anaheim, CA	8.8	9.0	9.5
San Francisco-Oakland-Hayward, CA	8.6	8.5	8.9
San Diego-Carlsbad, CA	7.9	7.8	8.1
New York-Newark-Jersey City, NY-NJ-PA	5.6	5.3	5.5
Denver-Aurora-Lakewood, CO	5.1	5.3	5.6
Seattle-Tacoma-Bellevue, WA	5.0	5.2	5.7
Boston-Cambridge-Newton, MA-NH	5.1	5.0	5.2
Austin-Round Rock, TX	3.9	4.0	4.0
United States	**4.0**	**4.1**	**4.2**
Washington-Arlington-Alexandria, DC-VA-MD-WV	4.1	4.1	4.1
Dallas-Fort Worth-Arlington, TX	3.3	3.5	3.7
Raleigh, NC	3.6	3.5	3.6
Chicago-Naperville-Elgin, IL-IN-WI	3.4	3.5	3.6
Atlanta-Sandy Springs-Roswell, GA	2.9	2.9	3.1
Detroit-Warren-Dearborn, MI	2.7	2.8	2.9

Figure 15
Source: *"State of the Nation's Housing 2018." Harvard Joint Center for Housing Studies, http://www.jchs.harvard.edu/state-nations-housing-2018*

While this may seem obvious, high housing costs divert a high percentage of your overall living expense budget. This leaves less for other spending and saving. While basic living expenses such as clothing, groceries, utilities, medical costs, auto insurance, and gas must be paid, high housing cost leaves less for discretionary out-flows, such as dining out, entertainment, hobbies, and vacations. And this estimated home ownership cost does not include annual home maintenance and periodic repairs, such as replacing the roof, changing the water heater, exterior painting, and the many other expenses involved in maintaining a home. And lastly, it does not in-clude any upgrades or remodeling to your new home. Even for high income households, buying and owning a home can be challenging.

Part of the cost of owning a home is tax deductible, which helps. Mortgage interest and property tax payments are deductible for federal and state income tax purposes. However, new tax rules for 2018 reduce some of the benefit as discussed below.

Is Your Home an Investment?

The value of your home as an investment is the equity you have in your home. Your home equity is the money you would have left if you sold your home, paid selling costs, paid off your home loans, and paid any capital gains tax owed.

You build equity in your home over time through appreciation of the property, by paying down your home loan, or both. Home prices have appreciated 6.5% annually on average in the U.S. over the last five years, continuing their rebound after the Great Reces-sion of 2008, with substantial variation by locality. Figure 16 shows annual appreciation in major metropolitan areas with a concentra-tion of technology industry.[3]

REGION	HOME PRICE APPRECIATION									
	2008	2009	2010	2011	2012	2013	2014	2015	2016	2017
United States	-12.0%	-3.9%	-4.1%	-3.9%	6.5%	10.7%	4.5%	5.2%	5.4%	6.3%
Atlanta	-12.8%	-3.9%	-7.9%	-12.8%	9.9%	18.1%	5.1%	5.5%	6.1%	5.4%
Boston	-7.0%	-0.5%	-0.8%	-2.6%	3.6%	9.7%	3.8%	4.5%	6.2%	5.5%
Chicago	-14.3%	-7.2%	-7.4%	-6.5%	2.2%	11.3%	1.2%	2.3%	4.2%	2.5%
Dallas	-4.4%	2.9%	-3.5%	-1.3%	6.5%	10.2%	7.5%	9.5%	8.1%	6.9%
Denver	-4.0%	-1.2%	-2.4%	-0.4%	8.5%	9.0%	8.2%	10.2%	8.9%	7.4%
Detroit	-21.7%	-10.3%	-6.2%	3.5%	15.2%	16.6%	2.5%	6.7%	6.1%	7.0%
Los Angeles	-26.5%	0.0%	-0.2%	-5.2%	10.2%	20.3%	5.5%	6.0%	5.4%	7.3%
New York	-9.2%	-6.3%	-2.3%	-3.3%	-0.3%	6.2%	1.6%	2.9%	3.1%	5.6%
San Diego	-24.8%	2.7%	1.7%	-5.4%	9.2%	18.0%	4.9%	7.0%	5.4%	7.4%
San Francisco	-31.2%	4.8%	-0.3%	-5.4%	14.4%	22.6%	9.4%	10.4%	6.1%	9.3%
Seattle	-13.4%	-7.9%	-6.0%	-5.6%	8.2%	12.4%	6.6%	9.7%	10.8%	12.7%
Washington D.C.	-19.6%	1.9%	2.3%	-2.5%	5.8%	8.1%	1.3%	1.4%	2.7%	2.8%

Figure 16
Source: Case-Schiller Home Price Index

Effects of Leverage

A home is a large asset. Because it is a large purchase, homebuyers typically finance the purchase of a home with a home loan. Common loan terms require a 20% down payment. By definition, when you finance the purchase of your home you make a leveraged investment, meaning you buy an asset worth more than the amount you have to invest. In this case you buy an entire home and invest only the 20% of the purchase price paid as down payment. You will earn appreciation on the entire home value, not just the 20% you invested.

For example, if you purchase a home for $1 million and you make a 20% down payment, you have invested $200,000. If your home appreciates 5% after one year, the value of your home grew $50,000. The value of your $200,000 investment grew by $50,000 also, which was a 25% return on your investment. Well, not exactly. You also have a loan on your home that you paid interest on at the rate of 4.5% per year. You paid total interest of about $36,000. If we subtract the cost of financing your investment from the amount the home appreciated for the year, you have a total return of $50,000 - $36,000 = $14,000. Your $200,000 investment earned $14,000, or 7% for the year. Notice that the home appreciated only 5%, but your investment earned 7%. That is the result of leverage.

If your home appreciated only 3% during the year, then your $200,000 investment would have lost $6,000 because the $36,000 of mortgage interest would have offset the $30,000 appreciation. In this case, you lost 3% on your investment even though your home increased in value by 3%. That also is the result of leverage. Leverage amplifies your investment return in both directions, up and down.

This is a simple example to demonstrate the effects of leverage. It does not take into account other costs of owning the home such as property tax. It also does not take into account the mortgage interest deduction for income tax, which has the effect of lowering the effective interest rate you pay on your loan.

Special Tax Treatment

Homes are unique investments because they receive special income tax treatment.

1. Mortgage interest tax deduction

You receive an income tax deduction for your mortgage interest payments. Mortgage interest on new loans up to $750,000 used to buy, build, or improve your home is deductible under the regular tax system and alternative minimum tax system. For mortgage loans in place on or before December 14, 2017, interest on loan amounts up to $1,000,000 remains deductible. Beginning in 2018, home equity line of credit, often called HELOC, loan interest is no longer deductible under the regular tax system, and it continues not to be deductible under the alternative minimum tax (AMT) system. With HELOC interest no longer deductible for federal income tax, you may want to reconsider taking on new HELOC debt and accelerating payoff of any existing HELOC loan.

The mortgage interest deduction has the effect of lowering the interest rate at which you can borrow money to buy a home. The deduction is particularly valuable for taxpayers in higher income tax brackets who receive a greater benefit from the deduction.

Other types of investments receive a deduction for interest on loans used to acquire the investment also, but there are limits on the deduction. You can only deduct investment interest up to the amount of investment income you earn during the year. Any investment interest left over can be carried forward to future years. However, investment interest expense is not deductible for AMT—unlike home mortgage interest, which is deductible.

2. Property tax deduction

Property tax on your home is tax deductible. However, new rules for 2018 limit your combined property tax and other state and local tax deduction to a total of $10,000 for federal income tax purposes under the regular tax system, and they continue not to be deductible under the AMT system. Before 2018, property tax deduction was unlimited. This new limitation will particularly affect people living in states with high income tax and high home prices such as California and New York.

3. Capital gain exclusion

The most valuable tax benefit is the capital gain exclusion. For single taxpayers, the first $250,000 of capital gain on the sale of your primary residence is excluded from income tax (capital gains tax). For married taxpayers, the first $500,000 of gain is excluded from income tax (capital gains tax). This is a huge benefit. No other investment allows you to not pay federal income tax on the first half-million dollars of investment gain. States generally conform to the federal rules and allow the exclusion as well.

Liquidity

Homes are fairly liquid investments, meaning that they can be sold reasonably quickly without impacting the price. Homes can be sold in a matter of weeks to months in most areas. This is not as quick as publicly traded mutual funds, which can be sold in one day. However, it is far more liquid than private equity or hedge fund limited partnership investments, which can tie up your money for as much as eight years or more with no opportunity to sell.

Divisibility

An important problem with considering a home as investment is that your home cannot be sold in pieces to pay for living expenses. It is an indivisible asset. Unlike mutual fund or stock investments, which allow you to sell a portion of your shares to raise cash for living expenses, you have to sell 100% of your home to raise cash to pay for living expenses or make other investments. There is no way to sell just the spare bedroom or the formal dining room you don't use any more. But if you don't mind having other people living in your home, you can rent a room to long-term tenant or rent part or all of your home occasionally, using a short-term rental brokering service such as Airbnb or VRBO (Vacation Rentals By Owner).

Use or Lifestyle Asset

Closely related to the divisibility problem is that your home is an asset that you use. You sleep there. You cook there. You keep your stuff there. It is an asset you use to facilitate your life, making it better defined as a lifestyle asset than an investment asset.

If you plan to never sell your home, it's difficult to consider it an investment asset. It may appreciate and generate income tax deduction for many years. However, if you never plan to sell your home, it can never serve the important function that your other investment assets serve—being available to pay for your expenses in retirement.

The important implication here is that if you plan to live in your home during retirement, you should not consider your home as part of your retirement portfolio. You must have other sufficiently liquid, divisible assets to pay for your living expenses.

Property Tax

Unlike your home loan, which typically will be paid off eventually through regular payments of principal and interest, the property tax payment on your home will continue for as long as you own your home. That may sound obvious, but it is a fact which many people overlook in making decisions about their home and where to live.

In most states, property tax is an asset-based tax levied on the value of your property. Most jurisdictions also have provisions for increasing your property tax as the value of your property increases over time. In some markets, property tax can increase based on budgetary needs of local taxing districts and are less predictable than if based on property value alone.

California's Proposition 13 modified the state's constitution in 1978 to limit property tax assessments to 1% of the value of the property and to limit annual increases to property tax to no more than an inflation factor, which cannot exceed 2% per year. Property in California generally appreciates at more than 2% per year, meaning that property tax assessments can fall behind market value assessments. Property is reassessed to market value when property changes ownership or construction takes place. This commonly means that people who have lived in their homes in California for many years pay less, often much less, property tax than people who purchased an equivalent property recently.

Because property tax is based on the value of your property, moving up in home size and property value increases your property tax bill. In addition, starting from a larger home value, annual increases in property tax assessment resulting from appreciation of your home will be larger in total dollars as well. This issue is particularly important in California if you have been in your current home for many years and your property tax is much lower than would be assessed now at the market value of your current home. Moving to a larger home could mean a large increase in property tax.

The additional property tax continues as long as you own your home. That extra expense in the years after full-time work adds weight to the cash flow scales, which must be balanced by more inflows during working years. Property tax is an important factor to consider in deciding whether to upgrade to a bigger home.

Should I Pay Off My Mortgage?

While you are working, there is a big benefit to the mortgage interest tax deduction, particularly in high income tax states like California and New York.

For example, if you are a two-professional household with taxable income of $200,000 and your filing status is married filing jointly, then you are in the 24% marginal tax bracket. That means that 24 cents of every dollar you earn in the income range between $165,000 and $315,000 goes to pay federal income tax. If you live in California, you are in the 9.3% marginal tax bracket for state income tax. That means 9.3 cents of every dollar you earn in the income range between $105,224 and $537,500 goes to pay state income tax. With $200,000 of income, you pay about 33 cents of each additional dollar you earn to federal and state income tax. When you deduct mortgage interest from your income on your tax return, you reduce your taxable income by the amount of mortgage interest you paid. The mortgage interest you deduct multiplied by your marginal tax rate is how much money you saved in income tax by claiming the mortgage interest deduction. In this example, if mortgage interest was $60,000, then the mortgage interest deduction saved you about $20,000 in total tax.

Another way to describe tax savings from the mortgage interest deduction is the tax adjusted interest rate on your home loan. The tax savings from the mortgage interest deduction effectively reduces your home loan interest rate by your marginal tax rate. For example, if your home interest rate is 4.5% and your combined federal and state marginal tax rate is 42%, then your effective home loan interest rate is 2.6%.

Borrowing to Invest

If you have investments which you could sell to pay off or pay down your mortgage, it may be better to keep those investments working and not pay off your mortgage immediately. For example, if your investments earn you an average annual return of 8% and you take some of those investments to pay off your home loan with a tax-adjusted interest rate of 2.6%, you just reduced your total return on that money by 5.4%. You saved interest expense at a tax-adjusted interest rate of 2.6%, but you gave up an investment return of 8%. The difference is 5.4% which you would have earned had you not paid off your home loan.

Essentially, by continuing your home loan when you have enough investment assets to pay it off, you are borrowing against your home to buy more investments. You have the option to use some of your investment assets to pay down or pay off your home loan at any time. Keeping your home loan leverages your investment portfolio and allows you to earn the return differential between your investment portfolio return and the after-tax interest rate on your home loan.

This is not something that everyone should do or will want to do. The idea is hotly debated among financial professionals, with many holding the view that paying down debt is a higher priority. There are real risks. For example, if you permanently lose money on your investments, you would have been better off using that money to pay down your mortgage. Also, continuing your home loan assumes that you can make loan payment from income and not access your investments. This sets an upper limit on how far you go with the approach. You don't want to need to access your investments to make home loan payments when your investments may be temporarily down due to stock market correction.

Assuming you have a common, fully-amortizing home loan, the amount of interest you pay with each payment declines over time. A higher fraction of your payment goes toward repayment of principal each month. As you get further into your loan repayment, you are paying less and less interest and receiving less and less benefit from the mortgage interest deduction. The value of keeping your loan to reduce income tax is declining all the time. As the amount of principal paid each month grows, more and more of your payments essentially become transfers from your investments. Once you stop working and your compensation income is gone, and depending on your other income sources, you may not receive much if any benefit from the mortgage interest deduction. In that case, paying off your home loan may make sense.

Home Loan Refinance

Refinancing your home loan usually refers to shopping for and obtaining a new home loan with a lower interest rate than your current loan. The key question in deciding whether to refinance your home mortgage and what type of loan to refinance with is this: Will your total financing cost be less over the time period you expect to have the loan? If the answer is yes, then it may make sense to refinance. To decide, compare the amount of money you'll save to the often considerable effort it takes to refinance and the value of your time.

The time element is important to your decision. In refinancing your home loan, you will incur upfront costs (including closing costs and possibly prepaying interest to reduce your interest rate on the new loan. i.e., paying points). It will take time before the monthly saving from a reduced interest rate allows you to recoup the amount you paid in upfront costs. The point in time after which you recoup upfront costs of a new loan through reduced interest rate is called "breakeven." You must keep the new loan a certain amount of time to breakeven on the refinancing, or the effort won't have been worth it. For example, if the breakeven point for a new loan is seven years and you believe you may move within five years, refinancing is probably not a good idea. Mortgage refinance calculators are available online to help with these calculations.

Time is also important in selecting the type of loan to refinance with. For example, if you know you will only be in your home for seven more years, until the kids graduate from college, then a loan which has a fixed interest rate for seven years and a variable interest rate after seven years might be a good choice. This type of loan is called 7/1 adjustable rate mortgage, or 7/1 ARM. The advantage of a 7/1 ARM is that the interest rate during initial seven year period will be lower than a traditional 30-year fixed rate mortgage. The interest rate is lower because the lender is taking less risk that interest rates will rise over seven years instead of 30 years. Lenders charge higher interest rates on loans that are riskier for them. Of course the disadvantage of a 7/1 ARM is that if you decide to stay in the same home longer than seven years, the interest rate may adjust to a higher rate at the end of seven years and the loan will be more expensive.

With traditional 30-year fixed rate home loans, a helpful rule of thumb is that a refinance may make sense if the interest rate on the new loan is 0.50% to 0.75% lower than your current loan. Of course the correct answer depends on the details of the specific loan and its upfront costs.

Be aware that refinancing your loan to obtain a lower interest rate also resets the term of the loan. For example, if you refinance a 30-year fixed interest rate home loan 10 years into the loan, you extend the remaining term from your current 20 years back out to 30 years. The total cost of the loan over 30 years instead of 20 years can be higher depending on the new interest rate. It may be worth shopping for 15- or 20-year loan, which may have a lower interest rate and lower total interest cost over the life of the loan.

Renting vs. Owning

In the United States, about 64% of households own the home they live in.[4] Home ownership in tech cities varies by city, which probably reflects home affordability in the region. Figure 17 shows home ownership percentage in the cities with largest tech industry employment.

METROPOLITAN STATISTICAL AREA	FIRST QUARTER 2018	MARGIN OF ERROR
Atlanta-Sandy Springs-Roswell, GA	67.4%	3.8%
Austin-Round Rock, TX	56.1%	6.8%
Boston-Cambridge-Newton, MA-NH	59.4%	3.7%
Chicago-Naperville-Elgin, IL-IN-WI	67.1%	2.9%
Dallas-Ft. Worth-Arlington, TX	62.0%	3.5%
Denver-Aurora-Lakewood, CO	53.0%	5.4%
Detroit-Warren-Dearborn, MI	65.0%	4.3%
Los Angeles-Long Beach-Anaheim, CA	51.9%	2.8%
New York-Newark-Jersey City, NY-NJ-PA	50.0%	2.2%
Raleigh, NC	67.8%	7.4%
Richmond, VA	60.0%	8.2%
San Diego-Carlsbad, CA	60.0%	5.2%
San Francisco-Oakland-Hayward, CA	52.6%	4.5%
San Jose-Sunnyvale-Santa Clara, CA	56.2%	6.9%
Seattle-Tacoma-Bellevue, WA	58.2%	4.5%
Washington-Arlington-Alexandria, DC-VA-MD-WV	62.6%	3.8%

Figure 17

Source: "Housing Vacancies and Homeownership," U.S. Census Bureau,
https://www.census.gov/housing/hvs/data/rates.html

Home ownership is an important goal for many people. However, owning a home may not fit your circumstances. Financially, it may be better to lease or rent a home. If you plan to live in the area only for a short time, leasing or renting a place to live may make more sense than buying a home. For example, if you are on a temporary assignment or if your company moves you around to different locations periodically.

Transaction costs on residential real estate are high and based on the value of the transaction. The seller typically pays the transaction costs, which include brokerage commission and closing costs. Selling a single family home or condominium will cost 5% to 10% of the sales price in most tech cities. For example, the total cost to sell the median-priced single family residence in Silicon Valley would be 7% of $1.4 million, or over $98,000. It takes several years of appreciation to cover just the round-trip transaction cost of buying and selling a home. If you don't plan on living in the area long enough for your home to appreciate enough to pay for the transaction cost, then it may make more sense to lease or rent a property for the time you are in the area.

If you do plan on living in the area for many years, it may make sense to lease or rent a home for a few reasons:

- **The cost of leasing or renting may be less than the cost of owning a home.** When you rent, you don't pay property tax or incur expenses in maintaining the property directly (although they may be passed onto you in the form of higher rent either now or in the future). The difference in cost between leasing or renting and owning is location specific.

- **You may be saving for a down payment on a home.**
  With reduced cost for housing, you're able to save more
  for your home purchase. Renting is typically cheaper
  than owning if you include full ownership costs of
  mortgage, property tax, insurance, and maintenance in
  the comparison.[5]

- **You may be waiting for your stock options or restricted stock units to vest.** Once your stock options
  or restricted stock units vest, you can sell shares and use
  sale proceeds to purchase your home. (You might also
  be waiting to receive money from other sources such as
  gifts or inheritance.)

- **You are keeping life simple.** Your work or travel
  schedule may not allow you time for home ownership
  right now.

With leasing or renting you will not be building equity in a
property. Furthermore, in an appreciating housing market, there is
a risk that home prices will continue to rise and you will be "priced
out" of market, meaning that as prices rise ultimately it becomes
too expensive for you to purchase a home in that market.

Renting Your Real Estate for Income

When moving to a new home, homeowners need to decide
what to do with their old home. The primary options are to 1)
sell the old home and use equity in the old home to help fund the
purchase of the new home or 2) turn the old home into an income
property by renting it out. If the old home has declined in value,

some homeowners might consider converting it to a rental property to avoid selling it at a loss while waiting for its price to go back up.

The prospect of developing an income stream separate from your day job can be appealing. There are plenty of books, websites, and free-seminars-coming-to-a-hotel-near-you promoting the idea of owning rental estate and creating lifetime income. Sometimes it's even described as an early retirement plan.

And it can be. But realize what it is: a separate investment discipline unto itself, pursued by deliberate real estate investors. Successful real estate investors carefully select properties for purchase that have strong cash flow or the potential to appreciate, or both. Many real estate investors develop a style around one or the other of these two investment goals, which impacts how their properties are financed. Developing the expertise to evaluate properties and their potential to be good investments takes considerable time and effort.

Would careful research identify your old home as the top candidate for your first rental property based on its potential for strong cash flow or appreciation? Maybe, but probably not because most people select their home based on different criteria than a real estate investor would use for selecting a rental property.

Owning rental real estate has the nature of owning a business. You own an asset that creates revenue which needs to be collected and that has expenses which need to be paid. Homeowners who are not real estate investors tend to overestimate the revenue potential, underestimate the expenses, and greatly underestimate the amount of work involved in rental real estate.

Managing Rental Income

While not an exhaustive list, here is a flavor of the issues you'll encounter related to the revenue portion of your business as a landlord:

- **You need to find tenants for your property.** That involves running ads, showing the property, accepting applications, conducting credit and reference checks, preparing a lease agreement, selecting a tenant and declining the other applicants (which is often the least fun part because you meet such nice people), arranging for key transfer and move-in. You may hire a real estate broker to help you find tenants. You need to be aware of the local, state, and federal laws related to discrimination and conducting credit checks.

- **You have to collect rents from tenants each month.** This can be a chore. Rather than waiting for paper checks, sending reminder emails or letters and knocking on doors to collect rents, encourage your tenants to set up an automatic direct deposit of their monthly rent. Maintain separate bank accounts for each of each your properties. Tenants don't always pay their rent. When that happens, you need to be familiar with local laws regarding evicting tenants.

- **In budgeting your monthly cash flow from your property, you'll need to plan for months when your property won't be rented, such as after a tenant moves.** You'll need to be able to turn your property quickly to get a new tenant moved in to keep loss of revenue to a minimum. This usually involves having maintenance, painting, and cleaning crews available on short notice unless you are able and willing to do the work yourself.

- **You will need to have a policy in mind for rental rate.** Will you price your rental at the high end of the range for your area, which is likely to attract demanding tenants who will require more service from you and will be intolerant of minor issues with the property? Or will you price your rental at the lower end of the market and let your tenants know you did that on purpose so they won't bother you (as much)? You'll need to decide how often to increase rents for existing tenants. If you live in a rent controlled area, you need to be aware of local laws dictating how much you can rent your residential rental property for and when you can increase rents.

Managing Rental Expense

As a landlord, you'll also need to consider the expenses involved in renting your property. Typical expenses include the following:

- Advertising
- Cleaning and maintenance (e.g., gardening service)
- Commissions (e.g., paid to real estate agents for finding tenants)
- Insurance
- Legal and professional fees
- Management fees
- Mortgage (only interest portion is deductible for income tax purposes)

- Property tax
- Repairs (e.g., replace dishwasher, replace garage door opener, new roof)
- Supplies
- Travel (including legitimate rental related over-night travel away from home)
- Utilities

As a rental property owner, you'll either be performing many of the tasks associated with these expenses yourself or you will be hiring service providers to do the work for you. Either way, it takes time and effort.

A certain amount of flexibility in dealing with issues that arise is helpful too. For example, I know a couple who moved from their large home to a smaller place when their kids went off to college. They rented out the old home to a local real estate agent. One day when the couple went to check on the property, they met a stranger at the house who was staying there. Apparently, the real estate agent posted the home on a short-term rental website (e.g., Airbnb, VRBO) and had been subleasing the property without the owner's knowledge or permission.

If you don't have time or inclination to manage the property yourself, you can hire a property manager to do most of the work for you. Property managers typically charge 7% to 10% of your monthly rental income to manage a property. If you'd prefer not to receive calls in the middle of the night about plumbing problems, hiring a property manager may be a good choice.

Rental Property Cash Flow

The way a property is financed affects its cash flow. Many single family homes are financed with a loan equal to 80% or 90% of the property value. Large loan payments often create a situation where that property will not generate positive cash flow. That is, the expenses of the property are greater than the monthly rental income received.

In such cases, the property owner has to "feed" the property using cash from other sources to make up the difference. The property is operating at cash flow loss. This may be a sound investment strategy if the property is also appreciating. But it does require the owner be able to fund the operating losses. In contrast, a real estate investor might make a 50% down payment on a property, reducing the monthly mortgage payments so that it has positive cash flow. Again the financing of a property depends on the investor's investment goals, cash flow, or appreciation.

Tax Rules on Rentals

If you haven't financed your rental property specifically to generate positive or at least neutral (zero) cash flow, you may be operating with a cash flow loss. Even if your cash flow is somewhat negative, you may be operating at a loss for income tax purposes. That's because of depreciation. For income tax purposes, you are allowed to deduct from your rental income a certain amount of depreciation expense each year along with your other cash expenses. Depreciation is an accounting concept meant to record the amount of an asset that is "used up" during the year and will ultimately need to be replaced. The value of the structure, not the value of the land, is depreciated over 27.5 years by IRS rules. With depreciation, you may be able to generate positive cash flow and still have a loss for income tax purposes.

Unfortunately, tax rules don't allow you to offset your rental property losses against your ordinary income. Losses from rental real estate are considered "passive activity losses" and have to be either offset with other passive income or accumulated until you sell the property and deducted against any gain on the sale of the property.[6] Owning and managing rental real estate is considered a passive activity under the tax rules unless you spend 50% or more of the time you work and more than 750 hours during a tax year on a real estate business in which you materially participate.

There is a special allowance that allows married couples filing a joint tax return to deduct up to $25,000 of loss from a passive real estate activity against ordinary income. Unfortunately, there is a limit on the allowance. The special allowance of $25,000 of loss is phased out based on your income. The amount of special allowance is reduced by 50% of the amount of your modified adjusted gross income that's more than $100,000 (married filing jointly). Once your joint income reaches $150,000, the special allowance is completely phased out and you get no benefit from it.

Another area of tax regulation that real estate investors should be aware of is Internal Revenue Code (IRC) Section 1031. If you have a lot of gain in a rental property, you can delay paying income tax on the gain when you sell the property by immediately buying another property in a "1031 exchange." The gain from the old property is rolled over into the new property and any tax payment on the gain is postponed until the new property is sold.

The new tax law for 2018 added a brand new feature to existing tax law that could prove to be beneficial to rental real estate owners. Section 199A, also called the pass-through deduction, allows a deduction equal to 20% of pass-through business income in calculating your taxable income on your personal tax return. While the 2018 tax law is still new, and the IRS has yet to issue guidance on interpretation of the new law, many tax professionals believe the new 20% deduction will apply to rental real estate. The deduction appears to apply to rental real estate that is held outside of an entity such as a limited liability company (LLC), subchapter S corporation (S-corporation) or partnership, as well as property held inside those entities. That means that rental property you own directly and report on Schedule E of your tax return appears to qualify for the new 20% deduction. As with many deductions, there are several complicated limitations on the new deduction, which may apply to your situation.

In summary, rental real estate owners need to be good at the business of operating rental real estate, which includes understanding tax rules. Like most other endeavors in life, becoming a good rental real estate investor requires effort, learning, and practice.

Private School vs. Property Tax

School quality is a key driver of single family home prices and appreciation, all other factors held constant. That fact is common knowledge among real estate professionals and has been well documented in economic research literature over seven decades.[7] Therefore, it follows that higher home prices also mean higher property tax payments in better school districts because property tax assessments are based on home value.

As an alternative to expensive housing in good school districts, buyers can also consider living in less expensive areas with lower quality schools and enrolling their children in private school. The cost of private school will be much higher than the free public school while the kids are in school. However, the annual property tax will be lower during the time the kids are in school and potentially long after that. There is a trade-off between the high cost of private school coupled with lower property tax versus free public education and the ongoing cost of higher property tax.

Of course you can always move to a good school district while your kids are in school and then move to a less expensive area when your kids leave home. But as discussed in this chapter, downsizing won't necessarily save money in the long term because property prices might have continued appreciating, resulting in higher property tax once you move. It's important to think this through ahead of time.

Whether it's better to send your kids to public school in a more expensive area or send your kids to private school while living in a more affordable area depends on the specifics or your situation and preferences. The point is to be aware of the different options available for your children to receive a great education.

Summary

- Because your home is one of your largest assets and housing costs are high in tech cities, take special care with decisions surrounding your home.
- Treat your home as an investment only if you plan to sell it and use the built-up equity to pay for living ex-

penses in retirement—otherwise your home is a lifestyle asset, not an investment asset.

- Property tax continues, typically increasing each year, even after your home loan is paid off, so carefully consider the cost of property tax before moving up to a larger home.

- In deciding whether to pay off your home loan, remember that you receive an income tax deduction for mortgage interest, effectively lowering your interest cost, and that pay-off money may be better left in your higher-earning investment portfolio.

- Explore the financial trade-off between living in a more expensive area and sending your kids to public school versus living in a more affordable area and sending your kids to private school.

- Refinance your home loan if the total financing cost over the time period you expect to keep the loan will be less, which often will be the case if the interest rate is 0.50% to 0.75% lower.

- Renting can make sense if the cost of renting is less than the cost of owning a home, you're saving for a down payment, you're waiting for stock options or restricted stock units to vest, or your travel schedule doesn't allow time for home ownership right now.

- If you're considering owning rental real estate, become familiar with what is required for success in that business including selecting properties, managing them, and understanding tax rules for rental real estate such as passive activity loss limitations, Section 1031 exchanges, and new Section 199A "pass through" deduction.

Homes are where we raise our families. We'll now move on from the place we call home to consider family life and other aspects of personal finance related to your personal well-being.

Getting Personal:
What Matters to You?

For 80 years, the Harvard Study of Adult Development has tracked the lives of 724 men, and later their families, to find out what keeps people healthy and happy.[1] Since 1938, the study has followed two groups: the first group entered the study when they were sophomores at Harvard College, and the second group were boys of about the same age from Boston's poorest neighborhoods who were not in college. The young men went on to a variety of careers, including factory work, law, bricklaying, medicine, and there was even one U.S. president. Tens of thousands of pages of data have been collected from questionnaires, interviews, doctors' reports, brain scans, blood tests, and genetic testing. Over 100 academic papers have been written on results of the study. Robert Waldinger, the study's current director and Harvard-trained psychiatrist, summarized the study's findings in a popular TED Talk: "The lessons aren't about wealth or fame or working harder and harder. The clearest message that we get from this 75-year study is this: good relationships keep us happier and healthier. Period."

Many people working in technology industries are strongly motivated by financial success. They're working hard to retire early and have enough money to enjoy a comfortable or luxurious lifestyle. Others are also driven by a desire to make a significant impact in society and become well-known entrepreneurs or leaders in their area of expertise. While tech culture and contemporary society contend that wealth, achievement, and notoriety lead to the good life, in fact they may not be the factors that bring the most happiness and meaning.

This chapter is different from the others. It focuses on your personal well-being as opposed to your finances. With a busy career, you can sometimes forget to take care of yourself and lose track of what's really important in life. Working in technology provides the opportunity for an intellectually stimulating and financially rewarding career. However, the intense work ethic and pressure to perform, particularly in startup companies, also present complications that need to be managed, or the emotional and financial costs can be substantial for you and your family. Socrates warned us over 2,400 years ago: "Beware the barrenness of a busy life."

Industry-Related Stress

While the number of hours per week worked in tech companies varies by position, company culture, and stage of development, the workweek is well above a traditional 40 hours. Founders and CEOs of startups typically work 80 hours or more per week and reports of 100 hour workweeks are not uncommon. The hours rival those put in by investment bankers, aspiring partners at top law and accounting firms, and doctors in residency. Executives and managers at startups and larger tech firms often work 60 to 70 hours per week, while software developers, scientists and other salaried professionals often work 50 to 60. Of course, hours can be greater in the early days of startup companies and around major product launches and releases. Working on weekends is expected at many companies. In areas where affordable housing is in short supply, long commutes add even more time to the workday.

Furthermore, staff are expected to work from home. Executives, managers, product development leads, and senior scientists keep up with emails and participate in conference calls with Europe or Asia at all hours. Sales and marketing professionals and executives may add extensive and exhausting domestic and international travel to that list of time demands. Vacations are interrupted by urgent work issues. In short, many tech professionals are expected to be on call nearly continuously. Even when they're not at work, tech professionals can be distracted and emotionally distant from family while physically present at home, which damages those relationships.

To the time demands, add the pressure to perform. Whether it's raising the next round of venture capital funding, getting an important design win, recruiting talented staff, closing an important deal with a beta customer, getting a drug through clinical trials, meeting quarterly earnings targets, launching a new web service, or releasing a minimum viable software product in a short period of time, there are pressures at all levels nearly continuously in tech companies.

A fundamental problem with working long hours is that it simply doesn't work. Research has shown productivity drops off after 50 hours in a workweek.[2] Plus, work tends to be of lower quality with more errors after many hours of sustained concentration. With overwork, we lose the ability to move forward, and we spin in circles instead. A *Harvard Business Review* article summarized research in this area well saying: "Keep overworking, and you'll progressively work more stupidly on tasks that are increasingly meaningless."[3]

Overwork and constant busyness also impair creativity. You need rest and quiet time to be creative. Many of our best ideas come to us during downtime. Solving difficult problems is next to impossible when you are tired and overworked.

Most importantly, working long hours under constant pressure to perform can lead to emotional and physical health problems, including serious issues like addiction, depression, divorce, and emotionally troubled children, each of which can also have major financial impacts.

Financial Cost of Divorce

Apart from the emotional costs, divorce can be financially devastating. While the cost of divorce varies by city and state, the average divorce costs between $15,000 and $20,000 in most tech cities and ranges up to $30,000 to $40,000 for difficult cases that go to trial to resolve child custody disputes or thorny property divisions.[4] Divorces in high-cost regions, such as New York City and Silicon Valley, can cost even more. In the case of high net worth couples with more complicated assets—multiple homes or other properties, a family-owned business, concentrated stock positions, or private investments, such as private equity, hedge fund or venture capital partnerships—anecdotally divorce costs can reach $40,000 to $100,000 per spouse or more.

There are other financial costs of divorce as well. Once a couple is divorced, their individual expenses increase as they no longer share the costs of housing, groceries, insurance, and a variety of other expenses. Family law attorneys typically estimate a "living-alone premium" of 20% to 40% for divorcing spouses when negotiating spousal support.

Once a marital settlement agreement between divorcing spouses has been reached and a divorce is finalized, there can be ongoing costs to monitor and enforce the agreement. One or both of the former spouses' circumstances may change over time, requiring the agreement to be modified. Post-divorce psychotherapy can also add to the costs of a marital breakup.

From a financial planning perspective, divorce creates a lot of collateral damage. Indirect costs can involve the sale of a couple's primary residence or liquidation of investments and capital gains tax on those sales. If real estate or investments are sold too quickly as a result of a divorce, investments may not be sold for their maximum value or may not grow to their full expected value. The operations of businesses or professional practices can be interrupted or disturbed, reducing their ability to produce income. The costs can reduce a couple's total net worth and make the whole less than the sum of its parts after divorce, making reaching retirement and other goals more difficult.

Generally, divorce cases that go to court are the most expensive, time consuming, and emotionally challenging. For couples who can work together while divorcing, as strange as that sounds, mediation or the collaborative law divorce process can save money and time, and leave divorced couples on better terms once the process is over.

In mediation, spouses may or may not be represented by attorneys. During the actual mediation, a professional mediator shuttles back and forth between the parties in different rooms to resolve differences and broker an agreement. The mediation process can span multiple meetings over several weeks or months.

In collaborative divorces, each spouse is represented by an attorney, and other experts (such as family counselors and financial planners) are brought in to help the couple through the process. Collaborative divorces have an expedited information exchange built in to the process, which can save time and money. With the collaborative process, the actual mediation takes place with all parties in the same conference room working together to resolve issues and come to agreement.

How to Deal with Overwork & Stress ... and Keep Your Job

To manage the demands of a tech career and perform at a peak level, while avoiding the most serious results of overwork and stress, you'll need to take care of yourself. You need strategies and routines designed to help you maintain your physical, mental, and emotional health. While you have probably read and heard these admonitions before, they are particularly important to countering the pressures of life working in tech.

- **Get enough sleep.** Most young adults and adults (18–25 and 26–64, respectively) require 7 to 9 hours sleep each night to be at full capacity and wide awake all day.[5] Only 5% of people can get by on six hours or less.[6] If you think you can survive on five or six hours of sleep, you might be fooling yourself. When you don't get enough sleep, your ability to think critically and be creative are diminished. Your memory and perception are impaired. To consistently perform at a high level, you need enough sleep.

- **Eat properly.** Maintain blood sugar levels throughout the day by eating smaller meals at traditional meal-times and adding healthy snacks between meals. Eat enough calories each day to maintain a healthy weight. Get enough protein in your diet each day along with generous portions of vegetables and fruits and adequate amounts of healthy fats such as avocado and olive oil. Enjoy the "white" foods (like bread, potatoes, rice, and sugar) in moderation. Consider reducing or eliminating caffeine, which interferes with sleep.

- **Exercise.** The enormous benefits of regular exercise for physical and mental health are well documented. Research suggests that regular exercise can improve concentration, help memory, enhance creativity, allow you to learn faster, and give you more mental stamina. Apps like Strava, the social network for people who run and bike, can allow you to have shared workout experiences. Group exercise classes can be a fun way to liven up your life outside of work and make working out more enjoyable.

- **Work on relationships.** Relationships are a major source of happiness and meaning in our lives and worth the effort they require to nurture and maintain. Enjoying your close relationships with your spouse or life partner, parents, children, and friends is vitally important to your emotional health. Invest in those relationships. Plan a date night with your spouse. Spend some time alone with each of your kids. Plan an adventure with your girlfriends or buddies. Pet your dog. Close personal relationships give meaning to our lives in ways a thousand work emails cannot.

- **Create a financially sustainable lifestyle.** Try not to bring unnecessary financial pressure on yourself and your relationships with unsustainably high levels of spending, debt or overly optimistic expectations about future income. Don't fall into the trap of comparing yourself to others and putting your own financial health at risk trying to match appearances. Live comfortably within your means. Be grateful for what you have.

- **Seek help**. If you're having trouble with substance abuse, depression, your marriage, or emotionally troubled children, please seek help from qualified counselors. If you are having thoughts about harming yourself, get help immediately. There is no weakness or shame in asking for help. On the contrary, it is healthy, and there is great strength in being able to ask for, and accept, support from others who care about you and your family.

Money & Happiness

If money and fame aren't what matter most in leading a happy and meaningful life, what does matter most?

The Harvard study mentioned earlier identifies relationships as a key source of happiness. Study director Robert Waldinger describes three main findings. The first is that social connections are important. People who are connected to family, friends, and community are happier, physically healthier and live longer than people who are less well connected. Second, it's the quality of your close relationships that matters most. Close relationships buffer us from the ups and downs of life and keep us happier even when, for instance, we experience physical pain. The third factor is that, as we age, good relationships protect our mind. People in close relationships maintain a good memory longer.

The study's findings about the importance of close relationships may provide some perspective on the use of social media. It's not really the number of casual friends that are important, it is quality of relationships that matters for personal happiness. Interestingly, new research is beginning to indicate that social media can negatively impact our well-being through either self-comparison or simply overuse or distraction from in-person relationship-building activities.[7] It seems that social media can be useful in supporting and reinforcing your real-world personal relationships, but in general, online interactions are not a good substitute for meaningful offline social experiences.

Relationships are clearly important to happiness and well-being. But what role does money play in personal happiness and satisfaction with life? Can money buy happiness? While earlier research in this area had been largely inconclusive, an important research paper published in 2010 by Nobel prize-winning economists Daniel Kahneman and Angus Deaton begins to tease out answers to that question.[8] Kahneman and Deaton looked separately at two aspects of well-being: emotional well-being and life evaluation. Emotional well-being refers to how often and how intensely you experience emotions in everyday life such as joy, stress, sadness, anger, and affection, and whether they make your life pleasant or unpleasant. Life evaluation refers to how you think about your life overall.

Interestingly, the authors found that emotional well-being rose steadily with household income until household income reached about $75,000 per year. Once household income reached that level, there was limited further improvement in emotional well-being. This is not to say that people would not be happy to receive a raise. They would. But above a certain level of stable income, the raise doesn't increase emotional well-being. Apparently, money does improve how often we feel joy and sadness but only to a point, with other factors such as personality and life circumstances having more impact above that point.

The other aspect of well-being—life evaluation—increased continuously with income. While money may not buy happiness, in general wealth contributes positively to our satisfaction with life. These findings are consistent with other research, which shows that people living in wealthier nations generally are happier than people living in poorer nations. But within wealthy nations, subjective measures of well-being have increased little over the last several decades, even as wealth has increased significantly. It seems that being wealthier does help us feel greater satisfaction with our lives, but above a certain amount, money doesn't make us any happier.

Creating Meaning in Your Life

In addition to happiness, we need meaning in our lives for personal well-being. We need to feel part of something larger than ourselves, whether that is family, work, faith, community, or in some way contributing to the betterment of humanity. Modern research on well-being has confirmed centuries-old truths about happiness and meaning. Whereas *happiness* is associated with receiving, *meaning* is associated with giving. Living in the moment can bring happiness, but creating meaning is about integrating past, present, and future to discern the purpose for our lives. Happiness is about satisfying needs and desires whereas meaning is about defining and expressing yourself.

In Abraham Maslow's well-known and still widely used psychological theory of a hierarchy of needs, self-actualization represents personal growth toward fulfillment of a person's highest needs, the need for meaning in life. At the highest level of Maslow's hierarchy, individuals are striving to maximize their potential, doing the best that they are capable of, creating, enjoying peak experiences, and defining themselves. In so doing, they find meaning in life. Self-actualization can be achieved in many settings such as parenting, athletics, education, creating art (painting, sculpture, composing music, writing literature, digital design), and in business. Developing new products or starting a company can be self-actualizing.

In Maslow's hierarchy of needs, lower level needs must be at least partially satisfied before higher needs can be met and self-actualization can be reached. On the lowest level are physiological needs such as food, water, warmth, and sleep. On the next level up are safety needs, such as security and personal safety. Belonging and love come next. On top of that are esteem needs, such as having feelings of accomplishment and self-respect.

Tech careers can interfere with the ability to progress up the hierarchy of needs at multiple levels. If you're not eating right, exercising, and getting enough sleep, you're not making it out of the basement. If your personal finances are not in good order, your security needs may go unmet and you're stuck at level two. Working long hours can interfere with intimate relationships and friends, leaving you stuck at level three. If you want to move up to self-actualization, you need to pay attention to your basic physiological and psychological needs first.

Excessive concentration on becoming rich and famous at the expense meeting your basic needs, having close relationships, and experiencing personal growth may prevent you from having the very happiness and meaning in your life you believed wealth and accomplishment would bring you.

Kids & Financial Literacy

Your close relationships are a key component of happiness. If you have kids, you already know your close relationship with them is one of the greatest joys in your life. You may be involved with them in all sorts of enriching activities outside of school that are fun for them and you. Another area for deepening your relationships with your kids and spending quality time with them is in learning about money.

The U.S. has a problem with money education. Personal finance is not taught in elementary school, middle school, high school, or college (except at a handful of universities that offer personal financial planning majors). Most adults have had no formal training in this area and learned about personal finance ad hoc from their parents, personal study, and life's hard lessons. Many don't learn it at all. A 2016 study found that two-thirds of Americans could not pass a basic financial literacy test.[9] Despite being one of the wealthiest nations on earth, the U.S. ranked only 14th in a global survey of financial literacy.[10] The consequences of a U.S. population largely uneducated in personal finance are enormous. The fact that we tolerate a U.S. national debt of over $20 trillion and growing (that's 20 followed by 12 zeroes, which is over $62,000 for every U.S. citizen, including babies), is one significant symptom of this huge problem.

You can help your children learn personal finance while having a fun activity to bond around at the same time. Talking about money with your kids is a good place to start. For many good reasons, make sure they understand that family finances are not to be discussed with people outside of the immediate family. Involving your kids in important money decisions such as buying major appliances or new cars can help them start to appreciate comparison shopping, financing, budgets, and the trade-offs all families make according to their financial constraints. When the kids are in late high school or college, help them create their own budget. Some experts recommend setting an allowance for kids so that they experience spending trade-offs and how far money can go.

Kids seem particularly fascinated with how quickly money can grow through the magic of compounding. Getting them started with a custodial brokerage account to learn about investing can spark an interest and help them on the way to developing a lifelong proficiency in investing.

High quality online classes are now available as well, which might fit in with their other extracurricular activities. Having children become proficient in managing their personal finances is critical to their success as adults and an important goal for parents in raising independently functioning human beings.

―――

Summary

- Be aware of diminishing returns to extra hours of work after 50 to 60 hours per week.
- Maintain creativity and ability to solve difficult problems with rest and quiet time.
- Deal with overwork and stress by getting enough sleep, eating properly, exercising, working on your relationships, creating a financial sustainable lifestyle, and seeking professional help when needed.

- Money does increase satisfaction with life but relationships and finding meaning are most important to our happiness and general well-being.

Taking care of yourself and working on your relationships will help you be more successful in your career and in achieving your financial goals. At the same time, paying attention to your physical, emotional, and spiritual needs will allow for personal growth and finding the true happiness and meaning in your life that a busy work-life by itself cannot provide.

Taxation Nation:
Minimizing the Burden

You probably know more about taxes than you want to already but maybe not as much as you need to. This chapter focuses on why taxes are relevant to your personal financial situation and includes a high-level approach for reducing taxes with several specific pointers that you might want to include on your tax savings checklist.

Taxes, Taxes Everywhere

When talking about taxes, most people mean income taxes. Your wages, salary, and bonus from work are taxed as income, and so is your stock-based compensation. In addition, the interest, dividends, and gains on your investments are taxed as income along, with pension payments and distributions from retirement accounts. Income is taxed in multiple jurisdictions, including at federal, state, and local levels. While that might seem like plenty of taxes to pay, there are more. In addition to income tax, you pay other personal taxes including these:

- **Payroll tax.** You (and your employer) pay federal payroll taxes on your earnings from work which fund Social Security and Medicare. Social Security tax is 6.2% of your earnings up to $128,400 (2018) and Medicare tax is 1.45% on all of your income up to $200,000 for single filing status and $250,000 for married filing jointly, after which the rate jumps to 2.35%.[1] States and local governments may have payroll taxes as well, for example for state disability insurance.
- **Sales tax.** You pay sales tax on items you buy at the state and local level. Sales tax ranges from about 5% to 9% across the U.S.

- **Excise tax.** You pay excise taxes when purchasing particular items such as gasoline, alcohol, and cigarettes. For example, the federal gas tax is about 18¢ per gallon and the average state gas tax is about 32¢ per gallon for a total of about 50¢ per gallon gas tax.
- **Property tax.** You pay property tax on real estate, vehicles, and other property you own. If you live in leased or rented housing, your landlord passes their property tax on to you in the form of higher rent.
- **Estate tax.** If you are fortunate enough to accumulate more than $11.2 million as an individual or $22.4 million with your spouse during your lifetime, you will pay 40% federal estate tax on the amount above those thresholds upon your death, and any state estate tax as well.

Not all jurisdictions have all of these taxes. For example, Texas has no state income tax, but property taxes tend to be higher in Texas than other states. When considering the tax burden of a particular city or state, it's helpful to look at the combined impact of income tax, property tax, and sales tax. The Tax Foundation's website is a good source of information on all three.[2]

Taxes are important for the simple reason that they reduce the amount of money you have available to save and invest. Of all the major taxes, you probably have most control over the amount you pay in income tax. For many people, income tax is also their largest tax in terms of total cash outflow for taxes. For that reason, this chapter focuses primarily on income tax planning. When you work, you pay income tax based on your wage income, and when you own investments, you pay income tax on your investment income.

These and all other types of taxes (except estate taxes, which apply at death) reduce the amount of money you have left over to save and invest each year. That's why ongoing tax planning is important in building and preserving net worth.

U.S. tax law is mind-bogglingly complex. The federal tax law itself spanned 3,728 pages before the changes for 2018.[3] Much of the law as written by Congress is general in nature and often difficult to apply to specific cases. The U.S. Department of Treasury provides more detail, and the official interpretation of U.S. tax law, in its Federal tax regulations. The Internal Revenue Service (IRS) also publishes official guidance on tax law and regulation.

Tax law compliance is complicated in part due to the sheer volume of rules to follow and in part because each important tax issue needs to be evaluated in the context of the overall tax code, the specific tax code section at issue, Treasury regulations, IRS guidance, and any court decisions which might interpret the relevant law. That's just federal tax law. Each state and municipality has its own parallel set of laws, regulations, and guidance from tax collection authorities for you to understand and comply with. Further complicating tax compliance is the need to keep track not just of current tax law but also older tax laws that may still apply or impact your income tax situation.

Complying with income tax laws involves filling out a set of numbered and lettered forms to report the income you earned and the tax you paid, plus any amount of tax still due to be paid. The set of completed forms is called an income tax return. You file income tax returns typically by April 15 each year with both the federal government and state government if your state has an income tax.

Waiting until just before the tax return filing deadline to start thinking about reducing your income tax bill is too late. At that point, you are simply documenting what has already happened and not planning for what's ahead. Proper tax planning takes place before the tax year ends. Good tax planning often requires looking several years into the future to minimize taxes over not just the current year, but over the next two, three, four, or five years, or longer.

Avoid & Delay

At a high level, there are two ways to reduce the amount of taxes you pay:

1. Avoid incurring tax liability
2. Delay incurring tax liability

Avoiding tax liability involves minimizing your taxable income, maximizing deductions and credits, and controlling the timing of income and deductions. Delaying tax liability involves arranging your transactions and accounts to defer taxable income until later, for example with retirement accounts.

There is a big difference between "tax avoidance" and "tax evasion." Tax avoidance is the legal use of tax law, regulation, official guidance, and court rulings to reduce the amount of tax you owe. Tax avoidance is completely legal and diligently practiced by people, corporations, partnerships, and trusts seeking to minimize their tax burden. Good tax planning is tax avoidance.

Tax *evasion* is the criminal practice of intentionally not paying your true tax liability. Tax evasion is largely a matter of intent to defraud. Some examples of tax evasion include concealing income, inflating deductions or expenses, and hiding income in offshore accounts. Tax rules and forms are complicated and mistakes can and do happen. **Making a mistake is not tax evasion, but if you intentionally underpay your taxes, you could face criminal charges.**

Because the income tax law is complex, there can be uncertainty about how the law, regulations, guidance, and court cases affect you. In some cases, your accountant or tax attorney may have a good sense of how the IRS or other tax authorities would view a particular issue. In other cases, the position you take in reporting income or deductions on your tax return may be open to interpretation, for example in the case of a uniquely structured corporate merger transaction affecting your equity compensation.

When your tax reporting requirements are unclear, and there is more than one option for how to properly report income or deduction on your tax returns, you and your tax preparer will need to decide where you want to be on the continuum between reporting in the most conservative manner possible and, at the other end, reporting in the most aggressive manner possible. By taking a conservative position, meaning one closer to what IRS or state tax authorities have agreed with in prior cases, your tax return is less likely to be audited and less likely to draw an "adjustment" by IRS or state if audited. By taking a more aggressive position, you increase your chance of audit and of having to pay additional tax if the IRS or state disagrees with your position. Your decision will likely be impacted by the dollar amounts involved and potential savings from a more aggressive stance. You will also want to consider the costs involved in defending your position to potential auditors and in tax court, and the amount of your time spent resolving the issue.

Basic Structure of Income Tax

U.S. federal income tax law received a major overhaul at the end of 2017 with the Tax Cuts and Jobs Act. The provisions of the Tax Cuts and Jobs Act, with a few exceptions, became effective on January 1, 2018. The new tax rules remain in effect until December 31, 2025, and after expiration will revert back to the pre-2018 law. The description and references here and throughout the book reflect the new tax law, with occasional notes about the prior law when relevant.

Ordinary Income

U.S. federal personal income tax compliance involves filing a completed set of forms called a tax return each year to self-report your taxable income and the amount of tax you owe. The flow of the tax return, which for individuals starts with the familiar 1040 form, mirrors the tax code.

1. First, income is reported. The U.S. requires that you report income from all sources worldwide.
2. Second, any required or allowed adjustments to your income can be made to arrive at Adjusted Gross Income (AGI).
3. Third, you list amounts for deductions from income. These are your "itemized" deductions. Deductions include mortgage interest, property tax, state income tax, charitable donations, medical expenses, and others. Some deductions have limitations. If the total of your itemized deductions doesn't exceed a threshold amount, you will use the default "standard" deduction instead,

which for 2018 was $24,000 for married couples and
$12,000 for individuals.

4. Next, you subtract your allowable total deduction
    amount (whether itemized or standard) from your
    adjusted gross income to arrive at a preliminary
    taxable income. After that, you subtract any amount
    from an important new deduction for income from
    "pass-through" businesses, which are businesses whose
    income you are required to include on your personal
    tax returns as opposed to corporate tax returns. (See
    below for more information).

5. After subtracting the pass-through deduction, you
    arrive at your taxable income. This is the amount of
    income on which you owe income tax.

Previously, you could also deduct an exemption amount from
your taxable income before calculating your tax owed. Before the
new tax law for 2018, a certain amount of income after deductions
was exempt from tax (i.e., you didn't have to pay tax on it). The
exempt amount was determined based on the number of people in
your household who qualified as dependents, for example, yourself,
your spouse, and the children who relied on your financial support.
After subtracting the exempt income, you arrived at your taxable
income. Exemptions were removed in the new law in exchange for
increased standard deductions, and a new deduction for business
income from pass-through entities was added.

Beginning in 2018, you can deduct 20% of "qualified business
income" from an S corporation, partnership, sole proprietorship,
and real estate investment trusts. Income from a limited liability
corporation (LLC) also qualifies for the 20% deduction if the LLC

is treated as an S corporation, partnership, or sole proprietorship for tax purposes and is not taxed as a C corporation. The deduction does not apply to C corporations.

The new deduction is known as Section 199A, after the numbered section of the law where it can be found. It is also known as the "pass-through" deduction because the definition of qualified business income includes only income from business entities such as S corporations, partnerships and sole proprietorships whose income is taxed on your personal tax return instead of the entity paying its own tax, as do C corporations—the income is said to "pass-through" to your personal tax return. On your tax return form, this new deduction is subtracted from your taxable income after your itemized or standard deduction to calculate your final taxable income. While generally equal to 20% of your pass-through business income, the new deduction is limited and you may not get to deduct the full 20%. If your taxable income is above $315,000 for married couples filing a joint tax return or $157,500 for all other taxpayers, then the deduction is reduced.

The amount of reduction depends on the type business. For certain "specified service businesses," the deduction reduces to zero when your taxable income reaches $415,000 for married couple filing joint tax returns and $207,500 for all other taxpayers. Businesses included in the specified business services definition include healthcare services, law, accounting, investment management, performing arts, consulting, athletics, and "any trade or business where the principal asset of such trade or business is the reputation or skill of one or more of its employees." Engineering and architecture are excluded from this definition. For all other types of businesses not "specified service businesses," the deduction may be reduced, but not to zero, according to a set of rules and calculations involving the W-2 wages paid by the business and the amount of capital used in the business.

Tax rates, standard deduction, and various other features and limits in the current and prior tax law are tied to your filing status. There are five filing statuses on a federal tax return. The most common are "Single," "Married Filing Jointly," and "Head of Household." If more than one filing status applies to you, choose the one which allows you to pay the least tax.

The U.S. federal income tax system is progressive, meaning that the rate of tax you pay on your taxable income increases as your taxable income increases. Beginning in 2018, the graduated rate of tax begins at 10% on taxable income up to $19,050 and tops out at 37% of taxable income on income over $600,001 for married taxpayers filing a joint tax return. The tax rates aren't continuous between 0% and 37%, instead they are broken up into rate "brackets," in which different rates apply to different ranges of taxable income. Tax brackets are important to understand in tax planning. Currently, there are seven federal income tax brackets as shown in Figure 18 below for two of the most common filing statuses.[4]

TAX RATE	TAXABLE INCOME— MARRIED FILING JOINTLY	TAXABLE INCOME— SINGLE
10%	$0–$19,050	$0–$9,525
12%	$19,051–$77,400	$9,526–$38,700
22%	$77,401–$165,000	$38,701–$82,500
24%	$165,001–$315,000	$82,501–$157,500
32%	$315,001–$400,000	$157,501–$200,000
35%	$400,001–$600,000	$200,001–$500,000
37%	$600,001 and over	$500,001 and over

Figure 18

To calculate the amount of tax you owe, you apply the rate for that bracket to your taxable income in that bracket. For example, if you are married and file your tax return jointly with your spouse and you have taxable income of $250,000, then you pay 10% on the first $19,050 of income, 12% on the amount of income between $19,051 and $77,400, 22% on the amount between $77,401 and $165,000 and 24% on the amount between $165,001 and $250,000. Your total tax is $48,579 and your average tax rate (the total tax divided by your taxable income) is 19%.

Notice that in this example the highest tax rate reached with $250,000 of income was 24%. We say that this taxpayer is in the "24% tax bracket," referring to the highest tax bracket which applied to that income. Even though the average tax rate on this taxpayer's total income was 19%, the tax owed on the next dollar of income earned is at the 24% tax rate, or $0.24. The flip side of that logic is that every dollar the taxpayer can reduce taxable income through good tax planning, reduces tax owed by 24¢. The taxpayer has extra incentive to reduce income to the next lower tax bracket because of the progressive tax system. One key goal of tax planning is to reduce taxable income in order to pay tax based on the lower rates in lower tax brackets.

The example above assumed that all of the income earned was "ordinary" income. Ordinary income is the income from salary, bonuses, hourly wages, self-employment, and other sources that you would normally think of as income. There are other types of income which are taxed at different tax rates.

Capital Gains

The most important other type of income is capital gain and loss. Gains and losses on your investments and other property you own are not taxable until you sell the assets. Once you sell the investment or property, any gain on the sale is known as a capital gain and is included in your income.

Capital gains on assets you owned for one year or less are taxed at your tax rate for ordinary income. Capital gains on assets you owned for more than one year are taxed at different rates. The capital gains tax rate depends on your total taxable income (not only the gain on the assets sold) and your tax filing status. Before 2018, capital gains tax rates were tied to particular income tax brackets. However, with the new tax law for 2018, the income thresholds for capital gains tax rates are independent of income tax brackets, which is extra confusing. The following table lists capital gains rates for 2018.

TAX RATE	TAXABLE INCOME— MARRIED FILING JOINTLY	TAXABLE INCOME— SINGLE
0%	$0–$77,200	$0–$38,600
15%	$77,201–$479,000	$38,601–$425,800
20%	$479,001 and over	$425,801 and over

Figure 19

You deduct any capital losses against capital gains in a tax year to reduce income from capital gains. If your capital losses are more than your capital gains, you can also deduct capital losses against up to $3,000 of ordinary income each year. You can carry forward any remaining unused capital losses to future taxable years indefinitely.

Investment Income

You pay additional tax on your net investment income, which is your investment income after investment expenses have been subtracted. The net investment income tax is equal to 3.8% of the lesser of your net investment income or the amount by which your adjusted gross income exceeds a threshold amount of $250,000 for a married couple filing jointly or surviving spouse, $125,000 for married person filing separately, and $200,000 for single individuals and all other filing statuses. What this means is that if your adjusted gross income is above $250,000 for a married couple filing a joint tax return, then your capital gains tax rate may be as high as 23.8% on some of your investment income, not the maximum capital gains tax rate of 20%.

Alternative Minimum Tax

All the rules just described are for the regular tax system. There is, in fact, a second tax system, the alternative minimum tax (AMT), which runs in parallel with the regular tax system. It has its own rules for income, deductions, and exemptions, and separate tax rate schedule.

When you or your tax preparer are completing your tax return, you are actually calculating your taxable income and tax owed under both the regular and AMT systems. If the amount of tax you owe under the AMT system is greater than the amount of tax you owe under the regular tax system, then the difference is simply included on your regular tax return. There is no separate tax return for AMT.

Under the AMT system, some income is recognized at different times. For example, income from incentive stock options is recognized upon option exercise in the AMT system and not until sale of exercised shares under the regular tax system.

Certain itemized deductions allowed under the regular tax system are not allowed under the AMT system, including state and local taxes, which is why people living in states with high state income tax and high property tax historically have found themselves having to "pay AMT" on their tax returns.

Under the AMT system, your taxable income below a certain threshold is exempt from tax, but the exemption is subject to a phase-out based on your taxable income. The new tax law for 2018 increased the exemption amount and phase out threshold, which will result in fewer people paying AMT. The exemption amount for a married couple filing a joint tax return was raised to $109,400 for 2018, up from $84,500 in 2017. Once your income reaches a threshold amount, your exemption is reduced 25¢ for every dollar that your income is above the exemption threshold. As the amount of your income increases, this has the effect of making more of your income subject to AMT as the exemption is reduced. Under the new tax law, the exemption threshold was raised significantly to $1,000,000 (from $106,900 in 2017) for married couples filing jointly, which means all except high income earners won't have their exemption amount reduced.

Tax rates under the AMT system for 2018 are 26% on alternative minimum taxable income below $191,100 and 28% on alternative minimum taxable income above $191,100. Capital gains tax rates under the AMT system are the same as under the regular tax system.

Tax Withholding

The income tax system is a pay-as-you-go system. You are required to pay your taxes as you earn income. Most people have income taxes withheld from their paychecks during the year. If you have income but don't receive a paycheck, you need to make quarterly estimated tax payments. After the end of the tax year, you calculate the amount of tax you owed for that year on your tax return. You also show on your tax return how much tax you paid through paycheck withholdings or estimated tax payments. The difference between what you owe and what you paid determines whether you receive an income tax refund or have to pay additional tax with your tax return. For example, if you have paid more through paycheck withholdings than you owe, you will receive a tax refund for the amount you overpaid. Your tax return is a "true-up" calculation to reconcile what you owe with what you paid during the year.

Fun fact: Some people actually pay extra tax voluntarily, but not many. The U.S. Bureau of the Fiscal Service accepts gifts to the U.S. government, including gifts made specifically to reduce the U.S. national debt. Over the last decade, about $3.5 million per year on average was donated by taxpayers to reduce the national debt.[5] While they are a nice gesture and appreciated by fellow citizens, those contributions are economically insignificant. The U.S. national debt *grows* by $3.5 million about every 7 minutes. For most people, paying as little tax as possible is an important personal financial goal.

Reducing Taxable Income

The simplest approach to think about for lowering your tax bill is simply to reduce your taxable income. While that's often easier said than done, here are three options that may be open to you, depending on when you started your tax planning.

Claiming All Deductions and Credits

If you've waited until it's time to gather information for your tax returns to start thinking about reducing your taxable income—after the end of the tax year—you won't be able to do much tax planning. Your best course is to be sure you claim all of the adjustments to income, deductions, and credits, and your first task is to know to which ones you are entitled.

Your tax preparer's "tax organizer" package will ask you for information to identify all available adjustments, deductions, and credits that apply to you. If you prepare your own tax returns, tax preparation software products such as TurboTax® include checklists to help you find expenses that are deductible or which qualify for an adjustment or credit.

Common adjustments (reductions) to income:

- Health Savings Account contributions
- Retirement account contributions
- Self-employment tax
- Self-employed health insurance premiums

Common deductions:

- Mortgage interest on loans up to $750,000 and up to $1,000,000 on loans in place before on or before December 15, 2017
- Loan points
- State and local taxes up to a maximum of $10,000 total annually, including for state and local income tax or sales tax, real estate property tax, and personal property tax such as vehicle license fees based on vehicle value
- Medical expenses over a 7.5% adjusted gross income threshold for 2018 and over a 10% threshold for 2019 through 2025
- Charitable contributions
- Pass-through business income deduction

Miscellaneous itemized deductions above 2% of your adjusted gross income are no longer deductible under the 2018 tax law. Miscellaneous itemized deductions included tax preparation fees, financial advisory fees, unreimbursed employee business expenses, home office expenses, job search expenses, certain legal fees, and others. Interest on home equity lines of credit is also no longer deductible.

Many states do not plan to change their tax laws to match the new 2018 federal tax law. Therefore deductions that may no longer be available on your federal tax return may still be allowed on your state tax return. For example, your state may continue to allow miscellaneous itemized deductions. For this reason, you should continue to track your spending on items which were deductible in prior years so that you can continue to claim those deductions on your state income tax return.

Common credits that may be available in your case:

- Foreign tax credit (e.g., for tax you paid through an international stock mutual fund)
- Child tax credit
- Residential energy credit (e.g., for solar panels)
- Lifetime learning credit
- American opportunity credit

Note that, dollar for dollar, tax credits are more valuable than adjustments or deductions because they directly reduce the amount of tax owed, whereas adjustments and deductions reduce taxable income to which a tax rate is applied.

The second part of your task is finding documentation for each adjustment, deduction, and credit that you plan to report or claim on your tax returns. Having well organized finances makes this part easier. However, regardless of how organized you are, this is a time consuming and usually unpleasant chore. Personal finance software and expense tracking applications are useful in identifying what documentation to look for, for example by generating a list of medical expenses. Some of the documentation will be in the form of paper statements and receipts. Other documentation you may have to track down online or through old emails. Diligence counts here. Work the checklists. Think about it this way: when you're looking for expense documentation, the amount you'll save in tax translates into tens, hundreds, or even thousands of dollars per hour for your labor.

Tax-Loss Harvesting

Tax-loss harvesting is a technique used by professional money managers and individual investors to reduce short-term or long-term capital gains in taxable investment portfolios within the current tax year. With tax-loss harvesting, you or your investment manager sell the investments within your portfolio that have unrealized losses (e.g., the selling price has fallen below purchase price) to create actual losses for tax purposes. The investments targeted for sale have already lost value for performance purposes, but a loss cannot be recognized for tax purposes until a sale transaction takes place. Existing losses are said to be "harvested" when they are sold to recognize a loss for tax purposes. The losses created using tax-loss harvesting offset capital gains generated by the portfolio (or other investments) during the year, for example, through rebalancing sales or mutual fund capital gains distributions.

Tax-loss harvesting does not necessarily require changing your investment portfolio in a way that changes its performance. Often, investments that are sold in tax-loss harvesting are replaced by similar investments. For example, suppose you held an S&P 500 index mutual fund in your portfolio (which holds stock in the 500 largest U.S. companies) that had lost value during the year. With tax-loss harvesting, you or your investment manager would sell that mutual fund and buy a similar investment, for example a Russell 1000 index exchange-traded fund (which like an S&P 500 index fund also holds stock in large U.S. companies). That way the portfolio continues to hold an investment that performs similarly while allowing losses to be realized for tax purposes.

One important note about tax-loss harvesting: you can't buy back the exact same investment. The IRS's wash-sale rule won't allow you to take a loss if you buy the same or substantially similar security within 30 calendar days. Selecting a replacement security with similar performance attributes that is not the same or substantially similar avoids the wash-sale rule. After 30 days, you or your investment manager can swap back to the original security by selling the replacement security and buying the original security. However, the replacement security may gain in value during the 30 days and selling it may create a taxable gain which partially or completely offsets the losses realized with tax-loss harvesting. You may get stuck holding the replacement security to avoid recognizing capital gains. For that reason, it's important to pick replacement securities that meet your asset allocation and long-term investment plan objectives.

Well diversified portfolios often have investments that have increased in value and some which have lost value. Not all investments perform the same across all economic and market conditions. That is the point of diversification. As a consequence, at any point in time there will often be some investments in a portfolio that can be loss harvested.

When reviewing an investment portfolio for tax-loss harvesting opportunities, it's important to look not only at the total unrealized gain or loss of an individual security or holding in your portfolio but also at the individual lots making up that holding and when they were purchased. For example, you may be holding shares of your company's stock that you acquired through your employer's employee stock purchase program. Certain quantities of shares were purchased on different dates at different prices; the quantities purchased on the same date at the same price are referred to as "lots" or "tax lots." Because each lot was purchased at a different price, some lots may have an unrealized gain and some may have an unrealized loss. This applies to mutual funds as well, for example when dividends are reinvested to buy more shares of the mutual fund, each purchase of new mutual fund shares is an individual tax lot.

The total of all the lots may be at an unrealized gain or loss position as well. Only by looking at the individual tax lots can you determine whether there are individual lots than can be tax-loss harvested. When tax-loss harvesting, you or your investment manager can choose to sell the entire position or sell only the lots which have unrealized losses. Even portfolios which appear at first glance to have only unrealized gains in all securities may in fact have individual tax lots that can be loss harvested. Individual tax lots can also be selected for sale based on their holding period. Selling lots held for less than one year creates valuable short-term capital losses that can offset short-term capital gains, which are taxed at a higher tax rate.

Tax-Efficient Investing

Generally, tax-efficient investing can reduce your taxable investment income over the long-term. The larger your investment portfolio, and the larger the fraction of your total income investment income represents, the more important this is.

One important technique that applies in investment tax planning is holding appreciated investments for greater than one year before selling so that appreciation in the investment will be taxed as a long-term capital gain rather than a short-term capital gain. Long-term gain is taxed at the favorable federal long-term capital gains tax rates, while short-term gains are taxed at higher ordinary income tax rates. Taking advantage of long-term capital gains tax rates is a key objective in tax-sensitive investment accounts and should be second nature to tax-aware institutional and individual investors alike.

Certain investment styles are inherently more tax efficient. Index investing can be significantly more tax-efficient than active investment styles in which securities are regularly bought and sold as a result of market timing decisions or stock picking. Active management typically involves higher turnover of securities in a portfolio, leading to more capital gains and, in particular, more short-term capital gains, which are taxed at higher ordinary income tax rates. Index style investing, also known as passive management, involves much lower turnover of securities within a portfolio, much lower short-term capital gains, and much lower capital gains altogether.

Certain investment vehicles also are inherently more tax efficient. Exchange traded funds may demonstrate greater tax efficiency than open-end mutual funds, due to their unique share creation mechanism discussed in Chapter 4. Institutional class index mutual funds (with multi-million dollar minimum purchase amounts) from firms that regulate short-term trading among their investors can rival exchange-traded funds (ETFs) in tax efficiency. However, most mutual funds are less tax efficient than exchange-traded funds, particularly those funds pursuing an active management style or attracting an active trading clientele.

Asset location is an investment technique that reduces tax drag and can lead to an additional 10% to 15% value of investment portfolio over an investor's lifetime.[6] With asset location, investments that generate higher amounts of income and dividends are placed or "located" in tax-deferred investment accounts. Investments that generate large capital gains and less income are located in taxable accounts. Placing income-generating investments in tax-deferred accounts, such as IRAs, shields the income they generate from taxation. Placing capital-gain generating investments in taxable accounts such as trust, joint or individual brokerage accounts allows income to be taken at the lower long-term capital gains tax rates and gives maximum control over when gains are taken.

In asset location, high income-generating asset classes and investments (such as high-yield bonds, corporate bonds, government bonds, real estate investment trust, and commodities) are placed in tax-deferred accounts, while U.S., international, and emerging markets stocks are placed in taxable accounts. In general, asset classes and investments are ranked in order from highest to lowest ordinary income generation and then placed first in qualified accounts, in that order, with remaining asset classes filling taxable accounts (spilling over) once qualified accounts are full. With asset location you defer tax on investment income—such as interest and dividends—which is taxed as ordinary income, while simultaneously paying tax on the portfolio at lower long-term capital gains tax rates with control over when that tax is paid. Asset location is discussed in Chapter 4.

Control Timing of Income and Deductions

Many tax planning techniques involve scheduling.

1. Spread Income

Because the U.S. income tax system is progressive, the more you earn in any given year the higher your tax rate. To avoid paying tax at the highest tax rates, it's helpful to try and spread large inflows of income over two or more years and pay tax in a lower tax bracket.

This isn't always possible, of course. If your private company is being acquired and your vested non-qualified stock options will be cashed out in a single year, you don't have any choice about when you receive the income from the stock options. You will have income when the deal closes. However, if your company has gone public and you can sell your vested stock anytime going forward, you may want to run tax projections to determine whether exercising and selling your options over two or three years could reduce your tax liability. Doing so will reduce your income to one-half or one-third of the total reported in each year, potentially resulting in your income falling into a lower tax bracket.

Of course, in deciding whether and when to sell stock, you should consider factors other than income tax, such as the company's prospects, your overall financial situation, and how much of your net worth is tied up in a single company's stock (i.e., do you have a concentrated stock position needing diversification?). Special considerations related to taxation of equity compensation are discussed in Chapter 5.

Anytime you have control over the timing of an irregular, large inflow of income, and if it can be done with little or no risk, it can be useful from a tax planning perspective to arrange for income to be spread out and paid over several years.

2. Timing Income

Similarly, if you can control the timing of at least some of your income, you can consider accelerating income into the current year if you expect your income to be lower this year than next year. Conversely, you can consider delaying income into next year if you expect your income to be lower next year than this year. For example, if you have an option to receive a bonus in December of this year or January of next year, you would choose to receive it in the year you expect to have lower income. Or if you work as an independent contractor and have the option to finish up a software development project late this year or early next year, you can consider timing completion of the project to coincide with the year you expect to have lower projected income. Staying up on your tax planning all year instead of reviewing your tax situation right before April 15 can help you pay less tax.

3. Match Large Deductions to High-Income Years

If you can't control the timing of a large inflow of income, another technique to reduce your taxable income is to increase your deductions in that year. Try to accelerate deductions into the high income year.

For example, a popular strategy is to make large charitable contributions in a high income years. Donor-advised funds are particularly useful for this. You can make a large contribution to the fund and receive a charitable deduction in the year of contribution, while also making grants from your donor-advised fund to your favorite charities over the next several years as you normally would have. For example, if you received a large bonus or sold employee stock options during the year, make a large contribution to your donor-advised fund in that year. With a donor-advised fund, you are essentially pre-funding your philanthropy for the next several years and receiving the charitable deduction all in one year. The donation can save you even more in tax if you contribute appreciated assets to the donor-advised fund instead of cash. When you contribute appreciated assets such as stock, you never have to pay capital gains tax on the donated stock. Because charities don't pay tax, the gain on your appreciated stock simply disappears when you donate it. Neither you nor the charity pay tax on the gain.

When high-income years occur periodically, timing your donor-advised fund contributions to coincide with those years can help smooth out taxable income. Income smoothing with donor-advised fund contributions is powerful because the timing of contributions to your fund is detached from the timing of your grants to charities. The two can happen independently. Timing strategies are more difficult to implement with direct gifts to charities. Using a donor-advised fund allows you to maintain steady giving despite fluctuations in income.

You can also try to accelerate other deductions into high income years. For example, you might make three property tax payments in a high income year and only one payment in the next year.

4. Bunch Deductions

If your income is relatively stable from year to year, bunching your deductions can help you claim deductions that you might not otherwise be able to claim. For example, medical expenses are deductible to the extent they exceed your adjusted gross income by 7.5% for 2018 and 10% for 2019 to 2025. Many high income households find their medical expenses don't typically exceed the threshold for deduction. By bunching deductions, you can claim more in a single year and, perhaps, get over the threshold. For example, you can concentrate elective medical procedures in a single year. Or if you have unexpected and expensive tests one year that don't quite get you over the threshold, think about having the full physical exam or knee surgery to repair a torn meniscus you've been putting off in the same year.

With the new tax law, bunching deductions becomes more important to be able to claim itemized deductions that don't exceed the standard deduction in a single year. For example, if your itemized deductions—including mortgage interest, state and local tax, and charitable donations—total $24,000, the standard deduction amount for married couples, you're not getting any benefit for your charitable deduction. However, if you bunch your charitable giving by using your donor-advised fund, you can push your itemized deductions up above the $24,000 standard deduction threshold in some years, lowering your tax in those years.

5. Roth Conversion in Low-Income Years

One of my personal favorite tricks in tax planning is to move funds from an Individual Retirement Account (IRA) to a Roth IRA, a so-called "Roth conversion," during low-income years. When completing a Roth conversion, you take a distribution from an IRA account and move the distributed funds to a Roth IRA account. Distributions from an IRA account for a Roth conversion are taxed as ordinary income, which means that the amount of the distribution is added to your income for the year. This is the main disadvantage of a Roth conversion. Otherwise, moving money to a Roth IRA account is desirable because the account grows tax free and later distributions are also tax free.

During low-income years, the additional income caused by a Roth conversion may be acceptable. In some cases, when taxable income is negative, Roth conversions can be completed with little or no income tax consequences. For example, maybe you've taken a year off between companies or projects and have no income in that year. However, you still have large deductions from mortgage interest and property tax. Your taxable income could be negative. Years when you have negative taxable income are great times for Roth conversion when you can convert enough IRA to Roth to bring your taxable income up to zero or even slightly positive and pay no or little tax.

Retirees with a mortgage might find themselves having negative taxable income and consider Roth conversion. Once you're over the age of 59 and six months and eligible to take distributions from an IRA account without penalty, this trick works well also. You can select an IRA distribution amount to bring your taxable income up to zero or slightly positive. Using this technique, you are able to withdraw IRA funds with little or no tax.

Deferring Income

Along with reducing taxable income and controlling the timing of income and deductions, deferring taxable income is a third mainstay of tax planning. Deferring taxable income means putting off receiving income and, hence, paying tax until sometime in the future.

1. Retirement Plans and Accounts

Retirement plans such as 401(k) plans and retirement accounts such as IRAs are great ways to defer income. Contributions to these traditional retirement savings vehicles are tax deductible, which lowers your taxable income in the year of contribution. You don't have to pay tax on income from, or growth of, the account while your money is in the account. When you take money out later in retirement, the amount you withdraw each year is considered income and adds to your other income for the year.

With these traditional retirement accounts, you defer income in two ways. First, you don't pay income tax on the amount you originally contributed. Second, you don't pay tax on any of income or growth in the account. All of the income is deferred until you withdraw from the account, so there is no "tax drag" on your investment return. There is also a good chance your income will be lower in retirement when you withdraw from these accounts, which means you will be paying income tax in a lower tax bracket (assuming tax brackets are similar to what they are now when you retire) as compared to when you contributed through the peak earning years of your career.

2. Deferred Compensation Plans

Some tech companies offer deferred compensation plans to executives and highly paid staff members. These plans provide additional opportunity to defer income into the future by contributing a portion of salary or bonus to the plan. These plans are similar to retirement plans in that contributions are deducted from taxable income in the year of contribution and funds contributed grow tax-deferred until they are withdrawn. Amounts later withdrawn are fully taxable as ordinary income.

Typically, deferred compensation plans require plan participants to begin taking distributions upon leaving the company or retirement. However, deferred compensation plans don't provide as many of the protections against loss that 401(k) and other retirement plans covered by the Employee Retirement Income Security Act (ERISA) provides and should be thoroughly reviewed before participating. If your company is acquired, there is a possibility the acquiring firm will terminate the deferred compensation plan forcing you to withdraw—and pay tax on—your entire balance in a single year, the exact opposite of the benefit the plan is intended to provide.

Unlike 401(k) plans, deferred compensation accounts cannot be rolled over to an IRA account when you terminate employment.

Summary

- Use the material in the chapter as an introduction to, or quick refresher on, the basic structure of income tax, including the major updates for 2018.
- Reduce your tax liability by using techniques to minimize income, maximize deductions and credits, and control the timing of income and deductions.
- Use timing techniques to reduce taxable income including spreading income over multiple years to pay tax in lower rate brackets, accelerating or delaying income into a lower-income year, matching large deductions such as charitable to high-income years, and bunching deductions to allow itemizing.
- Delay tax by using retirement accounts and deferred compensation plans to defer receiving taxable income.
- Consider an IRA to Roth IRA conversion in low-income years.
- Use tax-loss harvesting to reduce capital gains in your investment portfolio.
- Employ tax-efficient investing techniques such as holding investments for a year before selling to receive long-term capital gains treatment, use tax-efficient

investment products such as index mutual funds and exchange-traded funds, and shield ordinary income from tax with asset location.

Ongoing tax planning is important in reducing the tax you pay and allowing you to build and preserve net worth. Waiting until April 15 is too late to plan and tax law is complicated, so get help with this area of your finances if the complexity of your situation exceeds your understanding of the many rules that may apply. Taxes are important again in the next chapter on liquidity events, including acquisitions and initial public offerings.

Liquidity Events:
IPOs & Acquisitions

When the company you helped build has its initial public offering (IPO) or is acquired by a larger firm, your financial outcome could range from enough to fund a few nice dinners out to life-changing money.

The amount of money you receive as part of an IPO or acquisition depends on how many shares of company stock you own and the price at which your employer's stock is sold. You might own shares in the form of stock options, restricted stock, restricted stock units, or shares from stock options that you previously exercised.

In the case of an IPO, be aware that the company may adjust its number of shares outstanding with a "reverse stock split" prior to the IPO. The total value of your shares will remain the same, but you may have fewer total shares. Companies adjust their outstanding shares prior to IPO in order to adjust their share price to a range that will be attractive to investors. To estimate the value of your stock before the offering, multiply your stock-split-adjusted number of shares by the expected initial offering share price.

In the event that your company is acquired, which is the more common outcome, knowing what percentage of the company you own with your stock and option awards can help you roughly determine what your stake is worth. For example, if you have been awarded stock options with low strike price that, when exercised, will represent 0.50% of the company's total outstanding shares and the company is acquired for $200 million, then your stock options are worth about $1 million.

If the good fortune of an IPO or acquisition arrives and your potential payout is in the range of six or seven figures, here are a few thoughts to keep in mind as your make your way through the process.

Selling Restrictions & Payout Structures

One of the first considerations with a pending or imminent IPO or acquisition is how any selling restrictions (for an IPO) or payout structure (for an acquisition) will affect when you can sell your shares or receive cash proceeds.

IPO Lock-Up

When a company goes public, the securities firm managing the sale of shares to the public, called the underwriter, typically requires the company selling the shares to sign an agreement that prevents executives and employees from selling their shares immediately. The so-called lock-up agreement helps underwriters sell the company's stock to new investors by limiting the ability of current stockholders (executives and employees) to sell their shares, which limits a potentially competitive source of supply. Lock-up periods prevent company executives and employees from selling their shares for, typically, 90 to 180 days after the company goes public, sometimes longer.

Before committing to major purchases or other financial transactions after an IPO, be sure to understand when and how you can sell your shares. Savvy IPO investors are keenly aware of the end of lock-up periods, which can increase supply of available shares into the market and temporarily drive prices down. As an executive or employee planning to sell shares at the end of the lock-up period, be aware of the potential for your company's stock price to decline at that time as other employees begin to sell their shares. Research on share price movement around the time of lock-up expirations shows abnormally negative stock price returns beginning about 10 days or more before the expiration of the lock-up and peaking about two days after the expiration of the lock-up.[1] Selling some shares around the lock-up may still be prudent to diversify some of your concentrated stock risk despite the depressed stock price when you sell.

Acquisition Payout

While IPOs are straightforward and provide an opportunity for you to sell your shares almost immediately after the lock-up period, the structure of acquisitions is varied and unique to each specific transaction. You could receive cash, or stock in the acquiring company, or both. The acquiring company may require a certain portion of the sales price be held back and earned by the acquired company shareholders over time, based on accomplishing agreed-to milestones. Milestones might include meeting product development timelines, meeting particular customer acquisition goals, or attaining certain financial results. Milestone payments might span months to a few years, with 18 to 36 months being fairly common.

As part of an acquisition, executives and key employees also may be required to agree to continue working for the company for a period of time to earn their full payout. With various transaction-specific hold-back formulas, it can be hard to evaluate both the timing and amount of your milestone payments in an acquisition and, hence, the total value of the transaction to you. With an acquisition, it's even more important not to commit to major financial transactions based on your expected payout until you have a clear understanding of what the range of those payouts might be. Ask your human resources or finance department for a calculation of your portion of any milestone payments, including the range of those payments if their payment depends on company performance or other variable. Be sure to check the amount you receive against what you expected. Mistakes on complicated payout structures are more common than you would think.

After-Tax Proceeds

The second bit of math you should do after figuring out how much an IPO or acquisition will be worth to you and when you'll receive your payout, is to subtract taxes. It's easy to forget this important reduction in thinking about the money you will receive. Try not to underestimate your tax obligation. Avoid setting yourself up for disappointment, or worse, spending funds you owe to the government.

The amount of tax you owe depends on what type of options or stock you hold and the terms of the specific transaction. For quick mental math, you can use a worst-case scenario.

Here's an example:

Assume all of the income you receive will be ordinary income taxed at ordinary income tax rates.

- If your payout is in the high six figures or seven figures, some or most of your payout will be taxed at the highest federal tax rate of 37%.
- To that you need to add 2.35% federal Medicare tax, which includes the 0.9% Additional Medicare Tax on high income. That's about 39% total.
- On top of that, add any state and local income tax.

If you live in a high-tax state like California where the top income tax rate on income over $1 million is 13.3%, you could expect to pay over one-half of your earnings in federal and state taxes. If you're in a no income tax state like Texas, worst case would be about 40% shrinkage from taxes.

The tax consequences of exercising and selling incentive stock options (ISOs) depends on your specific situation. Avoid the temptation to assume you'll receive long-term capital gains treatment and a federal tax rate of 15%. At high income, the long-term capital gains tax rate jumps to 20%. To that you'll probably need to add the net investment income tax of 3.8%. Also, you will need to calculate your tax under the alternative minimum tax system with its top rate of 28%. There are other interactions on your tax return such as exemption phase-outs that make back-of-the-envelope calculations difficult.

A best practice is to assume the worst case until you can prepare or have prepared a complete income tax projection. For quick mental math on large payouts, assume 50% is gone to income taxes.

Estate & Gift Tax

Under current tax law, an individual can leave up to $11.2 million to heirs and pay no federal estate or gift tax. A married couple can leave up to $22.4 million to heirs without paying federal estate or gift tax. These limits apply in 2018 and the amounts will increase each year with inflation. Amounts above these limits are taxed at a flat tax rate of 40%. If an anticipated liquidity event will lift your net worth above these limits, you may want to consider estate planning techniques to move money out of your estate to avoid estate and gift tax.

A popular and effective estate planning technique for moving money out of your estate ahead of an IPO is to use a "grantor retained annuity trust" (GRAT). If you have a taxable estate (net worth greater than about $11 million individually or $22 million with your spouse) and are holding options or stock in a company expected to go public or be sold, you should consult a competent estate planning attorney about whether a GRAT (and other estate planning techniques) make sense in your case. Typically, GRATs and other techniques aimed at reducing or avoiding gift and estate tax must be completed well before the company's stock goes public or otherwise substantially increases in value.

GRATs involve complicated areas of estate and tax law. A simplified sketch of how they work goes like this: You transfer pre-IPO or pre-sale shares of stock to an irrevocable trust for a specific period of time, typically between two and 10 years. An irrevocable trust is a trust whose terms cannot be changed once it is created. The beneficiaries of the trust are people you want to transfer some of your net worth to, commonly your children, but other beneficiaries can be selected as well. The trust pays you a fixed payment (the annuity) during the term of the trust. The payment includes a portion of your contributed amount plus a rate of return on your contribution as required by IRS rules. The stock you transferred can be used to make the annuity payment. When the final annuity payment is made and the trust terminates, the remaining stock is given to your children or other beneficiaries.

If the value of the stock in the trust appreciates faster than the IRS required rate of return, then the excess appreciation is transferred to your children or other beneficiaries. In the case of an IPO, the appreciation in the stock will often be substantially greater than the growth rates assumed by IRS rules, allowing you to transfer a substantial amount of net worth out of your estate.

The difference between the value of the stock contributed to the trust and the value of the annuity payments you received back will be subject to gift tax. Most GRATs are designed to minimize or "zero out" the amount subject to gift tax by returning 100% of your initial contribution to you.

Emotional High

When contemplating or experiencing an IPO or acquisition, you may feel an emotional high as concerns about money fade into the background. Be aware that you may feel better off financially than you actually are. With vesting, lock-ups, hold-backs, and taxes, it can be challenging to determine what a liquidity event means for your net worth and cash flow in the short-term and over the longer-term. This is a good time to run some financial models to get an objective assessment of where you are financially. The purpose of financial modeling is to discover the boundaries of your financial situation and explore the limits of what is possible for you given likely scenarios. Knowing the limits will help you be realistic and keep you from overcommitting financially while you're still adjusting to your new situation.

It can take months to years to mentally and emotionally adjust to a significant liquidity or other event that increases your net worth substantially. Over the long term, your new financial resources can create opportunities for you to pursue new career interests, become involved in philanthropy, or work a few items off the list of things you've always wanted to do or places you've always wanted to go. It takes time to process the intersection of new opportunities available to you and new limits of your financial situation.

In the short term, pressures at work might increase. In the case of an IPO, the company will now be reporting its financial progress in quarterly earnings reports. Any slip in growth of customers, revenue or earnings can cause the stock price to drop sharply. There can be incredible pressure within the company to maintain the high rate of growth which preceded the IPO. After an IPO is no time to slack off. Also, with new capital raised during the IPO, the company will have more resources available to accelerate growth and begin new initiatives, such as developing follow-on products or entering new markets, which can translate into continued long work hours for employees. Understand it's all part of the process, and be prepared mentally and emotionally for what comes next after an IPO.

After an acquisition, the situation can vary depending on whether the acquired company will be left to run on a stand-alone basis or whether it will be integrated into the operations of the acquiring company. In the case of integration, after the acquisition, there can follow an intense effort internally to redraw organizational charts and blend teams and workflows together. This can be a stressful time for all involved, and the reorganization usually results in extra work hours for everyone. Some acquisitions go more smoothly than others with integrations taking anywhere from mere months to two years or more. Depending on the reason for the acquisition, the pressure to grow revenue or complete product development can be extreme, as management and staff alike work to meet milestones that are tied to payouts.

Early employees in startups receive more options and stock than later employees. The people that founded the company or started working there early make more money in an IPO or acquisition than people who joined the company later. This becomes evident in subtle and not so subtle ways after an IPO or acquisition. When the parking lot outside starts to look like a high-end Tesla showroom forecourt, you'll know that your fellow employees have started to make financial decisions based on their new wealth. This can trigger all sorts of feelings and thoughts, including envy, anger, frustration, excitement, and elation, which might cause you to make financial decisions you might not ordinarily make.

It's best to observe a cooling-off period of months to years before making any large financial decisions. While a new car might be a minor purchase for some of your colleagues, it could be a major financial disaster for others, depending on how much money they made during the IPO or acquisition. You don't know their financial situation, and it isn't relevant to you. Only your financial situation is a concern for you.

Successful Exits Are Rare

Many people working in technology don't fully appreciate the role that chance has played or will play in their company's financial success. Hard work and great ideas are necessary, but not sufficient. For a startup to emerge from incubation or for an established firm to avoid being disrupted into obsolescence, a good amount of luck is involved. It can be hard on your ego to admit, but often a successful outcome is as much about being in the right place at the right time as any factor under your direct control.

Human beings are wired to overestimate the odds of positive events and underestimate the odds of negative events. Entrepreneurs seem even more susceptible to optimism bias. As a result, it's easy to overestimate how easy it will be to repeat a successful exit, particularly those who found success early. If you've been part of an IPO or acquisition, be aware that life-changing liquidity events are rare and plan accordingly. It may never happen to you again. Adjust your lifestyle to your new financial situation without assuming or expecting another tech lottery win.

Deploying New Assets: Priorities

When you begin to receive proceeds from an IPO, an acquisition, or sale of shares that skyrocketed in value, you will need to
decide how to deploy the new cash. The following suggestions are
listed in rough order of priority.

Priority 1: Set Aside Cash for Taxes

The first priority for deploying your new cash is to set aside
enough cash to pay the income tax you will owe.

In calculating income tax, a best practice is to first model a
complete tax return for the year, including all of your income,
deductions, and any tax credits you are entitled to. Include income
from all sources, including compensation income such as salary and
bonus, proceeds from the liquidity event, and any other investment
income and other types of income. You will need to calculate your
federal income tax under the regular tax system and alternative
minimum tax system, including with the net investment income
tax overlay. You will also need to calculate the amount of state and
local income tax you will owe.

Run the calculations a second time, this time excluding the extra
income resulting from the liquidity event. The difference between
the income taxes calculated in step one and step two is the amount
of additional tax owed as a result of the liquidity event. You may
need to make estimated tax payments during the year to pay this
amount depending on the type of options or stock plans involved
and whether you paid sufficient tax through paycheck withholding.

It's generally best to hold the money for taxes in a federally
insured bank or credit union account, or a safe, low-volatility investment such as money-market mutual fund. If you will hold the

funds for several months, you might also consider a high credit quality, short-term bond mutual fund or exchange-traded fund. Money you are holding for taxes should not be invested in your risky retirement investment portfolio. This money needs to remain safe so that you can pay what you owe on time.

Priority 2: Charitable Account

To reduce income tax in a high-income year, you can accelerate charitable donations to reduce your taxable income in that year. For example, if you regularly give $10,000 per year to charity, you could consider giving 10 years' worth of donations all at once, or $100,000, in a liquidity event year (or other high-income year) to get a larger charitable deduction and reduce your taxable income. Accelerating your regular contributions (or beginning your philanthropy with a significant lump sum contribution) to a donor-advised fund can reduce your taxable income without impacting the timing of your normal annual giving. Whenever possible, it's best to donate appreciated assets, such as company stock, to your donor-advised fund to avoid paying capital gains tax on the gain in those assets. See Chapter 8 for more about this.

Outright donations to charity or creation of a charitable foundation are alternatives to donor-advised funds. Charitable foundations are covered in Chapter 11 on legacy.

Priority 3: Pay Off Debt

Another area you can deploy new cash is in paying off debt. To decide which of your loans and other debt to pay off, you should rank your loans in order of highest to lowest after-tax interest rate and pay off loans in order, starting with highest after-tax interest rate first.

For example, your ranked list might include credit card debt at 18%, car loans at 8%, student loans at 7%, home-equity line of credit at 5.5%, and home loan at 4.5%. In this example, you would pay off credit card debt first because it has the highest interest rate. Next you would pay off car loans and then student loans.

The after-tax interest rate of credit card debt, car loans, and student loans is the same as their stated interest rate because interest on those types of loans is not tax deductible. However, interest on home loans is tax deductible, which means their after-tax effective interest rate is lower than their stated rate. For example, if your home loan interest rate is 4.5% and you pay a combined average federal and state income tax rate of 34%, then the after-tax effective interest rate is about 3.0%. Interest on home equity lines of credit is no longer deductible for federal tax purposes as of January 1, 2018. If the after-tax interest rate on a loan is significantly lower than the rate of return you can earn on investments, you may consider keeping that loan in order to leave the cash you would use to pay off the loan in your investment portfolio.

Priority 4: College Savings Plans

A special provision in the tax law allows a single person to make a lump sum contribution to a 529 college savings plan equal to five years' worth of the annual gift tax exclusion amount. In 2018, the special five-year contribution could be as much as $75,000

(5 x $15,000). A married couple can together contribute $150,000 (2 x 5 x $15,000) to a single 529 savings plan. If a married couple has three children, they could contribute the maximum $150,000 to each child's 529 plan. The contribution grows tax-free until the money is used for college expenses. Contributing a lump sum early allows the magic of compounding to work so that less money needs to be contributed to fully fund a college education.

Priority 5: Cash Reserve

Another important category for deployment of liquidity-event proceeds is building or maintaining a cash reserve for living expenses and any near-term goals, such as home remodeling projects planned or major vacations. If you are in a position to retire and will no longer be earning regular income, you should consider keeping an amount of cash in reserve equal to two or three years' living expenses to avoid needing access to your liquid investments, or having to sell real estate or other illiquid investments, during a down market.

Priority 6: Taxable Portfolio

After all other priorities, the remaining proceeds from an IPO or acquisition can be directed to your taxable investment portfolio. Your taxable portfolio consists of investments you hold in taxable brokerage accounts (i.e., non-retirement accounts) and any private investments, such as real estate, private equity, or venture capital. For your taxable portfolio, follow the recommendations in Chapter 4 on investments to develop a proper asset allocation and select investments for your portfolio.

Summary

- Make a rough calculation of the after-tax proceeds you will receive from an expected IPO or acquisition, including any reverse stock-split adjustment to your shares in the case of IPO.

- Be aware of any selling restrictions such as lock-up period for an IPO or milestone-based payout structure for an acquisition before committing to major purchases or financial transactions.

- Learn about the popular and effective estate planning technique involving grantor retained annuity trusts (GRATs) before an IPO that may push your net worth close to or over the estate tax exemption amount.

- Give yourself time to adjust mentally and emotionally to a significant liquidity event that substantially increases your net worth before making major decisions.

- Because life-changing liquidity events are rare, adjust your lifestyle assuming you will never have another big payday from an IPO or acquisition.

- Deploy your new assets in the following rough order of priority: set aside cash for taxes, contribute to charitable account to reduce taxes, pay off debt, fund college savings plans, build a cash reserve, and direct remaining cash to your taxable investment portfolio.

Liquidity events such as IPOs and acquisitions can add to your net worth and help move you closer to retirement. But what exactly is retirement? And what are the logistics of making retirement work financially? That's covered next.

10

Quitting the Rat Race: Planning for Retirement

Retirement may be the most burdened word in use today. It's meant to deliver us the euphoric state of being that we've looked forward to our entire working career. We will be free to do as we please. Everything will be wonderful when we retire.

Expectations for retirement are high, yet retirement brings with it enormous anxiety. We worry that retirement is not attainable or sustainable. We worry that our accumulated wealth may not be sufficient to meet our spending needs. We face the great unknown of life after regular earned income. Across a wide spectrum of income and net worth, hopes and concerns about retirement are the same. Within the tech community, an early-retirement-or-bust mentality is a factor that adds even more pressure. Between high expectations and tremendous trepidation, poor retirement has a heavy load to bear.

To lighten the load, most people find it helpful to gain clarity in two main areas. First, what does retirement actually mean to you? And second, how does one actually live off of one's accumulated assets in retirement?

Making It Real

Retirement is such a vague, amorphous concept. By itself, it has no real meaning, other than as the absence of something—your day job. It's up to you to give your retirement shape and meaning. It's up to you to decide how you want to set up your life in retirement. Where will you live? What will you do? With whom will you spend time? To get more clarity on retirement and make it feel real to you, you'll need to think through the key features of the retirement you envision. Picturing your retirement is a creative design process. It's an act of will. It's something you do, not something that happens to you. And it can entail a little bit of work: you'll need to turn your indistinct notion about retirement life into concrete specifics, such as in what city and neighborhood you'll live, which family and friends you'll be close to, how much and where you will travel, and what hobbies and interests you will pursue.

A useful way to approach the prospect of retirement is to develop scenarios. Potentially, there will be many different retirement scenarios you are excited about that meet your financial constraints. For example, one scenario might be living in the same place and maintaining your current lifestyle, while another scenario might involve moving to a new city and planning for extensive travel. You might live in a different country for part of the year. You might split time in different cities. You might move closer to family. You might move from the city to the country or vice versa. You can build scenarios around any of these ideas and many others. It can be a lot of fun to let your mind wander and think about how you want to set up your life.

From those seeds, you can begin to grow solid scenarios. Fill in more detail. Make them more real. Focus on the three key drivers of retirement life: where you live, what you do, and with whom you spend time.

Where Will You Live?

If you plan on staying exactly where you are now once you reach retirement, then the location question is easy. If you are considering moving out of the area, then some investigation is in order. After doing online research, it's a good idea to spend time in the cities or places you're considering moving to. Go there and stay for weekends. Spend some of your vacation there. Drive the neighborhoods, look at open houses, shop at the grocery stores, and eat at the restaurants. Do the things you do now, at home, in the new location. Meet the people and visit family and friends in the area. The point is to make it as real as possible. Really experience the new place and imagine yourself living there. In the process of visiting your candidate retirement locations, you'll decide more unconsciously than consciously which place or places feel right for you and where you truly enjoy being.

One caution is to beware the vacation effect. Tropical islands aside, places we visit on vacation seem to feel a little better than they might feel if we were living there, going about our normal routine, and making our way through traffic on the way to the store.

What Will You Do?

For many of us, work is not just a source of income. Our chosen vocation gives purpose and meaning to our lives. It's a major source of contact with other people. In retirement, we may shift to other activities we find enjoyable and stimulating, that have meaning for us, and allow for social interaction.

Picturing what you will do in retirement is an important part of building your retirement scenarios. Many people travel in retirement, and that can take many forms: adventure, cultural, nature, cruises, or RV. You may volunteer at a school or for a nonprofit. You may learn a new language, take cooking classes or devote yourself to gardening, fitness, sports, or politics. You may have an active social calendar or become involved with a church or community service organization. You might learn to play piano or dust off your guitar and join a band. You might follow your favorite professional sports team to away games. The point, again, is to make it as real as possible. If you weren't working today, what would you be doing?

With Whom Will You Spend Time?

The people we plan to spend time with are the next consideration when clarifying our retirement scenarios. As we get older we value our close relationships more and more. If you can visualize where you'll be, what you'll be doing and who you'll be with, retirement starts to feel real.

With retirement, people and place are intertwined. In contemplating one, most people find themselves contemplating the other. For example, would you like to move closer to family? Or would you prefer to stay put in the community where you grew up and have deep roots? Do you have close friends nearby that you wouldn't move away from? Or is it time to set out to find new friends and acquaintances after your current relationships have run their course? Maybe you have friends scattered across the country and world you can now visit, or who can join you on adventures. Or maybe you'll pick a wonderful place with a resort feel to it where your family and friends will come visit you. Do you make friends easily and have "never met a stranger"? Have you adjusted well after moving several times in your life? Or does it take time for people to get to know you, which could leave you isolated after a move? These are important reflections in contemplating your retirement. Your social network of family and friends will have a big impact on your emotional well-being.

What Will Your Financial Constraints Be?

Financially, it's difficult to assess the feasibility of a retirement lifestyle you can't quite articulate. That's why it's so important to think through and research where you'll live, what you'll be doing, and who you'll be sharing your time with. Once you have developed three or four scenarios based on fairly specific answers to those questions, you'll be in a position to use financial modeling to put dollar amounts to the scenarios and compare them according to your financial constraints, which might include any wealth you plan to leave to family or charities.

Of course, like all design processes, creating a retirement lifestyle requires some iteration. You may need to adjust some aspects of your scenarios to make them affordable. You may need to discard one or more altogether, although that's usually not necessary if you've been realistic about your pre-retirement financial situation and post-retirement expectations. Or you may create a new scenario if your financial situation is better than you imagined.

Through this iterative process of defining what retirement means to you and comparing those scenarios to your financial constraints, you can develop a good understanding of the boundaries of your retirement space. You will begin to know that what's feeling more real to you is also attainable. Knowing where you are with retirement in such concrete terms is deeply comforting.

Within scenarios there can be a range of financial feasibility. College counselors often advise high school seniors to categorize schools they are applying to as either "safe, target, or reach," based on the likelihood of acceptance. Similarly, you can have safe retirement scenarios that are easily attainable or likely attainable, or reach retirement scenarios which include a more abundant lifestyle if your net worth accumulation allows. For example, you might easily be in a position to retire comfortably in your community if you downsized to a less expensive home, while being confident you'll be able to stay in your current home if you remain on track financially, and with the hope you'll be able maintain a second residence in a resort area if your stock options wind up being worth more than expected.

Be aware of the sensitivity of your scenarios to changes in standard of living. Does a small increase in living expenses greatly reduce the probability that your scenario is successful? If so, you may consider working an extra year or two, or reducing expenses a bit more to make your scenario more robust. Generally, it's preferable if small changes in inputs do not have a large change in the outcome.

Retirement scenarios allow you to try on retirement in your mind and see how it fits. Not from fantasy or speculation, but from facts obtained by the research you've done. Getting ready for retirement is the process of assessing where you are now, using your scenarios as a guide to where you want to be and filling in the steps in between.

This is not to say that you are locked into any particular scenario or set of scenarios. Plans can and do change. Planning for retirement is not an open-loop or set-and-forget process; you will make modifications along the way. When plans change, iterate the process. Develop new scenarios and compare them again to your constraints. This is a powerful technique for knowing where you are along your financial path.

New Retirement Paradigm

Retirement as traditionally conceived is an all-or-nothing concept. You're either working or not-working. That model has served well to this point in history. However, as we're living longer and staying healthier longer an opportunity for a different arrangement is presenting itself.

People who have had successful primary careers, or those who need to top off the financial gas tank before retiring, can now consider the possibility of scaling back their effort somewhat while still working. In the new retirement, you can work less intensely at something you enjoy for the latter part of your career. You can choose work that doesn't necessarily earn you a high income or demand achievement and accomplishment, but work which is meaningful or rewarding to you.

Working for 40 years and saving enough to spend for another 30 years with no income is challenging. With greater life expectancy, preparing for traditional retirement is harder than ever. People are working longer and that may represent a first generation response to increased longevity. In 2017, the percentage of people working past age 65 was nearly 19% compared to about 12% in 1998.[1]

With increased longevity, even different models of career income may emerge over time. Traditional retirement may become obsolete. People may begin to work more or less at different times during their lives, reaching a career peak later and spreading more leisure time throughout. Dramatically different, happier, and more fulfilled lives may be possible as a result of our increasing longevity.

While our ability to learn declines as we age, our general knowledge and specialized expertise allows us to maintain our ability to function at high levels. As we get older, our productivity can remain high as a result of our accumulated experience.[2]

Aside from the financial benefits of continuing to work less intensely in a meaningful role, there are potential emotional benefits as well. The first years of traditional all-or-nothing retirement can be anxiety provoking because you have no earned income. Having a post-career job or project can ease the anxiety and help you prepare mentally for full retirement by beginning to live partly on investment income and principal. Knowing how you will create cash flow from your assets can also help to ease your retirement anxiety.

Creating Cash Flow from Assets

The keys to building assets for retirement are to save plentifully, spend moderately, and invest prudently. Once you retire and begin to use your accumulated assets to live on, you'll need to convert your assets to an income stream to cover expenses. Even if you've done the math and are well prepared for retirement, the concept of living without a regular paycheck can be scary. For most people, it takes many months to a few years to get comfortable with living on investments without regular employment income. Going over a few of the mechanics of living on your investments can help you feel more comfortable in anticipating and beginning retirement.

In the past when pensions were common, professional investment managers were responsible for ensuring that the pension benefits promised to employees were delivered. Part of these investment managers' job responsibilities involved creating the income streams for individuals in the form of pension checks from a large pension plan investment portfolio. Today, individual investors and their advisors are responsible for creating that retirement income stream from their investment portfolios and ensuring it lasts. Investments in rental real estate as discussed in Chapter 6 can be another source of retirement income.

Sustainable Withdrawal Rates

How much money can you take out of an investment portfolio each year to cover living expenses in retirement without using up all of your investments too early or depleting them below a target fixed amount (for example, an amount you'd like to leave to heirs)? That's the question answered by research on maximum sustainable withdrawal rates from investment portfolios.

As a place to start thinking about withdrawal rates, studies have shown that you can withdraw about 3% to 5% of an investment portfolio's value each year and have it last the typical 25 to 30 years in retirement. Of course there are a number of assumptions, caveats, and potential adjustments that go along with this simple rule of thumb.

William Bengen's original article from 1994, which kicked off 20 years of research into sustainable withdrawal rates, assumed a 50/50 stock-bond portfolio, used historically observed rates of return and adjusted each years' withdrawal by the actual rate of inflation.[3] With the initial withdrawal set as a percentage of total portfolio value and increased or decreased each year by the rate of inflation, Bengen found that a 4% withdrawal rate was about the upper limit to maintain withdrawals for 30 years. Interestingly, Bengen found portfolios with asset allocations ranging from 50% stock to 75% stock were optimal for achieving maximum sustainable withdrawal rates. Bengen's original study has been repeated, verified, and expanded over the last 20 years. Rates of return on stocks and bonds have been lower on average since the original study, and many researchers (having run more withdrawal rate studies using current data) would advise shading to the lower end of the safe withdrawal rate range if using the same withdrawal rate formula.

It turns out that the sequence of annual returns earned on a portfolio is particularly important once annual withdrawals have begun. Starting withdrawals during a down stock market can have a significant and lasting effect on the ability of a portfolio to meet withdrawal targets. Research into sequence of returns led to development of withdrawal rules, which take into account stock and bond market performance. For example, in years when an investment portfolio delivers on-target or better investment returns, a full inflation adjustment (increase) can be made to the annual withdrawal amount. In years when investment performance is below target, no inflation adjustment should be made to the annual withdrawal amount. These adaptive withdrawal techniques can allow increases in initial withdrawal percentage of up to 50%.[4] If you are a risk-tolerant investor who can accept greater stock market risk in your investment portfolio during retirement, and along with that risk accept the possibility that you will need to cut spending at some point if stock market performance is weak, you may be able to increase your withdrawal rate slightly more.[5]

Total Return Concept

Generating income from a retirement portfolio isn't actually about earning income from investments as many people suppose. As opposed to an income investing approach, a best practice is to invest for "total return."

The definition of total return on your investments is the sum of the amounts you receive in the form of interest, dividends, unrealized gains (price appreciation), and realized gains. Total return is usually reported as a percentage over a certain time period—for example, an 8% annual total return. The income investing approach favors investments that pay interest and dividend income and puts less emphasis on the capital gain component of investment returns.

The total-return approach is indifferent to receiving return in the form of income or capital gain. In the total-return approach, you don't care how you earn your return, you're focused on earning the highest return possible for a given amount of risk.

In the income-investing approach, your interest and dividend income from your portfolio is your cash inflow for meeting living expenses in retirement. High dividend-paying stock portfolio strategies are based on this idea. In contrast, in the total-return approach, interest and dividends are typically reinvested into the portfolio, and cash for living expenses is raised periodically by selling some of the investments in the portfolio.

The key advantage of the total-return approach is that it allows you to invest in fully diversified portfolio using all asset classes, as opposed to focusing on a subset of higher income-producing assets or individual securities such dividend-paying stocks. An income-oriented portfolio may become distorted compared to a fully diversified portfolio. The fully diversified portfolio in the total return approach will earn a higher rate of return than the less diversified income-oriented portfolio for the same level of risk.

With the total-return approach, you or your advisor might plan, for example, to raise cash by selling investments for future spending needs once or twice per year. You can then transfer the cash to your savings or checking account all at once or set up regular monthly transfers of smaller amounts to mimic a paycheck. Raising cash more frequently than once or twice a year can increase your overall transaction costs and is usually unnecessary with proper planning. It's best to rebalance your portfolio at the same time you're raising cash. This reinforces the good portfolio management technique of selling the asset classes or investments that have increased in value and moving the portfolio back toward its target allocation, which reduces investment risk.

There isn't necessarily a big difference in income tax between income investing and total-return investing. Dividends from mutual funds can be "qualified," as are dividends received from individual stocks if certain conditions are satisfied. Qualified dividends are taxed at the favorable long-term capital gains tax rates. Whether mutual fund dividends are reinvested or not doesn't change the tax treatment. Dividends are taxable, whether received in cash or reinvested. When reinvested, dividends add to the cost basis of the mutual fund, which reduces your gain on future sale. When selling securities to raise cash, you'll want to sell investments you've held for longer than one year, which qualify for the lower long-term capital gains tax rates. Taxable income generated by sales under the total return approach may actually be lower than taxable income under the income investing approach because potentially more of the return is taken in the form of long-term capital gain as opposed to ordinary income.

Because the total return approach requires that you sell investments periodically to raise cash, it's important to have a cash buffer against market downturns. For retirees living on their investment portfolio, a good recommendation is to keep two to three years' worth of living expenses available in cash. This is particularly important during the first few years of retirement, when accessing your portfolio during a recession and market downturn can reduce the amount you'll be able to withdraw for the rest of your retirement.

Order of Withdrawals

Once you begin withdrawing from your investment portfolio in retirement, you'll need to decide which types of accounts to withdraw from first. Just as limiting taxes is an important goal when you are working and building your retirement portfolio, minimizing taxes in retirement when you are withdrawing from your accounts is vital as well. Tax-efficient withdrawals extend the life of your investment portfolio and preserve your assets further into the future.

There are three types of accounts to consider, each with different tax properties:

- Taxable – Brokerage accounts and bank accounts
- Tax-deferred – All types of Individual Retirement Accounts (IRA), 401(k), 403(b), 457
- Tax-free – Roth IRA, Roth 401(k)

Withdrawals from tax-deferred accounts such as IRA and 401(k) are taxed as ordinary income, whereas withdrawals from tax-free accounts such as Roth IRAs are not taxed. Unlike taxable accounts in which income earned is taxed immediately, in both tax-deferred and tax-free accounts income is not taxed, allowing the accounts to grow faster. Once you turn 70 and six months, tax-deferred accounts generally require that you take mandatory withdrawals each year known as required minimum distributions (RMD).

Absent considerations other than maximizing tax-efficiency, a good default order of withdrawal from your accounts is: RMD, taxable, tax-deferred, and then tax-free. With this withdrawal order, you ensure your mandatory RMDs are made, and you allow your tax-deferred and tax-free accounts to continue growing as long as possible by withdrawing from your taxable account first. Once your taxable accounts are depleted, you begin withdrawing from your tax-deferred accounts, leaving your tax-free accounts until last.

A variation on the default withdrawal order is to reverse the tax-deferred and tax-free accounts. If you predict ordinary income tax rates are lower now than they will be in the future, you'll prefer to take distributions from tax-deferred accounts now and pay the tax at lower current rates. If you believe ordinary income tax rates are high now and will be lower in the future, you will prefer to use tax-free money now and take distributions from a tax-deferred account when you can pay the tax at lower rates.

Another approach is to use a blended withdrawal strategy— taking money from each of the taxable, tax-deferred, and tax-free account types—based on your tax situation in any particular year. In this approach, you tune your withdrawals each year or over the next few years based on tax projections of your income, deductions, exemptions, cash needs, changing tax rates, embedded capital gains in taxable accounts, and other factors. For example, in some circumstances it may be beneficial to limit ordinary income from tax-deferred accounts in order to reduce the taxable portion of your Social Security benefit. Or you may have large income in one year and decide to withdraw from your Roth IRA account that year, instead of your IRA account, to avoid creating more taxable income.

The order of withdrawal effects not only the tax efficiency of withdrawals during your lifetime, it can also interact with your estate plan, affecting the taxes paid by your heirs. For example, if you follow the RMD/taxable/tax-free/tax-deferred order of withdrawals, your heirs may be left with a sizeable IRA or 401(k) account on which they'll pay ordinary income tax. Your heirs may prefer to receive taxable accounts, which receive a step up in cost basis on your passing, allowing them to inherit taxable assets tax free. Be sure to consider the tax efficiency of your withdrawal order over both generations if you intend to leave assets to heirs.

Summary

- Envision specific retirement scenarios to define what retirement means to you, including where you will live, what you will do, and with whom you will spend your time.
- Iteratively assess the feasibility of retirement scenarios compared to your financial constraints to develop an understanding of what's attainable.
- Consider new models of retirement, such as continuing to work less intensely in a role that is more personally meaningful to you.
- Use adaptive techniques, rather than a static percentage, to maintain sustainable withdrawal rates from your investment portfolio over your retirement.
- Invest for "total return" rather than an income approach to maximize the amount of retirement income your investments can produce.
- Follow a tax efficient withdrawal order from your accounts such as: required minimum distributions, taxable accounts, tax-deferred accounts, then tax-free accounts.

With retirement safely planned you can turn your attention to your heirs and legacy in the next chapter.

Leaving Your Mark:
Legacy Planning

There comes a point in life when you begin to think about your legacy—what you will pass on to future generations. Your reflections on legacy might be motivated by one or both of the following:

If you have succeeded in practicing good financial management principles, you realize you will have "leftover" net worth. What you do with your leftovers is one aspect of your legacy.

As you move into the second half of your life, there is a natural tendency to think more deeply about the meaning of your life. You may reflect on what more you want to contribute with your remaining time and resources.

The two aspects of legacy are related. Being financially prepared for your later years can allow you more opportunity to create and leave a legacy that includes both aspects.

This chapter begins with a broad discussion of what legacy means and why it's important. That is followed by an introduction to estate planning, which is important for many people who may not be aware of the actual legal mechanics for transferring their financial legacy and selecting guardians for minor children. The chapter concludes with a review of charitable giving including popular charitable giving vehicles.

What Is Legacy?

Originally, legacy related primarily to financial gifts upon death. Today, legacy has a broader definition involving making an impact on the well-being of current and future generations, and transmitting your values to family and community.

Leftover Net Worth

At the point when you are financially secure and relatively assured that your present net worth and projected earnings will more than cover your expenses through the end of your life, you may think about what you want to do with your surplus. This is the original definition of legacy, which dates from 15th-century Europe and had a narrow, legal meaning of a gift by will, especially of money or other personal property. Leaving a monetary or property gift to family or charity at the end of life remains an important part of what many people think about when considering their legacy.

For most people, their leftover net worth will go to one or both of two places: family members and charitable organizations.

Many parents consider their children and grandchildren to be the most important part of their legacy and likely the recipients of some, most, or even all of their financial legacy. In addition to inheriting from parents at their death, children may receive annual gifts from their parents, or ongoing income from trusts created for their benefit as part of the parents' estate plan.

Children and grandchildren of financially secure parents often receive other types of support, including college funding, private school tuition, and special tutors. The support may also include extracurricular activities, such as music lessons, sports clubs, robotics teams, dance classes, math competitions, science fairs, and summer camps. Many parents invest a lot of time, energy, and money in their children to give them a head start in life and, potentially, an advantage over peers. They hope this early advantage will translate into access to better schools, better jobs, and more rewarding and lucrative careers. Providing advantages to their children is part of these parents' legacies.

Most people leave a financial legacy to family, but you may not have family to receive your gift. Or you may choose not to leave money to family for many good reasons. For example, leaving money to a family member struggling with addiction could be destructive or even fatal. Or you may feel that family members would not use your bequest in a way that would honor your values. Or family members may be well-off themselves and not need or appreciate your gift. If family members are not a good choice to receive your assets, you can consider giving to a charity or nonprofit organization whose mission aligns with your values. Many people give to charity in addition to leaving property to family.

The National Center for Charitable Statistics counts 1.57 million nonprofit organizations in the U.S. alone. That total includes 1.1 million public charities, over 100,000 private foundations, and nearly 370,000 other types of nonprofits, including chambers of commerce, fraternal organizations, and civic leagues.[1] Charity evaluation website Charity Navigator assigns nonprofits to 11 broad categories according to their mission: animals, arts and culture, community development, education, environment, health, human and civil rights, human services, international, research and public policy, and religion. There are literally over a million nonprofit and charitable organizations working to make the world a better place and potentially worthy of your consideration.

Of course, not everyone wants to have leftover net worth. Many people carefully plan to allow for enjoyment of nearly all of their savings during their post-working years on travel, entertainment, and other fun and rewarding activities. While wonderful, not having any leftover net worth is trickier than it sounds. Because it is hard to predict how long a person will live, it is difficult to determine how quickly savings can be consumed without running out of money prematurely. Sophisticated financial planning techniques, such as statistical scenario analyses, are useful in these critical situations. Also, it is wise to leave a financial cushion for unexpected longevity or unexpected expense late in life (such as costly assisted living facilities for residents with dementia).

More Than Just Money

Today we think of legacy as more than just financial bequests. Your legacy is everything you hand down to future generations, and it can take many forms besides money or property. For example, transmitting your values to your children or other family members might be an important part of your legacy. Gifts of money or property are merely one of many ways to accomplish that objective.

In the broadest sense, your legacy includes your interactions with the people whose lives you have affected in a positive or negative way. It includes the relationships you have had with other people and what you have meant to them. It includes the recollections of all the people you have said a kind or ill word to. It includes the personal growth you have seeded in others because of something important you said in a teachable moment. The exceptional middle school math teacher who inspires 140 students every year has considerable leverage in her legacy. You may not even know the impact you are having on those around you, yet that impact is part of your legacy. When you are gone, people will remember you for the relationship and connection you had with them, not the size of your estate.

While many people consider their legacy later in life, you may reflect on yours earlier, particularly if you have significant net worth at an early age. Legacy can provide a useful compass for you in making choices about how to spend your time, energy, and material resources. Legacy results from the purpose with which you live and the meaning you give your life.

Professional Legacy

Your time at work is part of your legacy. Just because you are compensated for your work does not lessen its impact in the world. For example, medical researchers leave a legacy of foundational discoveries that others can build on to cure disease. Whether it is patients you have cured, code you have written, hardware you have designed, clients you have helped, deals you have closed, operational improvements you have made, or products you have launched: all that can be part of your legacy.

If you are an entrepreneur, your business experience and entrepreneurial skills are part of your legacy. You have created valuable businesses and technologies that did not exist before, and you have improved the lives of others through your products and services. You have created economic environments for families to flourish, and you have communicated your values through your businesses. This is part of your legacy.

Legacy at work is perhaps more important now than ever with the unprecedented electronic access each of us has to the work of other people in the same field—and the incredible technologies available now that allow us to find the helpful prior work that is someone else's legacy. Increasingly, because of new technologies, we have the potential to record our legacy at work and pass it on to future generations.

Passing On Values

While you are alive, you communicate your values continuously, through your words and actions to family members, coworkers, and members of the groups you belong to. Social media has significantly expanded the opportunity to create legacy, and never before in human history has a single individual had the means to communicate to millions, if not billions, of other people. Closer to home, your children pick up your values from you over time through your many interactions with them. This is part of our legacy to our children.

For explicitly educating future generations about your values, some thoughtful authorities have advocated the creation of a "personal value statement" that might be part of an estate plan. Personal value statements are also known as personal legacy statements, legacy letters, or ethical wills. Whereas an estate plan comprises legal documents to ensure the transfer of your outer, material assets such as property and financial assets to future generations in accordance with your wishes, a personal value statement helps transfer your inner, intangible assets, including your life experiences, values, family traditions and history, ethical beliefs, and observations about the themes and patterns of life.

With children and grandchildren, it may be important to teach your money values explicitly while you are alive. If your children and grandchildren will receive substantial inheritances, it makes sense to prepare them to receive the money. There is a lot for them to learn—not only about your money values but also about basic money mechanics and proper money management. This preparation is a critical piece of learning to be independent and avoiding feelings of entitlement.

Basic Estate Planning

The legal mechanics of leaving a financial legacy for family and charity is the topic of estate planning. It has never been easier to leave a financial legacy to your heirs.

Under the new tax for 2018, a single individual can leave up to $11.2 million to heirs without paying federal estate or gift tax; for a married couple that figure jumps to $22.4 million. Those are double the amounts for 2017 under the old law; however, the new tax law expires in 2025, at which time the amounts will be cut in half, back again to their original amounts. Some states also have an estate or inheritance tax or both. Nevertheless, with such a high federal estate tax threshold, not many households in the U.S. need to plan for estate tax. Internal Revenue Service statistics show that in 2016 only about 2,200 people who died during the year had taxable estates worth more than $10 million and only about 900 people had taxable estates worth more than $20 million.[2] Anecdotally, while a higher percentage of estates within the tech industry are taxable, the vast majority of tech professionals still will not pay federal estate and gift tax. For most people, estate planning is not about avoiding estate tax.

If estate planning is not about avoiding estate tax, what is the primary purpose of estate planning? Proper estate planning ensures that your assets are transferred to the people and organizations you want to receive them upon your death and provides for your minor children and other dependents when you are no longer able. If you have not yet accumulated enough assets to provide for your dependents, be sure to purchase enough life insurance to replace your lost income in the event of your death.

Estate planning and the administration of estates is governed by state law. Each state has its own set of laws and rules, which need to be taken into account when planning for transfer of your estate to heirs. Similarly, each state has its own procedures for settling the estates of people who have passed away. In addition, estate law is administered by courts at the county level, and each county has its own nuances in administrative procedure. Estate planning and administration is a specialized field of law practiced by licensed attorneys. When selecting an attorney to create your estate plan or help you administer an estate, it's important to work with someone for whom estate planning is their only or primary area of practice. Ideally, your attorney will be located, or practices frequently, in your state and be familiar with the procedures of the courts in your county.

If you don't have an estate plan, the state where you live has a default plan for you. If you prefer to direct where your assets will go upon your death, rather than having the state government direct them for you, then you'll need to have an estate plan in place to supersede your state's default plan. States' rules for who will inherit your assets typically follow your family lineage.

The most basic estate planning document is a will. Your will specifies how your property is to be distributed at your death. It lists which people and organizations are to receive your assets and how much. You can change your will at any time during your life, but at your death, your will becomes irrevocable—it's fixed and cannot be changed. Upon your death, the person you have named as executor of your will begins probate, the court-supervised process of collecting your assets, paying any outstanding debts and taxes, and distributing your remaining assets to the people and organizations you have named in your will.

One of most difficult decisions in preparing your estate plan is selecting guardians for your minor children in the event of your death or disability. If you have children, particularly young children, selecting guardians may be the most important reason for preparing an estate plan. Guardians are often named in your will and may also be named in a separate document.

Another option for specifying how your property will be disposed of at death is a revocable living trust. A revocable trust is a written agreement in which you appoint a trustee to manage your assets. You can revoke or cancel your trust at any time during your life, which is why these trusts are called "revocable living trusts." You can also change the trust's terms any time during your life, including the beneficiaries you've named to receive your assets. Typically, you name yourself as trustee during your life and name a successor trustee to take over those responsibilities upon your death. With a revocable living trust, your trustee will settle your estate at your death, paying your debts and taxes and distributing remaining assets from your trust. Revocable living trusts are funded by retitling your non-retirement account assets into the name of the trust. Revocable living trusts are "see-through" for income tax purposes. You report your income tax just as you would if you did not have a revocable living trust.

It is worth repeating that in order for the trust to be effective, your assets must be held in the name of the trust. Many people fail to complete this step, rendering their trust documents mostly worthless. Your revocable living trust will likely include a list of the assets held in your trust. Typically, you will also change the registration for each of your non-retirement brokerage accounts, bank accounts, and other investments to the name of the trust, and you will hold title to real estate in the name of the trust. Your attorney will give you instructions on how to include your assets in your trust, a process called "funding your trust."

With a revocable living trust, your assets do not go through the court probate process. Avoiding probate is the primary benefit of a revocable living trust over a will for distributing your assets upon death. Probate is a public process. Your financial situation and the amounts your heirs inherit becomes public record. In contrast, administering a trust is a private process. None of your financial information is made public.

The length of time to complete the probate process varies by state and depends on the types of assets involved. For example, probate can take a few months in Texas to more than one year in California. There are also fees associated with probate including court fees, attorney's fees, executor fees, accounting fees, and fees for appraisals and valuations. For example, attorney's fees in California are set by state law on a fee schedule, which allows attorneys to charge $23,000 on the first $1 million of gross estate value and 1% on gross estate value between $1 million and $10 million. For a $5 million estate, the statutory attorney fee is $63,000. Much of that cost can be saved using a revocable living trust.

Some assets including retirement accounts and life insurance benefits pass automatically by contract to your beneficiaries according to beneficiary designations. The transfer of those assets is not determined by your will or revocable living trust. This is why it is crucially important that you maintain up-to-date beneficiary designations on life insurance policies and 401(k), 403(b), 457, IRA, Roth IRA, Simplified Employee Pension (SEP) IRA, deferred compensation and other types of retirement accounts. Your attorney will give you instructions for completing beneficiary designations on these types of accounts.

In most states, a basic estate plan will include a revocable trust, will, financial power of attorney, and healthcare power of attorney.

For couples, each person will have a will, financial power of attorney, and healthcare power of attorney. When a revocable living trust is used in an estate plan, the will serves as a failsafe to put assets into the trust which were inadvertently left out. It's often called a "pour-over will" because assets pour over into the trust. The financial power of attorney is required to administer financial accounts, which are not governed by the trust including retirement accounts. The healthcare power of attorney allows for someone else to direct your medical care in the event you become incapacitated and includes your end-of-life wishes, such as whether you want to remain on life support.

Digital Assets and Intellectual Property

Access to your digital assets becomes critical at your death or if you become incapacitated. Without access to your bank and brokerage accounts and email, it will be difficult for your trustee, executor, and financial power of attorney to pay your bills and conduct other financial transactions. Most electronic accounts are linked to an email address. Access to email is needed for resetting passwords and user authentication. Security experts increasingly recommend two-factor authentication of financial and other sensitive accounts, but this can make accessing your accounts even more difficult for your authorized representatives.

In addition to financial accounts and email, your digital assets include social media accounts, professional networking accounts, online storage accounts for documents and photographs, gaming accounts, online software accounts, domain names, and virtual currency such as Bitcoin. Inability to access these accounts can create a problem in settling your estate or caring for you if you become disabled.

Most states have now passed the Uniform Fiduciary Access to Digital Assets Act, which gives your fiduciaries authority to act on your behalf in managing your digital assets.[3] However, this is still an unsettled area, and your representatives may have trouble accessing your accounts with online service providers who are in the process of changing their terms-of-service agreements and software to allow access by your legal representatives.

A best practice is to include provisions in your estate plan for who will manage and receive your digital assets. Your digital asset representative could be a different person than your trustee, executor, or financial power of attorney—someone with fluency in online technology. Keep an inventory of your digital assets including login IDs, passwords, challenge-question responses, two-factor authentication methods and other user-authentication security you've activated for your online accounts. Storing all of your online logins in one place is an obvious security concern. You can consider using one of the many good commercial password management applications to store logins.

Another important set of assets to include in your estate plan is any intellectual property which has value or could have value in future. Intellectual property includes copyrights, trademarks, patents, and trade secrets. Your trustee, executor or beneficiary will need to maintain your intellectual property according to the laws which apply to its property type in order to maximize and protect its value.

Charitable Giving

Your legacy, both in the financial and broader sense, is created during your lifetime. With both your financial resources and personal talents, you can have a great impact on the world during your life. Beyond family, you may want to serve your community or a global purpose with material resources and the time and expertise you can give by becoming involved with a charitable or nonprofit organization. By engaging during your lifetime, you get to see and enjoy the results of your gifts and efforts, and ensure that they are used in ways that match your values.

Charitable donations can be anonymous or in your name or the name of your family giving vehicle, whether that is a donor-advised fund or a family foundation. Many people prefer to give anonymously for the simple reason that nonprofit organizations are extremely effective in locating and soliciting potential donors. If your donations are public, having a mission statement and annual giving plan allows you to politely decline opportunities that are not areas of focus for you.

There can be great benefit to involving children in your charitable activities to teach them the value of service, giving back and a sense of community. Creating a family mission statement that details your charitable objectives can help you define and teach your core values to your children and other family members. You may have inherited assets or received support from someone or an organization during your life and you want to pass on those values to future generations as a good steward of those assets. A family mission statement can transmit those core values across generations.

Many people make charitable donations by writing a check directly to the charity or nonprofit organization during their lifetime. Other methods and vehicles allow for more tax-efficient contributions during your lifetime and as part of your estate planning.

Nonprofit Tax Basics

Tax considerations are important in charitable planning. Many types of nonprofit organizations are tax-exempt and do not pay federal or state tax on the income from their operations. However, not all nonprofit, tax-exempt organizations qualify for tax-deductible contributions.

Nonprofit, tax-exempt organizations that operate exclusively for charitable purposes, are defined in Section 501(c)(3) of the Internal Revenue Code, and contributions to these organizations are tax deductible. As a condition of qualifying for tax-deductible contributions, 501(c)(3) charitable organizations must be organized and operated exclusively for:

"Religious, charitable, scientific, testing for public safety, literary, or educational purposes, or to foster national or international amateur sports competition (but only if no part of its activities involve the provision of athletic facilities or equipment), or for the prevention of cruelty to children or animals."[4]

In addition, 501(c)(3) charities are restricted from political lobbying and from participating in or contributing to political campaigns. Importantly, any grants or other payments made from a 501(c)(3) must be for a charitable purpose and cannot be for personal or private benefit.

The IRS categorizes 501(c)(3) charitable organizations as either public charities or private foundations. A private foundation typically receives its funding from a family, an individual or a corporation, whereas a public charity typically receives funding from multiple sources, including individuals, government agencies, private foundations, and other public charities.

Donor-Advised Funds

A donor-advised fund is a charitable account you set up with a donor-advised-fund sponsor, which is a public charity. You create and fund an individual account by contributing to the public charity. You receive a charitable tax deduction for your donation in the year you make your contribution. Then you recommend grants to other public charities over time from the funds in your charitable account; we'll discuss recommending grants later in this section. Using your investment preferences, your donations grow tax-free while you decide which charities to support with your grants. Donor-advised funds can be opened with a minimum initial balance of as little as $5,000.

Donor-advised funds are the fastest-growing charitable giving vehicle in the United States—and for good reason.[5] Donor-advised funds are a simple, flexible, and tax-efficient way of supporting the charities you care about. With their ability to accept complex assets such as private company stock, real estate, and venture capital fund partnership interests, donor-advised funds are an important charitable planning tool for tech professionals. At year-end 2016, total donor-advised-fund assets stood at an astounding $85 billion.[6]

Donor-advised funds are available from a variety of sources, including mutual fund companies, brokerage firms, community foundations, faith-based charities, and independent providers. Fidelity Charitable sponsors the largest donor-advised fund, with 180,000 donors who recommended one million grants totaling $4.5 billion to support more than 127,000 nonprofit organizations in 2017.[7]

Sponsors provide essential services to their donor-advised funds, including receiving and selling contributed assets, ensuring that potential grants recommended by donors are to IRS-qualified charities, recording transactions in donor accounts, providing investment alternatives, and maintaining compliance with complex laws and regulations.

How Donor-Advised Funds Work

An important point to know about donor-advised funds is that your donations are completed gifts for estate planning purposes. What that means is that the money or assets you contribute to a fund are no longer your property; rather, they are owned by the sponsoring public charity. You cannot change your mind and later decide that you would rather have the money or assets back in your personal accounts. There are no exceptions to this rule. The assets you contribute are owned and controlled by the sponsoring public charity.

Even though you no longer own or control the money or assets you contribute, you retain two essential advisory privileges for your account that allow you to (1) recommend grants to other public charities and (2) select your investment preferences.

The grant process involves you making a grant recommendation to your fund sponsor for a grant to another public charity. The sponsor researches whether your recommended grant recipient is an allowable 501(c)(3) nonprofit organization. Depending on the donor-advised fund, you may be able to select from an online list of pre-approved 501(c)(3) organizations, which speeds up the process. If your recipient is allowable, the sponsor will follow your recommendation and make the grant. Sponsors honor grant recommendations in all but the rarest of cases. Despite the complicated-sounding process, in practice, the grant process is simple and will appear to you as if you made a grant to the charity of your choice from your account. The minimum grant amount from a donor-advised fund is as little as $50.

Knowing where you cannot donate from a donor-advised fund is as important as knowing where you can donate. You may not donate to individuals—all grant recipients must be 501(c)(3) organizations. Typically you cannot donate to foreign charities; however, there are U.S. nonprofits with operations in other countries to which you can contribute. Also, the rules against private inurement prevent you from making distributions that will benefit you or your family personally. You also cannot make contributions for which you receive something of value; for example, a ticket to a charity event that includes dinner in the ticket price would likely not be allowed.

Besides recommending grants, you also can recommend investments for your account. Depending on the donor-advised fund, you may have an online list of investment options similar to the way an online employer 401(k), 403(b), or 457 retirement plan works. You may also have the ability to use a third-party investment advisory firm to manage the investments in your charitable account. Typically, you will have enough options to create a well-diversified portfolio that meets your investment goals and time horizon for the funds in your account.

For their services, donor-advised-fund sponsors charge administrative fees. Pricing is typically based on the value of your account. The largest mutual fund and brokerage firm donor-advised funds have the lowest pricing, with fees ranging from about 0.6% of the value of your account per year on balances under $500,000 down to as low as 0.2% or less per year for balances of $1 million and more.

With a donor-advised fund, you get to select the name of your account. Many people have fun with this part of the process. You might name your account for your family—for example, the Washington Charitable Fund or Adams Family Foundation. You might name your account to reflect your family's charitable mission—for example, the Jefferson Cancer Research Source, Madison Educational Trust, or Monroe Philanthropic Fund for the Arts. Or you might create a donor-advised fund to honor the memory of someone who has passed away—for example, John Q. Adams Legacy Fund for Humanitarian Relief. There are few restrictions on what your account can be called, so have fun in coming up with a name.

What Assets Can Be Contributed?

Donor-advised funds can accept a wide variety of contributed assets, including cash and publicly traded securities, and complex assets, including private company stock, real estate, and partnership interests in venture capital funds, private equity funds, and hedge funds.

Cash is typically the worst asset to give to charity, which is why it is important that donor-advised funds can accept other types of assets. Many people make the mistake of selling an appreciated asset, such as a stock or mutual fund, paying income tax on the capital gain and then donating the after-tax proceeds to charity. For example, in California, with a top income-tax rate of 13.3% and a maximum federal long-term capital-gains tax rate of 23.8% (including the 3.8% tax on net investment income), the combined tax on sales of stock, mutual funds, or other appreciated assets could be as high as 37%, or over one-third of the value of your potential contribution.

By contributing an appreciated asset directly to charity, tax on embedded capital gain is never paid. You do not pay the tax because you donated the asset to charity rather than selling the asset and recognizing capital gain. The charity does not pay tax on the gain when it sells the appreciated asset because it is a tax-exempt nonprofit organization. Capital gains tax on appreciated assets disappears when you donate the assets to charity, including donor-advised funds. The net result is that you have more assets available to donate to charity, which is good for you and the organizations you donate to.

The same is true for complex assets, including private company stock, real estate, and limited or general partnership interests in private equity funds, hedge funds, and venture capital funds. These investments are private, complicated, and unique in their individual features. Many, if not most, charities cannot accommodate donations of complex assets because they lack the expertise or because the size of the donation would overwhelm the charity. Sophisticated donor-advised-fund sponsors play a valuable role, acting as an intermediary in accepting complex assets, selling them, or holding them until they are sold, and then leaving the cash proceeds in your account for you to distribute among as many charitable organizations as you like.

Timing your contributions is important, and they should be planned well in advance. For example, you might donate private company stock for which you paid little (low cost basis) to your donor-advised fund. The fund becomes a shareholder in the private company for as long as it takes to sell the company or until the company goes public. Once the company is sold or goes public, the cash proceeds are put into the charitable account from which you recommend grants.

Tax Deductions with Donor-Advised Funds

When you contribute to a donor-advised fund, you receive an immediate tax deduction in the year of your contribution. Your charitable tax deduction is the full market value of the assets you contributed, as long as you held the assets for one year or longer (long-term capital gain property). If you owned the contributed assets for less than one year, then your deduction is limited to the cost basis of the property you contributed. Notice that by contributing appreciated assets held for one year or longer, such as low-cost basis stock or mutual fund shares, you receive a charitable deduction for those assets' full value in addition to completely eliminating capital gains tax on those shares. It's a two-for-one tax deal.

There are limits on the amount of the charitable deduction you can use in any one tax year. The maximum allowable amount of your deduction is equal to 60% of your adjusted gross income for contributions of cash, and 30% of your adjusted gross income for contributions of stock, mutual funds, real estate, partnership interests, and other assets you owned for a year or more. If you cannot deduct all of your donation in the year you contributed it, a five-year carry-forward on contributions that exceed adjusted gross income limits is available. You can use the charitable deductions in future years.

Timing as a Tax Planning Opportunity

While you learned tax strategies around timing of contributions to donor-advised funds in Chapter 8, there are some important points to reinforce. Timing large contributions to your donor-advised fund for years when you have high income reduces income tax in those high income years. You can then make grants from your account in future years without having to make contributions. A donor-advised fund allows you to "delink" when you make charitable contributions for tax purposes from when you make contributions to your favorite charities. Starting in 2018, "bunching" charitable contributions using your donor-advised fund may be useful to get over the higher standard deduction to be able to itemize deductions and claim a charitable deduction.

The final few years before retirement are another time to consider "topping off" your donor-advised fund. Consider accelerating your future contributions into your final few working years when you will receive more benefit from the charitable tax deduction because of higher income.

Charitable Foundations

Private foundations offer more flexibility and control over the way donors pursue their charitable objectives than is possible with public charities and donor-advised funds. However, tax deductibility is limited compared with public charities, particularly for private company stock and real estate. In addition, private foundations are expensive to operate, so they are typically recommended for donors who expect to contribute in the range of at least $3 million to $10 million and who have net worth several times that amount.

Private foundations are more flexible than public charities in allowing donors to pursue their own charitable activities and in providing donors more control over how their contributions are used. While private foundations most frequently make grants to other 501(c)(3) organizations, they also can be used for hands-on charitable work directly, such as community aid work. Private foundations also allow giving internationally, which is more difficult with public charities. And private foundations allow giving to individuals, albeit under strict rules, such as for a scholarship or fellowship.

Tax Deductions with Charitable Foundations

Tax deductibility is a significant difference between public charities and private foundations, with donations to public charities (including donor-advised funds) receiving the larger tax benefit. Donations of cash to a public charity are tax deductible up to 60% of adjusted gross income, whereas cash donations to a private foundation are tax deductible only up to 30% of adjusted gross income. Similarly, donations of publicly traded securities to a public charity are deductible up to 30% of adjusted gross income, whereas donations of publicly traded securities to a private foundation are deductible only up to 20% of adjusted gross income.

The value of securities and other assets donated to private foundations is also different from the value of securities and other assets donated to public charities. For public charities, donors of appreciated assets held longer than one year receive a tax deduction of the fair market value of donated assets. For private foundations, only publicly traded stock held longer than one year receives a deduction of fair market value. Other types of assets, including private company stock, real estate, and limited partnership interests, receive a deduction only for the cost basis of the property. The reduced value of deduction (cost basis is often much smaller than market value for appreciated assets) can be a major disadvantage for giving through a private foundation.

With a 40% federal estate tax rate, private foundation donors with taxable estates (above $11 million for an individual and $22 million for a married couple) may prefer to give large amounts to charity rather than lose 40% of the taxable portion of their estate to tax.

Charitable Trusts

Advanced estate planning techniques for charitable giving involve the use of particular kinds of irrevocable trusts. One of the most useful charitable trusts is known as a Charitable Remainder Trust (CRT).

With a CRT, you contribute assets to the trust and the trustee makes payments to your non-charitable beneficiaries (such as you and your family) for a period of years. Once the payments to non-charitable beneficiaries stop, the charity receives the remaining amount in the trust. You receive an income tax deduction in the year the assets are contributed to the CRT. The amount of the deduction is equal to the present value of the ultimate gift to the charity. There are complicated rules around the amount and form of payments to beneficiaries and calculating the value of the charitable income-tax deduction.

CRTs can be useful to tech professionals with significant net worth and charitable intent. With a CRT, you can contribute highly appreciated assets (such as company stock, real estate, or limited partnership interests) to the trust. The trustee can then sell the assets. CRTs are exempt from federal income tax, so you therefore will not pay capital gains tax on the appreciation in the assets you contribute. The trustee will reinvest the assets, earning more than if you had sold the assets outside of the trust and paid capital gains tax. Thus, the non-charitable beneficiaries receive their payment based on the full value of assets contributed with no reduction for capital gains tax (which disappears upon contribution). Using a CRT also allows for diversification of contributed assets, which is, for example, safer than holding highly appreciated stock in a single company.

While receiving a charitable income tax deduction is an important part of using a CRT, it also helps reduce your estate tax obligation and can be an important part of your overall estate plan. Assets that you give to charity are out of your estate for estate tax purposes, and you will not owe tax (if you have a taxable estate) on amounts given to charity, or the growth on those assets had you not given them to charity.

Summary

- Have an estate plan prepared by a qualified estate planning attorney to provide for your minor children and to ensure your assets are transferred to the people and organizations you want to receive them.
- Ensure your estate plan is funded, including completing beneficiary designations for your retirement accounts.
- Maintain sufficient life insurance coverage to replace your income in the event of your death until you've accumulated enough net worth to support your dependents without the need for life insurance.
- Create a plan for access to your digital assets and maintenance of your intellectual property including patents, copyrights, and license agreements.

- To meet your charitable goals, contribute to a donor-advised fund, or create a charitable trust or charitable foundation depending on your specific needs and total net worth.
- Consider developing a personal value statement to pass on your life experiences, values, family traditions, and ethical beliefs to future generations.

We've covered a lot of material in the last eleven chapters. Now it's time to think about how you're going to get all of this done.

12

Who's in Charge of Your Financial Freedom?

Picture a meeting in which a prospective client is interviewing a well-qualified financial advisor. The interview lasts 50 minutes, and during that time, the advisor asks questions about the prospective client's current financial situation and future goals. The advisor also describes how the firm's suite of financial planning, investment management, tax planning, and other services could help the prospective client reach those goals. Toward the end of their appointment, prospective client asks the advisor what the services cost, to which the advisor replies with an industry-standard fee schedule. In response, prospective client says, "I can do all of those things myself. Why should I pay you?"

That's a valid question. It's also a common question from tech professionals who tend to be multi-talented, well-educated, and sometimes even experienced with investments, tax, and personal finance issues. When deciding whether to work with a professional financial advisor, you face a classic outsourcing question. Somebody has to do the work, so the right question is: will you do the work yourself or will you pay someone else to do it?

For most tech professionals, the issue to consider is not whether you *can* manage your own financial affairs (you probably can with enough study) but whether you *should* manage your own financial affairs. There are several challenges:

- Making objective decisions about your own money
- Mastering complex (and frequently changing) investment, tax, legal, and other subjects and developing sound judgment
- Finding time on a consistent basis

- Coping with the consequences of mistakes and the opportunity cost of not spending time on areas in which you are most productive

In deciding whether to work on your own or enter into an advisory relationship, you will need to decide the best way for you, knowing your unique situation and abilities, to address these challenges.

Remaining Objective

Money is personal. Money is emotional. Having enough money is important to our feelings of security. Fear of loss is deeply embedded in our psychology and is a powerful motivator. During stock market declines, people grow uncomfortable and strong feelings can drive actions to try and avoid the loss, even if those actions are counterproductive.

We also want more money. We want the things it can buy, the social status it brings, and the freedom it can give us. The desire to acquire more money can drive us to take imprudent and unproductive risks. Impatience with building net worth can lead to excessive spending and inadequate saving. Overspending within retirement can lead to leftover life at the end of the money. Fear and greed are such potent emotions, it's nearly impossible to make objective decisions about your own money.

In addition, the emerging field of "behavioral finance" is teaching us that our gut instincts, rules of thumb, and other ingrained thought processes for financial decision-making are often not helpful or just plain wrong. Behavioral finance is helping us understand our cognitive limitations around money choices. We're prone to wishful thinking about finance. We often don't correctly perceive what's good for us, and as a result, we have trouble acting in our own best interest.

Behavioral Coaching

With our innate susceptibility to emotional decision-making and often faulty thought processes involving money, one of the great benefits provided by an advisory relationship is behavioral coaching. An experienced and well-trained financial advisor or advisory team can act as your financial coach to improve your financial decision-making. Advisors can provide objective analysis and recommendations free from emotional bias and faulty logic. They help you maintain perspective during times of severe market volatility. Like a coach in sports, business and other disciplines, an advisor-as-coach can help you see your blind spots and become aware of issues you had not recognized.

Even experts themselves aren't immune to emotional decision-making, although they may be more alert to harmful behavioral biases. Experienced financial advisors find it necessary to consult with trusted colleagues about important financial decisions to get objective advice. By definition, you don't have an outside perspective if you're working alone.

A recent study by Vanguard, a large mutual fund company renowned for its index mutual funds and exchange-traded funds (ETFs), attempted to isolate and quantify the value of behavioral coaching with respect to investment performance. The study found that behavioral coaching can add as much as about 1.5% to an investor's annual investment return before fees.[1] Other Vanguard studies indicate a range of about 1% to 2% additional return before fees to investors whose advisors keep them from abandoning markets during periods of poor performance and chasing the next "hot" investment based on good recent performance.

Expect the Unexpected

We want to feel in control of our lives, including our financial lives. We feel secure when we feel in control. But being in control is an illusion. We live in a random world. Stock markets fluctuate unexpectedly, sometimes violently. Economic variables such as gross domestic product, length of recessions, interest rates, and inflation befuddle expert forecasters. Geopolitical risks appear out of nowhere. Even tax laws are random, created at sporadic intervals as the precarious outcome of epic, unseen battles between powerful interest groups in Washington D.C. and state capitols nationwide.

With your personal finances, it can be liberating to accept the fact that investment markets and economic forces fluctuate randomly. You may take actions that help you feel in control, but to a large extent, you are not in control, which can cause a great deal of consternation. To be a successful investor, you will need to come to grips with this emotionally. You should design investment portfolios and an overall wealth allocation that can weather financial storms—because there will be storms. Try to control the variables you can control, and get as comfortable as possible with the residual variability in your financial life. Things you can control are:

- How much risk you take with your investments
- How much you pay for your investments (e.g., ongoing expense ratio)
- How you manage your equity compensation
- How long you work, assuming no special circumstances

- How much you spend on discretionary items and services
- How much you save
- How much you give to charity
- How much you earn at your job (which is somewhat within your control)

An experienced and well-trained financial advisor can help with both randomness and control. In particular, reviewing historical market performance and creating stress-tested financial plans that take into account market volatility (using Monte Carlo simulation techniques to model hundreds of possible outcomes) can provide reassurance that your finances are structured to withstand the randomness. Often, just having the calming presence of someone who's been through it all before and knows what to do can be comforting.

Accountability

As in all forms of coaching, part of the work of a financial coach is acting as an accountability partner. An accountability partner helps you keep your commitments. This is important in the areas of your financial life that you can control. For example, your financial advisory team can help you keep commitments to save more, monitor your spending, participate in ESPP, fund a college savings account, max out your 401(k), manage your stock-based compensation, and prompt you to look for a new job when it's time to move on. People vary in their self-discipline, particularly in difficult areas such as spending control. A financial advisory relationship can provide an environment of accountability to help keep you on track toward meeting your financial goals.

Competence

Perhaps the most important consideration in deciding whether to manage your own finances is the question of competence. Do you have background in these areas or a keen interest to learn? The investment, tax, and legal subjects involved are complex. They take years to learn initially and require ongoing study to stay current.

Well-qualified financial advisory professionals earn specialized credentials to learn these subjects. For example, the top certifications for financial planning and investment management take years to earn and require thousands of hours of study and completed work experience. To obtain the Certified Financial Planner (CFP®) designation, candidates must have earned a bachelor's degree; completed six or seven college-level courses, including a capstone course designed to demonstrate proficiency; passed a seven-hour test; completed either 6,000 hours of work experience or 4,000 hours of a closely supervised apprenticeship; and agreed to a strict code of conduct. Maintaining the CFP® credential requires completing 30 hours of continuing education every two years, including two hours of ethics training. One highly-regarded professional association for financial planners requires 60 hours of continuing education every two years.[2]

To obtain the Chartered Financial Analyst (CFA) designation, candidates must have earned a bachelor's degree; finished an in-depth three-level course of study on investments, which requires more than 300 hours of study per level; passed a six-hour exam for each level; completed four years' relevant work experience; provided three professional references; and agreed to a stringent code of ethics.

True expertise is developed over time with practice and the experience gained from hundreds of real-life situations. Experts are better at recognizing issues in any situation because they can compare a current set of facts to patterns they've seen before. Experience provides a starting place to clarify and interpret potentially ambiguous situations or data. Nonprofessionals will usually operate at a disadvantage to experienced professionals because they do not have a library of historical cases to draw on in crafting solutions or—more importantly—the experience to recognize important issues to begin with.

Not all financial advisors are familiar with the issues facing tech professionals, particularly around stock-based compensation, such as stock options, restricted stock, restricted stock units, and employee-stock purchase plans. A financial advisory team with deep experience in the tax and investment issues around equity compensation can be even more valuable to the tech professional.

On a more practical level, professional financial advisors typically have access to a variety of software programs, tools and databases that may be cost-prohibitive for individuals, programs that are also difficult to learn and use properly without solid training. For example, professional financial planning software costs several thousands of dollars per user and takes months to gain basic proficiency and years to become an expert user. Perhaps this is why there is no retail equivalent of financial planning software for nonprofessionals. Tax planning software is another category designed for experts, although some tax planning can be accomplished in user-friendly TurboTax®.

While experienced advisors may be able to do the work in a fraction of the time that it would take you, they have many clients to take care of and can't spend as much time on your finances as you can. With enough time and interest, you may be able to learn the subjects needed to adequately manage your finances. If you are retired, semiretired, or simply enjoy these subjects and are prepared to engage deeply, you can probably make more time to work on your finances than a professional advisor. Once you have a basic competence in, familiarity with, and focus on personal finance topics relevant to your specific situation, the extra time you can spend on your finances can offset some of the advantage of a professional advisor's greater experience and access to professional-grade tools.

Assessing the Value of Advisors

Two recent studies by Morningstar and Vanguard attempt to quantify the value of professional financial advisors.

The study by Morningstar, published in *The Journal of Retirement*, is the most ambitious study of its kind to date.[3] The authors calculated the additional value achieved by individual investors making more intelligent financial planning decisions. The study focused on retirees and measured the percentage increase in retirement income that could be achieved over a base case when using five specific financial planning techniques: dynamic withdrawal strategies; tax-efficient decisions, such as asset location in investment portfolios; taking into account income sources such as Social Security and pensions; using guaranteed income products, such as annuities; and explicitly accounting for the risk of a particular goal. The authors note there are other financial planning techniques that might be equally or more important than the five selected, particularly for investors at different stages in their life.

The results of the study showed that retirees could earn an estimated 22.6% more retirement income per year than the base case which featured 4% static withdrawal rate and 20% stock allocation portfolio. This equated to an increase of 1.59% in annual rate of return, which is substantial. The authors note that this increase in annual rate of return has nothing to do with investment performance or beating the market. The results flowed exclusively from the benefits that good financial planning decisions in these five areas can bring to investors. Many other financial planning and tax planning techniques are not included in the study which almost certainly also would show additional benefit to investors.

Interestingly, the Morningstar study measured the benefit of performing five particular financial planning techniques. Those techniques could be implemented by advisors and do-it-yourself individual investors alike. In deciding whether to outsource or work on your own, you can ask yourself whether you would be able to implement these five techniques or whether you would need the help of a professional advisor. Who implements the techniques is not important, only that they get implemented. Also, if you decide to outsource, the ability to implement these techniques and others could be a metric in evaluating advisors you may work with.

The Vanguard study similarly examined seven best practices that professional advisors can bring to their client relationships and attempted to quantify the additional value to investors in terms of annual investment return averages. The seven best practices are developing a suitable asset allocation, cost-effective portfolio implementation (i.e., low expense ratios), rebalancing, asset location, optimal withdrawal order from accounts, total return verses income investing, and behavioral coaching. Overall, the study showed an increase of about 3% in average annual return by following best practices in these seven areas.

The study further broke down the 3% extra return in each of the seven areas. The largest contributor at 1.5% was behavioral coaching, discussed previously. All of the techniques except behavioral coaching could be implemented by individual investors themselves. Working on your own and following best practices, you earn up to about 1.5% more return than if you did not use these best practices. The authors found that two of the best practices—selecting a suitable asset allocation and following a total return approach—added return and are part of the value added by professional advisors, but those best practices are widely accessible to investors and the authors assigned no value to them. That means that the 3% additional average annual return does not include any amount for those two best practices.

The Vanguard study's authors note that while some of the value from the seven best practices could be expected to yield a benefit every year, some of the most significant opportunities to create additional value will occur intermittently over the years. The authors don't expect the 3% additional return to be earned annually; they expect extra return to be quite lumpy. They also note that the applicability of the best practices and expected additional value will vary according to an investor's individual circumstances, such as time horizon, risk tolerance, portfolio composition (taxable accounts vs. qualified accounts, asset allocation), tax bracket, and financial planning goals.

With the two studies, Morningstar and Vanguard made important contributions to quantifying the value of applying intelligent financial planning techniques and investment best practices. These techniques and best practices are typically implemented by professional advisors but are available to individual investors working on their own as well.

More Outsourcing Considerations

Time Commitment

Finding time to manage your finances on a regular basis over the long-term is critical. The set of principles and planning techniques covered in these pages need to be applied consistently over time. You or your advisor need to be alert to changes in your situation and the financial environment, and be prepared to apply the correct planning technique at the right time. This requires ongoing attention. It's like stoking a campfire—it takes skill to keep a fire burning, and fires need tending. If the fire goes out, it can be hard to get restarted.

For your best financial health, it's better not to think of personal finance as a hobby or a sometime interest. It's not a fad. It can't be something you're into right now before moving on to the next thing. Your money requires your attention on a steady basis while you are alive and, potentially, once you are gone as well. The commitment is for decades not days. It's real work that needs to be performed well on a consistent basis for a long time.

Personal Interest

Your interest in personal finance topics will have a big impact on your commitment to doing the work on a regular basis. If you're not interested in these topics, you will find it hard to make time for your finances. There will always be other activities that you find more interesting and where you'd rather spend your time. If that's the case for you, then outsourcing should be a serious consideration.

Consequences

One final point in deciding whether to outsource or not is considering the consequences of not doing so. If you don't have background in these subjects or a keen interest to learn, or if you don't have time available on a regular basis to work on your finances, it's likely your best case outcome will be subpar results. You could miss out on the additional value an advisor brings or the value you could bring by applying techniques used by experienced advisors. If you're unable to create and stick to sound financial and investment plans during bad or sky-rocketing investment markets, you could seriously impair your odds at reaching your major financial goals with emotional investing. Worst case would be making a major mistake, such as triggering a big tax bill or permanently losing value in your investment portfolio.

Cost

A downside to hiring an advisor is that it costs money. It's not always easy to quantify the benefit you receive from professional finance advice, but you do know how much you're paying for it. That cost is either cash out-of-pocket, which is money you could otherwise be saving, or it's a reduction in your investment portfolio rate-of-return, which compounds over time. There can be an emotional cost too if you find yourself having hired a not-right-fit financial advisor.

Of course, if you hire yourself to manage your personal finances, your services are not free either. You incur opportunity cost—the cost of missing the alternative activities you gave up. That cost could be financial if managing finances is not the highest and best use of your time. That time could be spent in your primary career, where you are more productive and your efforts are worth more in real dollar terms. The cost could also be more intangible, such as missing out on weekend family time after an already long work week.

Introvert or Extrovert

In psychology, the terms introvert and extrovert, as used by Carl Jung, describe how a person gets energy and how a person directs their attention, either outwardly or inwardly. Interestingly, research shows that introverts can be just as outgoing as extroverts; however, social interactions are draining for introverts, who need time alone to recharge after being social. Extroverts, on the other hand, get their psychic energy from social interactions and use those interactions to recharge.

The introvert/extrovert energy test and reading this material may be a good metaphor for deciding whether to outsource your personal finance work. If this book exhausted you like an introvert at a large party, you may not be a good candidate for do-it-yourself personal finance. However, if you finished the book in less time than you can binge-watch a Netflix series, downloaded and read the referenced articles, and have already ordered more books on Amazon to continue your study, you might not only be candidate for do-it-yourself, you might consider a career in the financial services industry.

Summary

If you decide to outsource your personal financial management, be sure to hire a well-trained, credentialed advisor who is acting only in your best interest (i.e., a "fiduciary"). You can use what you've learned to help you differentiate between advisors and find the most qualified candidates.

Either way, for your best financial health you'll need to apply the techniques and best practices in this book yourself or hire someone who can help you.

Moving Forward

As a technology professional, you have additional needs in your personal financial life that the general population doesn't have. There are specific issues you need a working knowledge of that most other people don't, and this book has discussed them in depth with the goal of increasing your awareness and deepening your understanding of the issues and complexities surrounding these subjects.

It's likely that as a tech professional you did not receive much training in finance while you were in school. Personal finance is typically not taught in school at any level outside of certain college majors. It's particularly true of education in the fields of science, technology, engineering, and mathematics (STEM), which simply do not include finance topics. While a lot of math and statistics are used in finance, their application to financial problems is not covered in STEM curricula. There is no F in STEM. As a result, you're learning personal finance on your own when issues arise.

If you've read straight through, it's been a journey through concepts, research, and practical advice you may not have been familiar with and hopefully have enjoyed learning about. This book covered the basics and then some, in order that you can use this knowledge to improve the lives of you and your family. The goal of this book and for you going forward is for you to have a robust enough understanding of personal finance to better work with your advisors or to manage your own finances.

This book also provided suggestions for taking care of yourself, for achieving personal growth, and for finding meaning in your life beyond making money. While this may seem out of place in a finance book, the two are connected. You cannot separate the human elements from the numbers. They must be considered together to have success in both areas.

Of course, all of the knowledge and education in the world isn't useful unless you do something with it. After reading this material, you may have come to the conclusion that paying attention to your finances may be more important than you realized. It's not enough to understand the material and think about it, you actually need to take action to ensure you're financially healthy.

Specific actions you can take include:

- **Review the checklists and recommendations provided throughout the book.** Be sure you understand the issues behind each recommendation and review it with respect to your particular situation. If you're working with an advisor, discuss the recommendation with him or her. While common for tech professionals, the list of issues covered is not exhaustive, and there may be other issues important to your financial situation.
- **Continue your study.** If you will be managing your own finances, this book provides an introduction and background to many of the topics faced by tech professionals. With this as an outline, you can continue your study and deepen your understanding, particularly on the more complex topics of equity compensation, tax,

and investments. Some of the issues covered are more long range in nature. You can continue thinking about potential long-term adjustments and optimizations to your financial situation as you learn more.

- **Interview financial advisors.** If you've decided to work with an advisor, you can move forward by setting up informational interviews with three to five financial advisors over the next month and finding a firm and advisor whose business is a good fit for your needs. Your tax preparer or estate planning attorney may be able to provide a referrals for you. Top professional organizations for financial planners are also good sources of prospective financial advisors. The National Association of Personal Financial Advisors (NAPFA) offers a consumer referral service on their website at www.napfa.org. The Certified Financial Planner Board of Standards also offers a financial planner search engine at www.letsmakeaplan.org.

Final Thoughts

I attend several conferences and seminars every year to keep up with developments in personal finance. The sessions range from highly technical subjects, such as investments, tax, and estate planning, to softer topics, such as how to be a better communicator. Typically, I am grateful to learn one or two big new ideas at a conference that I can take back with me and use to better serve the people who have entrusted me with their finances. Likewise, I hope that, at a minimum, you have been able to take away at least one or two good ideas that will improve your life. If you're like many people I meet, the section on what to do with your old 401(k) accounts alone was worth the price of the book.

Besides providing education and updates on a variety of topics, conferences and seminars are valuable for another reason. After attending, I know what it is that I didn't know before. Conferences provide an opportunity to find the gaps in my knowledge. Similarly, I hope that the topics covered in this book have been helpful to you in recognizing potential issues in your finances for the first time, or have helped you more fully understand the issues you thought you understood better than you actually did.

In closing, I want to leave you with one final thought. You may read and hear recommendations from a variety of sources, including blogs, social media, magazines, websites, colleagues, family, and trusted professionals about how to manage your financial affairs. Yet at the end of the day, it's still your money. **Ultimately you are responsible for keeping your finances in good order, for your own financial well-being, and for the well-being of the people who depend on you.** A good portion of that responsibility involves learning enough about these topics to ensure you're making good decisions with your money. I hope this book will help you with that by pulling together financial information for tech professionals in a way that, to the best of my knowledge, has never been done before. Going forward, I wish you the best of luck in reaching your career goals and creating a financially healthy, happy, and meaningful life for yourself and your family.

Appendix
Summary of Key Recommendations

Chapter 2 – Buy Now, Pay Later: The Big Trade-Off

- Spending is the most important aspect of your personal financial life to focus on because it is the area in which you have most control.
- Strike the right balance between spending and saving over your lifetime to avoid a sharp reduction in lifestyle at retirement.
- Use a budget to track your spending, or, if budgeting is difficult, track the amount you're saving instead.
- Be aware of behavioral biases that can increase your spending such as present bias (feeling that goods purchased now are worth more than goods purchased in the future), believing that buying things will make you happy, and social spending to keep up with a peer group.
- Use a "cooling off" period before making big, un-planned purchases.
- Conduct an annual expense review to look for money wasted on unused services, monthly bills that have crept

up over time, better deals on your regular expenses, and ways to reduce spending on "nice to haves."

- If an annual expense review doesn't bring spending in line, consider longer-term structural changes to your spending, such as scaling back on your housing costs.

Chapter 3 – Saving: Playing the Long Game

- Compare your assets-to-income ratio and current savings rate using the guidelines in this chapter for a quick assessment of whether you are on track with your saving.
- Review the recommended order of savings, and accounts types to use, for various goals including emergency fund, major purchase, retirement, college, and charity.
- Contribute the maximum amount your cash flow allows to your employer's 401(k) retirement plan and review your investments at least once per year.
- Consolidate 401(k) plans from former employers to make ongoing management easier.
- Use Section 529 College Savings Plans to save for kids' college education.

Chapter 4 – Investing for Financial Success

- Review historical investment performance to become familiar with what is possible to earn and to properly set your expectations for your investment performance.
- Select or develop an asset allocation for your investment portfolio that is appropriate to your stage of life and that suits your willingness, ability, and need to take risk.
- Rebalance your portfolio at least annually to maintain proper risk level.
- Use asset location across your accounts to reduce the tax drag on your investments.
- As a starting place, build your investment portfolio with traditional stock and bond asset classes using low expense, tax efficient index mutual funds or exchange-traded funds.
- For more diversification, look to alternative asset classes, such as real estate, commodities, and managed futures.
- If you are a high net worth investor, consider adding private equity, venture capital, or hedge funds to your portfolio to increase return.
- If you will be investing in private securities, such as private company stock or venture capital partnerships, learn the federal and state requirements for accredited investors and qualified purchasers.

Chapter 5 – Taking Stock: Equity Compensation

- Become familiar with the features and tax treatment of major types of equity compensation available to you including non-qualified and incentive stock options, restricted stock, restricted stock units and employee stock purchase plans.
- If your employer's ESPP has favorable features, earn the nearly risk free, built-in investment gain by enrolling in the plan, maxing out your contribution, and selling your shares when you receive them.
- With restricted stock and RSUs, there is no tax benefit to holding shares so generally it's best to sell your shares as they vest to diversify your investments.
- Avoid becoming dependent on an equity compensation subsidy to your income.
- Be sure to include any gain from the sale of ESPP, restricted stock and RSU shares in your income tax planning.
- For ISOs, run tax projections to determine whether an exercise-and-hold strategy is beneficial under regular and AMT tax systems, and consider selling some shares upon exercise to pay taxes.
- For NSOs, run multi-year tax projections to determine whether spreading income over several years can reduce your tax liability by paying tax in lower rate brackets.
- Keep in mind that technology stocks are often risky and volatile. Balance tax considerations with investment considerations: the risk of holding technology stock and

suffering a large price decline may outweigh any benefit from a particular tax strategy.

- Be aware when your company's trading window is open for sales of shares from exercised stock options, restricted stock, RSUs, and ESPP.

- With restricted stock subject to vesting and early-exercise eligible stock options, consider making an 83(b) tax election.

- If you are regularly in possession of "material nonpublic" information and want to sell or buy your employer's publicly traded stock, a 10b5-1 trading plan can provide protection against insider trading charges.

Chapter 6 – Home Truths About Real Estate

- Because your home is one of your largest assets and housing costs are high in tech cities, take special care with decisions surrounding your home.

- Treat your home as an investment only if you plan to sell it and use the built-up equity to pay for living expenses in retirement—otherwise your home is a lifestyle asset, not an investment asset.

- Property tax continues, typically increasing each year, even after your home loan is paid off, so carefully consider the cost of property tax before moving up to a larger home.

- In deciding whether to pay off your home loan, remember that you receive an income tax deduction for mortgage interest, effectively lowering your interest cost, and that pay-off money may be better left in your higher-earning investment portfolio.

- Explore the financial trade-off between living in a more expensive area and sending your kids to public school versus living in a more affordable area and sending your kids to private school.
- Refinance your home loan if the total financing cost over the time period you expect to keep the loan will be less, which often will be the case if the interest rate is 0.50% to 0.75% lower.
- Renting can make sense if the cost of renting is less than the cost of owning a home, you're saving for a down payment, you're waiting for stock options or restricted stock units to vest, or your travel schedule doesn't allow time for home ownership right now.
- If you're considering owning rental real estate, become familiar with what is required for success in that business including selecting properties, managing them, and understanding tax rules for rental real estate such as passive activity loss limitations, Section 1031 exchanges, and new Section 199A "pass through" deduction.

Chapter 7 – Getting Personal: What Matters to You?

- Be aware of diminishing returns to extra hours of work after 50 to 60 hours per week.
- Maintain creativity and ability to solve difficult problems with rest and quiet time.

- Deal with overwork and stress by getting enough sleep, eating properly, exercising, working on your relationships, creating a financial sustainable lifestyle, and seeking professional help when needed.
- Money does increase satisfaction with life but relationships and finding meaning are most important to our happiness and general well-being.

Chapter 8 – Taxation Nation: Minimizing the Burden

- Use the material in the chapter as an introduction to, or quick refresher on, the basic structure of income tax, including the major updates for 2018.
- Reduce your tax liability by using techniques to minimize income, maximize deductions and credits, and control the timing of income and deductions.
- Use timing techniques to reduce taxable income including spreading income over multiple years to pay tax in lower rate brackets, accelerating or delaying income into a lower-income year, matching large deductions such as charitable to high-income years, and bunching deductions to allow itemizing.
- Delay tax by using retirement accounts and deferred compensation plans to defer receiving taxable income.
- Consider an IRA to Roth IRA conversion in low-income years.
- Use tax-loss harvesting to reduce capital gains in your investment portfolio.

- Employ tax-efficient investing techniques such as holding investments for a year before selling to receive long-term capital gains treatment, use tax-efficient investment products such as index mutual funds and exchange-traded funds, and shield ordinary income from tax with asset location.

Chapter 9 – Liquidity Events: IPOs & Acquisitions

- Make a rough calculation of the after-tax proceeds you will receive from an expected IPO or acquisition, including any reverse stock-split adjustment to your shares in the case of IPO.
- Be aware of any selling restrictions such as lock-up period for an IPO or milestone-based payout structure for an acquisition before committing to major purchases or financial transactions.
- Learn about the popular and effective estate planning technique involving grantor retained annuity trusts (GRATs) before an IPO that may push your net worth close to or over the estate tax exemption amount.
- Give yourself time to adjust mentally and emotionally to a significant liquidity event that substantially increases your net worth before making major decisions.
- Because life-changing liquidity events are rare, adjust your lifestyle assuming you will never have another big payday from an IPO or acquisition.
- Deploy your new assets in the following rough order of priority: set aside cash for taxes, contribute to charita-

ble account to reduce taxes, pay off debt, fund college savings plans, build a cash reserve, and direct remaining cash to your taxable investment portfolio.

Chapter 10 – Quitting the Rat Race: Planning for Retirement

- Envision specific retirement scenarios to define what retirement means to you, including where you will live, what you will do, and with whom you will spend your time.
- Iteratively assess the feasibility of retirement scenarios compared to your financial constraints to develop an understanding of what's attainable.
- Consider new models of retirement, such as continuing to work less intensely in a role that is more personally meaningful to you.
- Use adaptive techniques, rather than a static percentage, to maintain sustainable withdrawal rates from your investment portfolio over your retirement.
- Invest for "total return" rather than an income approach to maximize the amount of retirement income your investments can produce.
- Follow a tax efficient withdrawal order from your accounts such as: required minimum distributions, taxable accounts, tax-deferred accounts, then tax-free accounts.

Chapter 11 – Leaving Your Mark: Legacy Planning

- Have an estate plan prepared by a qualified estate planning attorney to provide for your minor children and to ensure your assets are transferred to the people and organizations you want to receive them.
- Ensure your estate plan is funded, including completing beneficiary designations for your retirement accounts.
- Maintain sufficient life insurance coverage to replace your income in the event of your death until you've accumulated enough net worth to support your dependents without the need for life insurance.
- Create a plan for access to your digital assets and maintenance of your intellectual property including patents, copyrights, and license agreements.
- To meet your charitable goals, contribute to a donor-advised fund, or create a charitable trust or charitable foundation depending on your specific needs and total net worth.
- Consider developing a personal value statement to pass on your life experiences, values, family traditions, and ethical beliefs to future generations.

Chapter 12 – Who's in Charge of Your Financial Freedom?

If you decide to outsource your personal financial management, be sure to hire a well-trained, credentialed advisor who is acting only in your best interest (i.e., a "fiduciary"). You can use what you've learned to help you differentiate between advisors and find the most qualified candidates.

Either way, for your best financial health you'll need to apply the techniques and best practices in this book yourself or hire someone who can help you.

Glossary

401(k) plan – Retirement plan offered by employers that allows employees to contribute a portion of their earnings to an individual investment account. Contributions are excluded from taxable income and investments grow tax-deferred. Withdrawals are included in taxable income. Withdrawals prior to age 59 and six months may incur an additional tax penalty.

529 plan – Tax-advantaged educational savings plan sponsored by a state. After-tax contributions are invested and grow tax-deferred. Withdrawals are tax-free if used for allowed educational expenses such as tuition, books, and housing.

83(b) election – A tax election under Section 83(b) of the Internal Revenue Code to have income from restricted stock taxed in the year shares are received instead of the year shares become vested.

Alternative investments – Non-traditional asset classes such as commodities, hedge funds, managed futures, private equity, real estate, and venture capital.

Alternative Minimum Tax (AMT) – Income tax calculated under a second tax system that runs parallel to the regular tax system and that has its own rules for income, deductions, and exemptions, along with a separate tax rate schedule.

Asset allocation – The process of combining asset classes in different proportions to create diversified portfolios.

Asset class – Groups of investments with similar characteristics that behave similarly during changing economic and market conditions. Examples of asset classes include small stocks, large stocks, corporate bonds, government bonds, inflation protected bonds, international stocks, emerging markets stocks, and real estate.

Asset location – The placement of particular asset class investments into certain types of investment accounts to reduce taxes. For example, by locating corporate bonds in an IRA account, interest income is shielded from taxation, which can increase return.

Behavioral bias – Taking action based on incorrect thought processes or feelings rather than facts. This can lead to poor financial decision making, such as feeling overconfident in one's own abilities leading to excessive risk-taking.

Bond – An investment in which an investor loans money to a corporation or government for a specified length of time at a fixed or variable interest rate.

Capital gain (loss) – The amount an investment has increased (decreased) in value above (below) its purchase price at the time of its sale. Gain (loss) is recognized for tax purposes when an investment is sold and is included in taxable income.

Certified Financial Planner (CFP®) – A top professional designation for financial planners requiring a bachelor's degree, completion of up to seven college level courses, passing a seven-hour test, up to 6,000 hours of work experience, and agreeing to a strict code of conduct.

Charitable remainder trust (CRT) – An irrevocable trust used for charitable giving in which non-charitable beneficiaries first receive payments for a period of years and then a charity receives the remaining amount in the trust. The donor receives a charitable income tax deduction equal to the present value of the ultimate gift to the charity.

Chartered Financial Analyst (CFA) – A top professional designation for investment managers and analysts requiring a bachelor's degree, completion of an in-depth three-level course of study on investments that requires more than 300 hours per level, passing a six-hour exam for each level, four years' relevant work experience, providing three professional references, and agreeing to a stringent code of ethics.

Distribution – In the context of retirement accounts, a distribution is a withdrawal of cash or other assets from an account, usually with income tax implications. In the investment context, a distribution refers to payment of interest, principal, or dividend to shareholders.

Diversified portfolio – A mix of investments from different asset classes. It often includes stocks and bonds from many companies and government entities. Diversification reduces overall portfolio risk and helps avoid reductions in investment return caused by poor performance of a single asset class, industry, sector, country, stock, or bond.

Donor-advised fund – A charitable account set up with a sponsoring public charity. Donations to the account receive a charitable tax deduction in the year of contribution. Grants can be made from the account over time to other public charities.

Employee Retirement Income Security Act (ERISA) – A federal law enacted in 1974 that regulates employee pension and health plans to protect the rights of participants.

Employee stock purchase plan (ESPP) – An employee benefit plan that allows employees to buy employer stock over time through payroll deductions, often at a discount to market price.

Equity compensation – Employee pay in the form of company stock, or options on company stock, instead of cash. Equity, or "stock-based," compensation is granted under a stock plan and may include restricted stock, restricted stock units, non-qualified stock options, incentive stock options, or participation in an employee stock purchase plan.

Estate plan – A set of legal documents that provide for the transfer and management of your assets in the event of your death or incapacitation.

Estate tax – A tax on the total value of property an individual transfers to heirs upon death and the value of gifts made during an individual's lifetime. Under federal law, beginning January 1, 2018, an individual can transfer or gift up to $11.2 million or up to $22.4 million with their spouse without incurring estate tax.

Above those thresholds, a 40% federal estate tax applies. State estate tax may also apply.

Exchange-traded fund (ETF) – An investment product that contains a large number of individual stocks, bonds, or both. ETF shares are bought and sold like stock in transactions with other investors on an exchange, and their price fluctuates throughout the trading day. Because of their unique share creation mechanism, ETFs can be more tax efficient than mutual funds.

Fiduciary – A person or organization acting on behalf of another person or group of people, often involving finances. Fiduciaries are in a position of trust and must not exploit their position for personal gain. A financial advisor working in a fiduciary capacity has a legal duty to act only in the best interests of the client.

Fixed-income investment – Investments that pay a return on a fixed schedule. The phrase "fixed-income" is often used interchangeably with bonds or bond investments.

Grant (award) date – The date on which a company gives restricted stock, RSUs, or stock options to an employee.

Grantor retained annuity trust (GRAT) – An irrevocable trust created as part of an estate planning technique aimed at avoiding or reducing gift and estate tax by moving money out of an estate prior to an initial public offering or company sale.

Home equity line of credit (HELOC) – A type of home loan that allows a homeowner to borrow against the equity in their home (current value minus outstanding loans). With a HELOC, the homeowner can borrow up to the maximum loan amount as needed, for a certain period of time, instead of all at once.

Incentive stock options (ISOs) – A type of stock option with potential tax-saving features. ISO shares held for two years from date of grant and one year after date of exercise may receive long-term capital gain tax treatment.

Index funds – Mutual funds or exchange traded funds that are constructed to replicate the performance of a market index such as the Standard & Poor's 500 Index (S&P 500) or the Bloomberg Barclays U.S. Aggregate Bond Index.

Individual retirement account (IRA) – A tax-advantaged retirement savings account in which investments grow tax-deferred. Pre-tax contributions and investment growth are fully taxable as ordinary income upon withdrawal. For after-tax contributions, only investment growth is taxed on withdrawal.

Initial public offering (IPO) – The process of registering a company's shares with the U.S. Securities and Exchange Commission and marketing its shares to investors when a company prepares to sell its stock to the public for the first time.

Life expectancy – The number of additional years an average person is expected to live, given their current age. Life expectancy at birth refers to the average number of years a person born that year is expected to live.

Liquidity – A measure of how quickly an investment or asset can be bought or sold without significantly changing its price.

Lock-up – The period of time after an initial public offering when executives and employees are prevented from selling their shares. Lock-up periods typically last 90 to 180 days.

Money market mutual fund – A mutual fund that invests in short-term, money market securities such as U.S. Treasury bills, certificates of deposit, and commercial paper. Money market funds are often used as an alternative to cash.

Mutual fund – An investment product that contains a large number of individual stocks, bonds, or both. With mutual funds, the share price is set, and all purchase and sale transactions occur at the close of trading each day. Investors buy or sell mutual fund shares directly from the mutual fund company, and the fund's manager then buys or sells underlying investments to invest or raise cash for the transaction.

Non-qualified stock options (NSOs) – A type of stock option that does not qualify for special tax treatment. Any gain on a non-qualified stock option (market price minus strike price) at the time of exercise is taxable as ordinary income.

Payroll tax – Federal and state taxes paid by employees and employers based on the wage or salary of employees. Payroll tax is in addition to income tax. Federal payroll tax is used to pay for the Social Security and Medicare programs.

Rebalancing – The process for restoring an investment portfolio to its target asset allocation by buying some investments and selling others. Rebalancing helps maintain the proper risk level in an investment portfolio.

Required Minimum Distribution (RMD) – Mandatory withdrawal from a retirement account each year once the account owner reaches age 70 and six months.

Restricted stock – Company stock awarded to an employee that cannot be sold or transferred until certain conditions have been met. Ownership in the stock vests, meaning its restrictions are removed, over time, or as company or individual performance goals are met.

Restricted stock units (RSUs) – A pledge by an employer to transfer shares of company stock to an employee when certain conditions have been met. As with restricted stock, RSUs vest over time or when company or individual performance goals have been met.

Return – Rate of return is the measure of compound rate of growth of an investment or portfolio of investments over a period of time. The phrase "rate of return" is often shortened simply to "return." Investment returns are typically expressed as a percentage. For example, U.S. large company stocks earned a return of 10.2% per year for the 92 year period that ended December 31, 2017.

Risk – Investment risk refers to uncertainty about the rate of return on an investment or the potential to experience an investment loss. Many factors can create investment risk and affect investment returns, such as inflation, interest rate changes, currency fluctuations, and poor financial performance of an individual company or industry.

Roth IRA – A tax-advantaged retirement savings account in which investments grow tax-deferred and both contributions and earnings can be withdrawn tax-free after age 59 and six months. Contributions are after-tax and do not reduce taxable income.

Rule 10b5-1 – The U.S. Securities and Exchange Commission rule that allows company insiders to set up a trading plan to sell a pre-determined number of shares of company stock at a predetermined time as a defense against insider trading charges.

Section 199A deduction – A new income tax deduction under the Tax Cuts and Jobs Act. Also known as qualified business income deduction and pass-through entity deduction, it allows a deduction of up to 20% of pass-through business income from a partnership, S corporation, or sole proprietorship in calculating taxable income on a personal tax return.

Security – A certificate or other financial instrument that represents proof of ownership or debt that has monetary value and may be bought or sold. For example, common stocks are equity securities and corporate bonds are debt securities.

Stock – An investment in which an investor pays cash for ownership of a fraction of a company. Ownership typically confers the right to receive future dividends and to vote on company directors and other important matters.

Stock option – A legal agreement that gives the option holder the right to buy a specific number of shares of company stock at a specific price, known as the exercise price or strike price, for a specific amount of time.

Strike price – The stock price at which a stock option can be exercised to buy shares of company stock. Also known as the exercise price or grant price.

Tax avoidance – The legal use of tax law, regulation, official guidance, and court rulings to reduce the amount of tax owed. Tax planning is tax avoidance. In contrast, tax evasion is the illegal practice of intentionally not paying tax actually owed.

Tax Cuts and Jobs Act (TCJA) – Major tax legislation signed into law on December 22, 2017, that amends the Internal Revenue Code of 1986. Most features of this new tax law took effect January 1, 2018, and will terminate on December 31, 2025.

Tax loss harvesting – A technique used to reduce short-term or long-term capital gain in a taxable investment portfolio within the current tax year by selling investments that have unrealized losses to create realized losses for tax purposes.

Time-value of money – The concept that an amount of money today is more valuable than the same amount of money in the future because money today can be invested and grow to a larger amount in the future.

Total return – The sum of the amounts received from an investment in the form of interest, dividends, unrealized gains (price appreciation), and realized gains.

Trading window – A period of time when companies allow employees to sell or buy the company's stock. Employees may not sell or buy company stock when the trading window is "closed." Companies enforce trading windows to prevent insider trading, whether deliberate or inadvertent, by employees who possess insider information.

Volatility – Variation in the rate of return of an investment over time. Generally, riskier investments are more volatile than less risky investments.

Withdrawal rate – The amount of money taken out of an investment portfolio over time, usually expressed as a percentage of the total value of the portfolio.

References

Chapter 1: Finally! A Personal Finance Book for Tech Professionals

1 "Key Findings," Cyberstates, CompTIA, March 2018, http://www. cyberstates.org/.
2 "Key Findings."
3 "Key Findings," "National Snapshot."

Chapter 2: Buy Now, Pay Later: The Big Trade-Off

1 Hal E. Hershfield et al., "Increasing Saving Behavior through Age-Progressed Renderings of the Future Self," *Journal of Marketing Research* 48 (November 2011): S23–S37.
2 Richard H. Thaler, *Misbehaving: The Making of Behavioral Economics* (New York: W. W. Norton & Company Ltd., 2015), 100–102.
3 Jeffrey R. Stevens, Elizabeth V. Hallinan, and Marc D. Hauser, "The Ecology and Evolution of Patience in Two New World Monkeys," *Biology Letters* 1, no. 2 (October 2004): 223–226.
4 Miriam Tatzel, ed., *Consumption and Well-Being in the Material World* (New York: Springer, 2014).
5 Marsha L. Richins, "When Wanting Is Better than Having: Materialism, Transformation Expectations, and Product-Evoked Emotions in the Purchase Process," *Journal of Consumer Research* 40, no. 1 (June 2013): 1–18.
6 Juliet B. Schor, *The Overspent American: Why We Want What We Don't Need* (New York: Harper Perennial, 1999).
7 Marianne Bertrand and Adair Morse, "Trickle-Down Consumption," Chicago Booth School of Business Research Paper Series (Research Paper No. 13-37), March 5, 2013, http://dx.doi.org/10.2139/ssrn.2237640.

Chapter 3: Saving: Playing the Long Game

1   Nick Murray, noted author and speaker, has been prominent in creating awareness of this idea within the financial planning profession.

2   Elizabeth Arias, Melonie Heron, and Jiaquan Xu, "United States Life Tables, 2012," *National Vital Statistics Reports* 65, no. 8 (November 28, 2016): 48 (Table 19), https://www.cdc.gov/nchs/data/nvsr/nvsr65/nvsr65_08.pdf.

3   Ker Than, "The Truth on Longer Life Spans," *Live Science*, May 23, 2006, https://www.livescience.com/10464-truth-longer-life-spans.html.

4   Arias, Heron, and Xu, "United States Life Tables, 2012," 53 (Table 21).

5   *Health, United States, 2016: With Chartbook on Long-Term Trends in Health*, National Center for Health Statistics (Hyattsville, MD: U.S. Department of Health and Human Services, 2017), 116 (Table 15).

6   Paul Ausick, "10 U.S. Cities with the Longest Life Expectancies," *24/7 Wall St.*(blog), December 26, 2016, https://247wallst.com/healthcare-economy/2016/12/27/10-us-cities-with-the-longest-life-expectancies/; Jody Meacham, "San Jose Metro Area Has Longest Life Expectancy of All U.S. Metro Areas, Report Says," *Silicon Valley Business Journal*, December 24, 2015, https://www.bizjournals.com/sanjose/news/2015/12/24/san-jose-area-has-longest-life-expectancy-of-all-u.html.

7   Joseph Brownstein and ABC News Medical Unit, "Most Babies Born Today May Live Past 100," *ABC News*, October 1, 2009, http://abcnews.go.com/Health/WellnessNews/half-todays-babies-expected-live-past-100/story?id=8724273.

8   Brendan McFarland, "A Continuing Shift in Retirement Offerings in the *Fortune* 500," Willis Towers Watson, *Insider*, February 18, 2016, https://www.towerswatson.com/en-US/Insights/Newsletters/Americas/insider/2016/02/a-continuing-shift-in-retirement-offerings-in-the-fortune-500.

9   "Establishments Offering Retirement and Healthcare Benefits: Private Industry Workers, March 2017," *Employee Benefits Survey*, U.S. Department of Labor, Bureau of Labor Statistics, September 2017, https://www.bls.gov/ncs/ebs/benefits/2017/ownership/private/table01a.pdf.

10   *The 2017 Annual Report of the Board of Trustees of the Federal Old-Age and Survivors Insurance and Federal Disability Insurance Trust Funds*, Board of Trustees of the Federal Old-Age and Survivors Insurance and Federal Disability Insurance Trust Funds, July 13, 2017, https://www.ssa.gov/oact/tr/2017/tr2017.pdf.

11 Follows the methodology described in a series of research papers by Massi
De Santis, PhD, and Marlena Lee, PhD, of Dimensional Fund Advisors. For
a summary of their work, see "How Much Should I Save for Retirement?,"
Dimensional Fund Advisors, June 2013 (http://www.smartretirement.com.au/
wp-content/uploads/2015/06/Dimensional-How-Much-Should-I-Save-For-
Retirement-White-Paper-Lee.pdf).

12 "Retirement Assets Total $28.2 Trillion in First Quarter 2018," Investment
Company Institute, June 21, 2018, https://www.ici.org/research/stats/
retirement/ret_18_q1.

13 I.R.C. § 72(t)(2)(A)(v).

14 This rule does not apply to IRA accounts. Leaving your money in your
employer-sponsored 401(k) plan allows you to access your money four years and
six months earlier than an IRA without incurring the early withdrawal penalty.
If you are between the ages of 55 and 59 and six months, consider leaving your
money in your 401(k) plan and not rolling over to an IRA until age 59 and
six months to take distributions without incurring the 10% early withdrawal
penalty.

15 I.R.C. § 72(t)(2)(A)(iv); I.R.C. § 72(t)(3)(B).

16 *2018 Investment Company Fact Book*, Investment Company Institute, 2018,
https://www.ici.org/pdf/2018_factbook.pdf.

17 For example, this is an important consideration for physicians.

18 A particularly useful resource is www.savingforcollege.com.

Chapter 4: Invest for Financial Success

1   Andrew Whitten, "Why Are There So Few Public Companies in the U.S.?,"
The National Bureau of Economic Research, accessed September 16, 2017,
http://www.nber.org/digest/sep15/w21181.html.

2   Bloomberg Barclays U.S. Aggregate Bond Index included 9,706 bonds
and the Bloomberg Barclays U.S. Corporate High-Yield Index included 1,830
bonds as of 12/31/2017. Data taken from Vanguard's website on pages for
the Vanguard Total Bond Market Index Fund Admiral Shares (VBTLX) and
Vanguard High-Yield Corporate Fund Investor Shares (VWEHX) from the tab
for Portfolio and Management (https://investor.vanguard.com/mutual-funds/).

3   "Trends in Mutual Fund Investing," Investment Company Institute,
December 2017, https://www.ici.org/research/stats/trends/trends_12_17
(document no longer available online); "Closed-End Fund Assets and Net
Issuance, Third Quarter 2017," Investment Company Institute, January
30, 2018, https://www.ici.org/research/stats/closedend/ci.cef_q3_17.
print (document no longer available online); ETF Assets and Net Issuance,
Investment Company Institute, January 30, 2018, https://www.ici.org/research/
stats/etf/ci.etfs_12_17.print (document no longer available online).

4   Financial economists define the value of a corporation as the present value
of all future cash flows plus the value of its present assets minus liabilities.
It is difficult to predict future cash flows for corporations, which results in
uncertainty about the true value of a company and disagreements about its
correct stock price.

5   Treasury bills are represented by 30-day U.S. Treasury bills. Government
bonds are represented by 20-year U.S. Government bonds. Large stocks are
represented by the Ibbotson Large Company Stock Index. Small stocks are
represented by Ibbotson Small Company Stock Index. Inflation is represented
by the Consumer Price Index.

6   International stocks are represented by the Morgan Stanley Capital
International Europe Australasia Far East Index (MSCI EAFE). Real estate is
represented by the Financial Times and Stock Exchange National Association
of Real Estate Investment Trusts Index (FTSE NAREIT). Commodities are
represented by the Morningstar Long-Only Commodity Index. Large stocks are
represented by the Ibbotson Large Company Stock Index.

7   A groundbreaking research paper published in 1986 (Gary Brinson,
Randolph Hood, and Gilbert Beebower, "Determinants of Portfolio
Performance," *Financial Analysts Journal* 42, no. 4 [1986]: 39-44) was widely
misinterpreted to mean that over 90% of an investment portfolio's return could
be attributed to its asset allocation. Subsequent research (Roger G. Ibbotson,
"The Importance of Asset Allocation," *Financial Analysts Journal* 66, no. 2
[2010])) has clarified that across a large sample of institutionally managed
portfolios, about 75% of performance derives from the decision to invest in the
market as opposed to holding cash, and the remainder of the performance was
attributed about equally to asset allocation and active management.

8   Calculated using Fama-French Large Growth, Large Value, Small Growth,
and Small Value Total Return Indices for the period January 1, 1928 through
December 31, 2017.

9   Robert M. Dammon, Chester S. Spatt, and Harold H. Zhang, "Optimal
Asset Location and Allocation with Taxable and Tax-Deferred Investing,"
Journal of Finance 59, no. 3 (June 2004).

10 Eugene Fama won the 2013 Nobel Prize in Economics for his Efficient Market Hypothesis.

11 Tim Jenkinson, Robert Harris, and Steven Kaplan, "How Do Private Equity Investments Perform Compared to Public Equity?," *Journal of Investment Management*, Vol. 14 (3), Third Quarter 2016, 1-24.

12 *Report on the Review of the Definition of "Accredited Investor,"* U.S. Securities and Exchange Commission, December 18, 2015, 1, https://www.sec.gov/files/review-definition-of-accredited-investor-12-18-2015.pdf.

13 17 CFR 230.501(a)(6).

14 17 CFR 230.501(a)(5).

15 U.S. Securities and Exchange Commission, Securities Act Rules Compliance and Disclosure Interpretation 255.14.

16 U.S. Securities and Exchange Commission, Securities Act Rules Compliance and Disclosure Interpretation 255.11.

17 *Report on the Review*, 2.

18 17 CFR 230.501(a)(8).

19 17 CFR 230.501(a)(7).

20 17 CFR 230.506(b)(2)(ii).

21 17 CFR 230.501(a)(8).

22 Investment Company Act of 1940, § 3(c)(1).

23 Investment Company Act of 1940, § 3(c)(7).

24 Investment Company Act of 1940, § 2(a)(51).

Chapter 5: Taking Stock: Equity Compensation

1 Tax-qualified ESPPs meet the requirements and receive the special treatment of I.R.C. § 423. These plans are sometimes referred to as Section 423 plans.

2 I.R.C. § 423(b)(6).

3 I.R.C. § 423(b)(6).

4 I.R.C. § 423(c).

5 I.R.C. § 423(b)(8).

6 Barbara Baksa, "Silicon Valley vs. the Nation," *The NASPP Blog*, NASPP, March 3, 2015, https://www.naspp.com/blog/2015/03/silicon-valley-vs-the-nation.

7 A change in accounting rules in 2005 led public companies to prefer restricted stock and restricted stock units over stock options for their equity compensation plans. FASB 123 required companies to begin expensing stock options as compensation expense.

8   Paul Sloan, "Three Reasons Facebook Has to Go Public," CNET, January 31, 2012, https://www.cnet.com/news/three-reasons-facebook-has-to-go-public/; Owen Thomas, "The Other Challenge of Facebook's Stock Swoon," *Business Insider*, May 21, 2012, http://www.businessinsider.com/facebook-ipo-stock-price-recruiting-2012-5.

9   "Notice 1036, Early Release Copies of the 2018 Percentage Method Tables for Income Tax Withholding," IRS, revised January 2018, https://www.irs.gov/pub/irs-pdf/n1036.pdf.

10   The value of private company stock is typically determined by an independent appraisal firm that prepares a 409A valuation analysis. Section 409A of the Internal Revenue Code regulates tax treatment of non-qualified deferred compensation including stock options.

11   This is the maximum time allowed after termination for incentive stock options by I.R.C. § 422(a)(2).

12   This is the maximum option term allowed for incentive stock options by I.R.C. § 422(b)(3).

13   Technology start-ups across the full spectrum of sectors that venture capitalists would typically invest, including social media, networking, semiconductor, cloud software, biotechnology, medical devices, etc.

14   I.R.C. § 422.

15   For additional reading, tax attorney Kaye A. Thomas provides a detailed discussion of incentive stock options and Alternative Minimum Tax in his excellent book: Kaye A. Thomas, *Equity Compensation Strategies, A guide for professional advisors* (Elgin, IL: Fairmark Press Inc., 2014).

16   Kaye A. Thomas, *Equity Compensation Strategies, A guide for professional advisors* (Elgin, IL: Fairmark Press Inc., 2014), 235-36.

17   I.R.C. § 83(b).

18   I.R.S. Rev. Proc. 2012-29.

19   SEC Rule 10b5-1 codified at 17 CFR 240.10b5-1.

20   15 U.S.C. § 78u-1.

21   15 U.S.C. § 78ff.

22   Our office is occasionally in possession of material nonpublic information, and we have safeguards in place to ensure employees and clients don't inadvertently trade on that information. Also, as a frontline product manager and later executive in technology companies, I was often aware of material nonpublic information and learned about the importance of this issue early in my career.

23 Affirmative defense means that the accused presented evidence that eliminates criminal or civil liability even if the accused committed the alleged acts. In this case, even though an employee was aware of material nonpublic information when a trade was executed, because the trade instructions were given before the employee was aware of material nonpublic information as part of a 10b5-1 plan, the employee will not face penalties for insider trading as a result of the trades.

24 17 CFR 240.10b5-1—trading "on the basis of" material nonpublic information in insider trading cases.

Chapter 6: Home Truths About Real Estate

1 As of June 2018. (For updated information, go to "100 Best Places to Live in the USA," U.S. News, http://realestate.usnews.com/places/rankings/best-places-to-live.)

2 "Current Sales & Price Statistics," California Association of Realtors, May 2018, https://www.car.org/en/marketdata/data/countysalesactivity; "Existing-Home Sales," National Association of Realtors, May 2018, https://www.nar.realtor/sites/default/files/documents/ehs-05-2018-overview-2018-06-20.pdf.

3 "S&P CoreLogic Case-Shiller Home Price Indices," S&P Dow Jones, accessed February 8, 2018, https://us.spindices.com/index-family/real-estate/sp-corelogic-case-shiller.

4 "Quarterly Residential Vacancies and Homeownership, First Quarter 2018," U.S. Census Bureau (Release CB18-57), April 26, 2018, https://www.census.gov/housing/hvs/files/currenthvspress.pdf.

5 Emily Starbuck Crone and Daniel Tonkovich, "How Much More It Costs to Own vs. Rent in Your State," NerdWallet, March 22, 2017, https://www.nerdwallet.com/blog/mortgages/cost-homeownership-vs-renting/.

6 "Publication 925, Passive Activity and At-Risk Rules," IRS, 2017, https://www.irs.gov/pub/irs-pdf/p925.pdf.

7 Abbigail J. Chiodo, Rubén Hernández-Murillo, and Michael T. Owyang, "Nonlinear Effects of School Quality on House Prices," Federal Reserve Bank of St. Louis Review 92, no. 3, May/June 2010, 185–204.

Chapter 7: Getting Personal: What Matters to You?

1 Robert Waldinger, "What Makes a Good Life? Lessons from the Longest Study on Happiness," TEDx Beacon Street, November 2015, https://www.ted.com/talks/robert_waldinger_what_makes_a_good_life_lessons_from_the_longest_study_on_happiness/transcript.

2   John Pencavel, "The Productivity of Working Hours," The Economic Journal 125 (October 9, 2014): 2052–2076.

3   Sarah Green Carmichael, "The Research Is Clear: Long Hours Backfire for People and for Companies," Harvard Business Review, August 19, 2015, https://hbr.org/2015/08/the-research-is-clear-long-hours-backfire-for-people-and-for-companies.

4   "The Cost and Duration of Divorce," Lawyers.com, accessed February 17, 2018, https://www.lawyers.com/legal-info/family-law/divorce/cost-duration/.

5   Max Hirshkowitz et al., "National Sleep Foundation's Sleep Time Duration Recommendations: Methodology and Results Summary," Sleep Health, Journal of the National Sleep Foundation 1, no. 1 (March 2015): 40–43, https://doi.org/10.1016/j.sleh.2014.12.010.

6   Katherine Harmon, "Rare Genetic Mutation Lets Some People Function with Less Sleep," Scientific American, August 13, 2009, https://www.scientificamerican.com/article/genetic-mutation-sleep-less/.

7   Holly B. Shakya and Nicholas A. Christakis "Association of Facebook Use with Compromised Well-Being: A Longitudinal Study," American Journal of Epidemiology 185, no. 3 (February 1, 2017): 203–211, https://doi.org/10.1093/aje/kww189.

8   Daniel Kahenman and Angus Deaton, "High Income Improves Evaluation of Life but Not Emotional Well-Being," Proceedings of the National Academy of Sciences 107, no. 38 (September 2010): 16489–16493, https://doi.org/10.1073/pnas.1011492107.

9   Judy T. Lin et al., Financial Capability in the United States 2016, FINRA Investor Education Foundation, July 2016, https://www.usfinancialcapability.org/downloads/NFCS_2015_Report_Natl_Findings.pdf.

10 Leora Klapper, Annamaria Lusardi, and Peter van Oudheusden, Financial Literacy Around the World: Insights from the Standard & Poor's Ratings Services Global Financial Literacy Survey, Responsible Finance Forum, November 27, 2015, https://responsiblefinanceforum.org/publications/financial-literacy-around-the-world-insights-from-the-standard-poors-ratings-services-global-financial-literacy-survey/.

Chapter 8: Taxation Nation: Minimizing the Burden

1   "Fact Sheet, Social Security: 2018 Social Security Changes," Social Security Administration, https://www.ssa.gov/news/press/factsheets/colafacts2018.pdf

2   For more information, go to the Tax Foundation's website at https://taxfoundation.org/.

3   26 U.S.C. Internal Revenue Code.

4   "Overview of the Federal Tax System as in Effect for 2018," Congress of the United States, Joint Committee on Taxation (JCX-3-18), February 7, 2018, https://www.jct.gov/publications.html?func=startdown&id=5060.

5   "Gift Contributions to Reduce Debt Held by the Public," U.S. Department of the Treasury, Bureau of the Fiscal Service, TreasuryDirect, https://www.treasurydirect.gov/govt/reports/pd/gift/gift.htm.

6   Dammon, Spatt, and Zhang, "Optimal Asset Location."

Chapter 9: Liquidity Events: IPOs & Acquisitions

1   James Brau et al., "Market Reaction to the Expiration of IPO Lockup Provisions," Managerial Finance 30 (2004): 75–91, doi:10.1108/03074350410768859; Clifford Stephens and Christopher Dussold, "An Examination of Multiple or Staggered Lockups and Rule 144 Trading Restrictions," Department of Finance, E. J. Ourso College of Business, Louisiana State University, March 2007, https://slideblast.com/an-examination-of-multiple-or-staggered-lockups-and-rule-144-_598031b61723ddcdeadd6417.html.

Chapter 10: Quitting the Rat Race: Planning for Retirement

1   "Employment Status of the Civilian Noninstitutional Population by Age, Sex, and Race," Labor Force Statistics from the Current Population Survey, U.S. Department of Labor, Bureau of Labor Statistics, last modified January 19, 2018, https://www.bls.gov/cps/cpsaat03.htm; "Employment Status of the Civilian Noninstitutional Population by Age, Sex, and Race," Labor Force Statistics from the Current Population Survey, U.S. Department of Labor, Bureau of Labor Statistics, 1998, https://www.bls.gov/cps/aa1998/CPSAAT3.pdf.

2   Simon Biggs, Laura Carstensen and Paul Hogan, "Social Capital, Lifelong Learning and Social Innovation," chap. 7 in Global Population Ageing: Peril or Promise? (PGDA Working Paper No. 89, Harvard Initiative for Global Health), January 2012, http://mfile.narotama.ac.id/files/Jurnal/Jurnal%202012-2013/International%20Migration%20and%20Population%20Ageing.pdf#page=42.

3   William P. Bengen, "Determining Withdrawal Rates Using Historical Data," Journal of Financial Planning, October 1994.

4   David M. Zolt, "Retirement Planning by Targeting Safe Withdrawal Rates," Journal of Financial Planning, Financial Planning Association, October 2014, https://www.onefpa.org/journal/Pages/OCT14-Retirement-Planning-by-Targeting-Safe-Withdrawal-Rates.aspx.

5   Michael Finke, Wade D. Pfau, and Duncan Williams, "Spending Flexibility and Safe Withdrawal Rates," Texas Tech University, National Graduate Institute for Policy Studies, November 5, 2011, https://mpra.ub.uni-muenchen.de/34536/1/MPRA_paper_34536.pdf.

Chapter 11: Leaving Your Mark: Legacy Planning

1   "Quick Facts about Nonprofits," National Center for Charitable Statistics, accessed June 23, 2018, http://nccs.urban.org/data-statistics/quick-facts-about-nonprofits.
2   "SOI Tax Stats—Estate Tax Statistics Filing Year Table 1," IRS, 2016, https://www.irs.gov/statistics/soi-tax-stats-estate-tax-statistics-filing-year-table-1.
3   Revised Uniform Fiduciary Access to Digital Assets Act (2015). For more information, go to http://www.uniformlaws.org/shared/docs/Fiduciary%20Access%20to%20Digital%20Assets/2015_RUFADAA_Final%20Act_2016mar8.pdf.
4   I.R.C. § 501(c)(3).
5   *2017 Donor-Advised Fund Report*, The National Philanthropic Trust, 2017, https://www.nptrust.org/daf-report/.
6   *2017 Donor-Advised Fund Report.*
7   *2018 Giving Report*, Fidelity Charitable, 2018, https://www.fidelitycharitable.org/docs/giving-report-2018.pdf.

Chapter 12: Who's in Charge of Your Financial Freedom?

1   Francis M Kinniry Jr. et al., "Putting a Value on Your Value: Quantifying Vanguard Advisor's Alpha," Vanguard, September 2016, https://www.vanguard.com/pdf/ISGQVAA.pdf.
2   National Association of Personal Financial Advisors (NAPFA) requires 60 hours of continuing education every two years for its NAPFA-Registered Financial Advisors, all of whom hold the CFP® credential, work on a fee-only basis, and take a fiduciary oath.
3   David Blanchett and Paul Kaplan, "Alpha, Beta, and Now… Gamma," *The Journal of Retirement* 1, no. 2 (Fall 2013): 29–45, DOI: https://doi.org/10.3905/jor.2013.1.2.029.

About the Author

Bruce Barton, CFP® CFA is a practicing wealth manager in Silicon Valley, and owner of a boutique wealth management firm he founded 15 years ago. Bruce brings a unique perspective to personal finance after a full career as a technology professional and years of experience as advisor to families and individuals whose personal finances are tied to technology industries.

In a tech career spanning 15 years, Bruce worked as system design engineer, product manager, director of product management, and vice president of marketing. He worked in three venture capital-backed tech startups, including one that went public, one that was acquired, and one that failed. His employers also included a large, publicly traded U.S. company and a large, foreign multinational company. The early days of the startups were always the most fun.

Bruce's multidisciplinary approach to financial advisory work requires a broad background in finance and expertise across a wide range of disciplines spanning retirement planning, investments, tax, equity compensation, and estate planning to ensure all areas are coordinated in achieving clients' goals. He works in a fiduciary capacity, acting only in the best interests of clients. Because there has not been a standard, go-to resource for tech professionals who want to better manage their personal finances, Bruce created this book to provide an introduction to, and practical advice on, the personal financial issues facing this influential group of people.

Bruce earned a Master's of Business Administration in Finance from the University of Chicago, Bachelor of Science in Engineering from Harvey Mudd College, and Bachelor of Arts in Liberal Arts from Claremont McKenna College. He holds the Certified Financial Planner (CFP®) and Chartered Financial Analyst (CFA) designations. Bruce served on the Board of Directors of the National Association of Personal Financial Advisors (NAPFA) and is past president of the NAPFA West Region Board of Directors. He is co-inventor on a patent for performance monitoring of telecommunication systems.

Bruce and his wife Alicia, whom he met at Harvey Mudd College, live with their dog, Romeo, in Los Gatos, California. They have two great kids away in college who are studying biology and electrical engineering.

Acknowledgments

Creating a great tech product or company requires the skills and hard work of many talented people. And so does creating a book to help those tech professionals better manage their personal finances. I am grateful to have had such a capable team contributing to this project.

Stacy Ennis is a creative consultant, editor, author, and coach extraordinaire—she's also the person I relied on most to help me write this book. Stacy helped me clarify my goals, create a reader-friendly structure, and develop a writing schedule that meshed with my already more-than-full-time job. She coached me regularly to improve my writing and sharpen my ideas, offered content suggestions and edits that improved the quality of the book, and helped me navigate the complex publishing industry, which is evolving rapidly as a result of new technologies. Most importantly, she provided unending positive reinforcement to keep me going during the eight months it took to complete a first draft. Stacy, I couldn't have done this without you. I owe you gigantic thanks.

At Mascot Books, CEO Naren Aryal saw the potential of this project and lent his enthusiastic support. Editor Lorna Partington applied her considerable talent in smoothing the manuscript's rough spots large and small, trimming excess, identifying areas needing development, refining awkward phrases, and generally transforming the text to its final polished state. Ricky Frame developed the eye-catching cover and interior design that so well matches the tone of the book. Daniel Wheatley and Kristin Perry expertly led me through the many-step process of getting a book into production. Thanks to the whole Mascot team.

Editor Kim Foster did an amazing job of thoroughly reviewing and meticulously formatting all of the cited references to complete the manuscript first draft. Thank you, Kim.

Chris Missirlian, CFP®, provided research and diagrams for Chapter 4 on investing, double-checked the math throughout the book, and critically reviewed the entire manuscript, catching errors and suggesting improvements in explanations of key concepts. Sheac Yee Lim-Hamilton provided research and tables for Chapter 7 on housing, compiled references, applied her technical writing expertise in reviewing the manuscript, and assisted in managing the entire project. Thanks so much to you both, Chris and Sheac Yee.

Special thanks to my professional colleagues who read portions of the manuscript, suggesting improvements and helping to ensure the content was as accurate as possible. Any errors left in the book are on me. Contributing review time from their already busy professional and personal lives were Scott Bryning, CPA; Vadim Gorin, CFA; Barbara Hamrock, CRTP; Bridget Harkins, CFP®; and Raymond Sheffield, JD LLM.

Thanks also to Kristen Luke and Brittany Peña at Kaleido Creative for their encouragement to take on this project, and their valuable suggestions and expertise in design and marketing. Kaleido graphic designer Mario Salinas performed magic turning rough spreadsheet diagrams into the great looking figures throughout the text.

At home, I'm grateful for the support and encouragement of my wife, Alicia Barton, who is still the same brilliant and full-of-life girl I first met during a party at Harvey Mudd College thirty-two years ago. I appreciate her many suggestions for the book as well as her patience with this project, which impinged on quite a few weekends. My kids, Claire and Reid, also have encouraged me and are mildly impressed with their dad, which doesn't happen often and may be the most rewarding part of the whole experience. Thanks also to my brother, Craig Barton, for proofreading and discussing the manuscript, and finding more than his share of typos. And lastly, I appreciate the companionship of my dog, Romeo, who kept me company during many an early morning writing session, sleeping soundly at my feet.

Index

NOTE: Page references with an *f* are figures.

T